Heath's Brief Handbook of Usage

9th edition

Heath's Brief Handbook of Usage

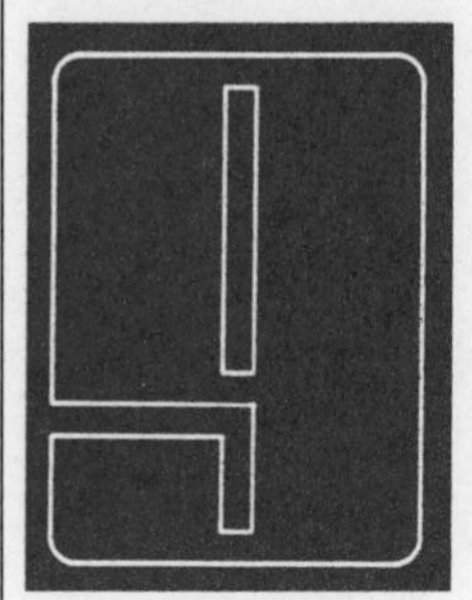

Langdon Elsbree
Claremont Men's College

Frederick Bracher
Pomona College

Nell Altizer
University of Hawaii

D. C. Heath and Company
Lexington, Massachusetts Toronto

Cover design by Leonard Preston,
inspired by the *Book of Kells.*

Published simultaneously in Canada.

Printed in the United States of America.

International Standard book Number: 0-669-00588-6

Library of Congress Catalog Card Number: 76-55461

Acknowledgments

WILLIAM COLLINS + WORLD PUBLISHING COMPANY, from *Websters New World Dictionary of the American Language,* Second College Edition. Copyright © 1976 by William Collins + World Publishing Co., Inc.

THOMAS Y. CROWELL COMPANY, from *Funk & Wagnalls Standard College Dictionary*. Copyright © 1963, 1966, 1968, 1973 by Funk & Wagnalls Publishing Company, Inc. Used by permission of the publisher.

HOUGHTON MIFFLIN COMPANY, from *The American Heritage Dictionary of the English Language*. Copyright © 1969, 1970, 1971, 1973, 1975, 1976, Houghton Mifflin Company. Reprinted by permission.

LANGSTON HUGHES, from "The Negro Artist and the Racial Mountain." Copyright 1926 by Langston Hughes. Renewed. Reprinted by permission of Harold Ober Associates Incorporated.

G. & C. MERRIAM COMPANY, from *Webster's New Collegiate Dictionary*. Copyright © 1976 by G. & C. Merriam Co., Publishers of the Merriam-Webster Dictionaries. By permission.

DAVID C. STEWART, from "The Movies Students Make" copyright © 1965 by Harper's Magazine Inc. Reprinted from the October, 1965 issue of *Harper's Magazine* by permission of the author.

Contents

8

9

10

The Long Paper 189

Heath's Brief Handbook of Usage

9th edition

1 Sentences

1a Elements of a Sentence

This section is a highly simplified summary of the Grammar 2 of English. That is, it attempts to analyze the language you use every day (your Grammar 1) and make a generalized description of the way it operates. For any kind of grammatical analysis, it is necessary to *classify* the words and groups of words that make up a sentence. To classify means simply to group together words that are alike in some respects and to give names to the classes thus formed.

Let's start with a kind of classification you may never have thought of, though structural linguists use it all the time. *Pen, telephone, tax,* and *fluid,* for example, are alike in that they often appear after words like *the, a,* or *this: a pen, the telephone, this tax.* Words of this class also take inflectional endings to indicate the plural, usually a suffix including the letter *s: telephones, fluids, taxes.* Another class is made up of words to which inflectional suffixes like *-ed* can be added: *ask, asked; cry, cried; walk, walked.* A third class consists of words to which *-er* and *-est* can be added: *happy, happier, happiest; swift, swifter, swiftest.*

As names for these classes, let's adopt the ones used by traditional grammar: we'll call the first class NOUNS (words that name something), the second class VERBS (words that assert something), and the third class ADJECTIVES (words that describe or limit the meaning of a noun). However, as we go on to classify more and more words, it will become apparent that these classes must be broadened. Traditional grammar will suggest that a word like *man* should be put in the first class, even though the plural is *men*, not *mans*. Similarly, in the second class we will want to put such a word as *weave*, even though, instead of taking an *-ed* ending, it is inflected *wove*. The third class will be widened to include some words which do not add *-er* and *-est*, like *beautiful*, which is inflected *more beautiful*, *most beautiful*.

In widening the classes, traditional grammar makes use of another set of similarities: it puts words into classes not merely by their position in a sentence or by their forms (the way they can be inflected), but by their *functions* in a sentence. That is, traditional grammar says that *man*, *pen*, and *tax* belong together in a class because they name something; whereas *rich* and *beautiful* and *cold* belong together in another class because they modify (that is, describe or limit) something.

Modern linguists have proposed alternative classifications which may well provide a more accurate and complete analysis of grammatical structures and relationships than the categories of traditional grammar do. But for the limited sort of analysis needed in a handbook, which tries merely to explain why certain constructions are "grammatical" without offering a complete system of grammar, the traditional classifications and the old names have the advantage of simplicity and familiarity. And they can be made consistent enough to be relevant and usable.

Many of the supposed inconsistencies of traditional grammar are caused by the fact that most English words can function in more than one way, and hence fit into more than one class. The word *poor* belongs in the class with *happy* and *swift* because it can take the suffixes *-er* and *-est* to make *poorer* and *poorest*. But the sentence "The poor usually eat poor food" shows that *poor* can also be used like words of the first class described above. *The poor* belongs with *the telephone*, *the pen*, etc., even though it does not take an *-s* suffix like *telephones*.

Into what class, then, do we put the word *poor?* The answer is no class, until we see the word used in a sentence. In a sentence, the form and position will indicate the word's meaning and grammatical function. *The poor* names an economic class; in this construction, the word belongs with other names like *telephone* or *fluid*. In the construction *poor food*, *poor* describes the quality of food; it belongs in the class with *rich*, *hot*, and *good*.

Once it is clear that grammatical analysis deals not with isolated words but with words used in sentences, various systems of classification are possible. For the present purpose, classifying words by their *functions* in a sentence provides a simple and usable tool, adequate for the needs of a composition course.

There are four functions of words in sentences: to name things, to assert things, to modify (describe, identify, or limit) other words, and to connect other parts of a sentence. Groups of words (what linguists call *constructions*) may have the same functions as single words: such groups are called PHRASES or CLAUSES—see 1a(5) and 1a(6).

class	*function*	*types*
substantive	to name	nouns, pronouns, gerunds
predicative	to assert	verbs
modifier	to describe or limit	adjectives, adverbs, participles
connective	to join elements	conjunctions, prepositions

Note that a GERUND (a verb form used as a noun, like *swimming* in "Swimming is good exercise") is classified along with nouns and pronouns, and that a PARTICIPLE (a verb form used as an adjective as in "*floating* beer can" or "*torn* paper") is put with the modifiers.

The basic unit of discourse, and the starting point of grammatical analysis, is the sentence. Sentences do a number of things: ask questions (INTERROGATIVE SENTENCE) or answer them, issue commands or requests (IMPERATIVE SENTENCE), or, most often, make statements. In speech they are not always explicitly complete. The single word "Going?" may serve in place of the full question "Are you leaving the party already?" and the answer may be the single word "Yes," just as the answer to the question "Where do you live?" may be no more than "On Elm Street." These answers are abbreviated sentences—a short way of saying "I am leaving the party," or "I live on Elm Street." Questions and answers, commands or requests are special types of the sentence, with their own grammatical characteristics. (Commands usually omit the subject; questions are indicated by a peculiar word order.) But the typical sentence in written English is a statement.

(1) Subject and Predicate

A statement says something about something, and to make a statement you need to *name* what you are talking about and *assert* something about it. The grammatical term for the word or words that name what you are talking about is the SUBJECT. The PREDICATE is the assertion you make about the subject.

subject	*predicate*
Edison	invented the light bulb.
The storm	cut off our lights.
A coyote	howled all night.
I	like spices.
My younger brother	does not like spices.

The subject is usually a noun or PRONOUN (a word used in place of a noun), though it may be a phrase or clause, as will be explained later. The predicate may contain a number of different words used in different ways, but the essential part is a VERB, a word that asserts something.

(2) Modifiers

It is possible to make a complete sentence of two words, a subject and a verb:

Rain fell.

Few sentences, however, are as simple as this. We usually add other words whose function is to describe the subject or the verb:

A gentle rain fell steadily.

Here *gentle* describes rain and *steadily* describes how it fell. Such words are called MODIFIERS, and they may be attached to almost any part of a sentence. Although modifiers usually describe, they may also indicate how many (*three* books, *few* books), which one (*this* pencil, *the* pen, *my* pencil), or how much (*very* gently, *half* sick, *almost too* late).

Modifiers are divided into two main classes: ADJECTIVES and ADVERBS. Any word which modifies a noun, pronoun, or gerund is an adjective in function; an adverb is any word which modifies a verb, an adjective, or another adverb.

Very hungry men seldom display good table manners.

In this sentence, *hungry, good,* and *table* are adjectives, describing or indicating what kind of men and manners. *Very* is an adverb since it modifies the adjective *hungry; seldom* is an adverb modifying the verb *display.*

Adjectives and adverbs have different forms to indicate relative DEGREE. In addition to the regular, or "positive," form (*slow, comfortable, slowly*), there is the COMPARATIVE degree (*slower, more comfortable, more slowly*), and the SUPERLATIVE degree (*slowest, most comfortable, most slowly*). The examples illustrate the rule: adjectives with more than two syllables form the comparative and superlative degrees by the words *more* and *most*, instead of the suffixes *-er* and *est.* All adverbs ending in *ly* use *more* and *most* to indicate degrees of comparison.

(3) Identifying Subject and Verb

The analysis of any sentence begins with the identification of the simple subject and the verb. Look first for the verb: a word or group of words that often states an action or happening. Some forms or tenses of a verb are really phrases, including one or more AUXILIARY VERBS—I *was hit,* I *have been hit;* I *had taken,* I *shall have taken.* Verbs which do not add *-ed* to form the past tense are called IRREGULAR VERBS—*swim, swam; eat, ate,* etc. A person learning English remembers these verb forms by memorizing their PRINCIPAL PARTS—*swim, swam, swum; eat, ate, eaten,* etc.

> I ***sprained*** my wrist.
> Joe Miller ***wrote*** me a letter.
> The fire ***burned*** out.
> He ***has*** never ***painted*** landscapes before.
> *(In this sentence the two parts of the verb are separated by the adverb* never.*)*

Some verbs merely assert, with varying degrees of certainty, that something is—or looks or sounds or seems or appears to be—something. These are called LINKING VERBS, or COPULAS.

> He ***is*** a fine mechanic.
> She ***seems*** intelligent and dependable.
> There ***were*** two reasons for believing his story.
> The troops ***looked*** weary.

When you have found the verb, ask yourself the question, "Who or what ....?" putting the verb in the blank space. The answer to the question is the subject, and if you strip away the modifiers you have the SIMPLE SUBJECT.

> A long, dull speech followed the dinner.

What followed the dinner? A *long, dull speech.* But *long* and *dull* are adjectives describing *speech;* the simple subject is *speech.*

This method is especially helpful when the normal order of the sentence is inverted (that is, when the subject comes *after* the verb) or when the sentence begins with an introductory word like "there." In the sentence "Across the Alps lies Italy," the verb is *lies.* What lies across the Alps? The answer is the subject, *Italy.*

Consider the sentence "There was a serious error in the first paragraph." The verb is *was,* and the predicate asserts that something "was in the first paragraph." What? The word *there* does not name anything and hence cannot be the subject. The answer to the question is "a serious error," and *error* is the simple subject.

Note that in a sentence which asks a question the subject often follows some form of the verb *have* or *be,* or a form of an auxiliary verb.

verb	*subject*	
Have	***you***	a match?
Is	***he***	dependable?

auxiliary	*subject*	*verb*	
Have	***you***	***returned***	the books?
Did	***she***	***buy***	a lock?
May	***they***	***come***	in?
Has	***the purse***	***been found?***	

	auxiliary	*subject*	*verb*
What kind of lock	***did***	***you***	***buy?***

In an imperative sentence the subject is not expressed. Since a command or request is addressed directly to someone, that person need not be named.

subject	*verb*	
( )	***Come***	in.
( )	***Shut***	the door.

	subject	*verb*	
Please	( )	***take***	this to the post office.

A sentence may have several nouns as its subject, since it is possible to make one assertion about several things. Such a construction is called a COMPOUND SUBJECT.

compound subject	
The ***trees and plants***	were dying.
Richmond, Wills, and Hyatt	have been elected.

Similarly, it is possible to use a COMPOUND PREDICATE—that is, to make several assertions about one subject.

	compound predicate	
The car	***swerved, skidded,*** and ***ran***	into the ditch.
Marilyn	***washed*** her face and ***dressed***	for dinner.

Exercise 1

Pick out the simple subjects and the verbs in the following sentences. Note that either the subject or the verb may be compound.

1. After locking the door, the flight attendant sat down at the rear of the plane.
2. Invisible to us, the pilot and copilot were checking the instruments.
3. Signs warning passengers not to smoke and to fasten their seat belts flashed on.
4. Directly beneath the signs was a door leading to the pilot's compartment.
5. Altogether there were about sixty passengers on the plane.
6. In a few moments the plane moved, slowly at first, and then roared into life.
7. After taxiing out to the airstrip, the pilot hesitated a moment to check the runway.
8. Then with a sudden rush of speed the plane roared down the runway and gradually began to climb.
9. Below us, at the edge of the airport, were markers and signal lights.
10. The football field and the quarter mile track enabled me to identify the high school.

(4) Complements

Some verbs, called INTRANSITIVE verbs, require nothing to complete them; that is, in themselves they make a full assertion about the subject.

After meeting all the relatives, my cousin ***left.***
In a heavy rain, cabbage ***may explode.***

TRANSITIVE verbs, however, are incomplete by themselves. If one says only "I bought," the reader is left hanging in mid-air and is apt to ask "What did you buy?" Words which answer such a question, and thus complete the assertion, are called *complements* of the verb.

subject	*verb*	*complement*
I	bought	a scarf.

The commonest type of complement is the DIRECT OBJECT of a transitive verb, illustrated in the sentence above. The direct object is usually a noun or pronoun, though it may be a phrase or a clause, and it usually names the thing acted upon by the subject.

subject	*verb*	*direct object*
My niece	built	a water clock.
They	chased	the soccer ball.

The easiest way to identify a direct object is to say the simple subject and verb and then ask the question "What?" My niece built what? The answer *clock*, is the direct object of the verb *built*. Note that the direct object may be compound.

subject	*verb*	*direct object*
I	borrowed	a tent, a sleeping bag, and a gas stove.

In addition to a direct object, certain verbs (usually involving an act of giving or telling), may take an INDIRECT OBJECT, a complement that receives whatever is named by the direct object. Consider the sentence "The Constitution grants us certain rights." What does the Constitution grant? *Rights* is the direct object. Who receives them? *Us* is the indirect object—the receiver of what is named by the direct object. Note that the same meaning could be expressed by a phrase beginning with *to* or *for:*

The Constitution grants certain rights ***to us.***
I told ***her*** a lie = I told a lie ***to her.***
I wrote ***him*** a check = I wrote a check ***for him.***

Linking verbs, or copulative verbs, sometimes require a SUBJECTIVE COMPLEMENT, a word which completes the predicate by giving another name for the subject, or by describing the subject. In the sentence "Floyd is the clerk," *clerk* cannot be called the direct object since it is merely another name for Floyd, and it can be made the subject of the sentence without changing the meaning: "The clerk is Floyd." (Contrast "Floyd fired the clerk," in which the direct object, *clerk*, names another person, who is acted upon by Floyd. Making *clerk* the subject of this sentence changes the meaning entirely.) A noun which serves as a subjective complement of a linking verb is usually called a PREDICATE NOUN.

Linking verbs may also be completed by an adjective which describes the subject. Such a subjective complement is called a PREDICATE ADJECTIVE.

The concert was ***routine*** and ***unimaginative.***

Routine and *unimaginative* describe concert, but instead of being directly attached to the noun ("a routine, unimaginative concert"), they are joined to it by the linking verb *was* and become predicate adjectives.

Exercise 2

Pick out the subjects and verbs in the following sentences. Identify direct objects, indirect objects, predicate nouns, and predicate adjectives.

1. As a wedding present, my uncle gave us a picture.
2. It was an original sketch by Dufy.
3. The technique was interesting, since Dufy had used only a few simple lines.
4. It seemed an early work, according to a friend to whom I showed it.
5. We hung it in the living room and it looked good.
6. I wrote my uncle a note and thanked him for the picture.
7. We enjoyed it for several months, until my friend told us its value.
8. Then we worried about burglars, and we wrote my uncle again asking if he would give us a less valuable picture.

(5) Phrases

A group of words may have the same function in a sentence as a single word. For example, in the sentence "The train to Boston leaves in ten minutes," the group of words *in ten minutes* modifies the verb *leaves* in exactly the same way as an adverb like *soon.* Similarly, *to Boston* functions like an adjective: it describes and identifies *train.* Such groups of words, which do not make a complete statement but which function like a single word, are called PHRASES. Phrases may be named for the kind of word around which they are constructed—prepositional, participial, gerund, or infinitive. Or they may be named by the way they function in a sentence—as adjective, adverb, or noun phrases. *To Boston* in the sentence above is a prepositional phrase used as an adjective.

Prepositional Phrases

A PREPOSITION is a word which, by connecting a noun or pronoun (its object) to the rest of the sentence, forms a modifying phrase. Prepositions are good examples of what linguists call "structure words": that is, their primary function is to hold structures together, rather than to convey lexical meaning. More specifically, they produce PREPOSITIONAL PHRASES, which function as modifiers. The following are prepositions in phrases:

> an agreement ***between us,*** a motel ***in New Orleans,*** a piece ***of paper,*** slid ***under the table,*** walked ***for an hour,*** try ***with all my strength.***

Some of the most common prepositions are *of, by, with, at, in, on, to, for, between, through, from.* Prepositional phrases usually modify nouns or verbs, and they are accordingly described as adjective or adverb phrases.

> *adjective* / *adverb*
> The lyrics ***in the musical*** were written ***by Stephen Smith.***

Verbals and Verbal Phrases

A VERBAL is a verb form used as some other part of speech. *Fishing* may be used as part of a verb in a construction like "We were fishing for perch," but it may also be used as an adjective, to modify a noun: "a fishing rod." A verbal which modifies a noun is called a PARTICIPLE. Note that a participle may be in the past tense, as well as in the present—"a *used* car with *cracking*, *worn* upholstery." When a verb form ending in *ing* is used as a noun, it is called a GERUND: "Hunting is his hobby." In this sentence, *hunting* is the subject of the sentence. Gerunds may also be used as the objects of verbs or of prepositions.

> *obj. of verb* / *obj. of prep.*
> He loves ***hunting*** and supports himself by ***training*** dogs.

One other type of verbal is common: the INFINITIVE. This is the ordinary form of the verb preceded by the preposition *to* (to run, to see). Infinitives are frequently used as nouns—as subject or object of a verb.

> *subject* / *object*
> ***To win*** is his chief concern, and he hates ***to lose.***

Since they are verb forms, participles, gerunds, and infinitives may take objects and they may be modified by adverbs or by prepositional phrases. A verbal with its modifier and its object, or subject, makes up a verbal phrase and functions as a single part of speech, but it does not make a full statement.

PARTICIPIAL PHRASE ***Flying some strange foreign flag,*** a ship was entering the harbor.

Here the participle "flying," *with its object and the modifiers of the object, describes* "ship."

GERUND PHRASE ***Scaling a long slippery barracuda*** takes strong hands.

Here the phrase—gerund, object, and the modifiers of the object—is the subject of the sentence.

INFINITIVE PHRASE The rules required us ***to arrive at 7:30.***

The infinitive has a subject, "us," *and a modifying prepositional phrase,* "at 7:30."

Absolute Phrases

An ABSOLUTE PHRASE consists of a participle with a subject (and sometimes a complement) grammatically unconnected with the rest of the sentence but usually telling when, why, or how something happened.

The floodwater having receded, people began returning to their homes.
I hated to leave home, ***circumstances being as they were.***

Appositive Phrases

An APPOSITIVE is another name for something already indicated—a noun added to explain another noun: "Helen Fitzgerald, *the novelist,* was guest speaker." Appositives with their modifiers make up phrases, since they function as a unit to give further information about a noun.

APPOSITIVE PHRASE Her subject was "Male Chauvinism," ***a surprising choice for that audience.***

Note that appositives are ordinarily set off by commas. For exceptions, see page 132.

Exercise 3

Pick out the phrases in the following sentences. Identify them as prepositional, participial, gerund, infinitive, or appositive, and be ready to describe their function in the sentence.

1. On Tuesday I came home expecting to drive my car, a shiny new convertible, into the garage.
2. To my surprise, I found a ditch between the street and the driveway.
3. A crew of men had begun to lay a new water main along the curb.
4. Hoping that I would not get a ticket for overnight parking, I left the car in the street in front of the house.
5. For three days a yawning trench separated me from my garage.
6. Finding a place to park was difficult, since all the neighbors on my side of the street were in the same predicament.
7. By Friday the workmen had filled up the ditch, but my car, stained with dust and dew, looked ten years older.
8. I had to spend the weekend washing and polishing it.
9. My wife, a strong advocate of justice, suggested sending the city a bill for the job.
10. My refusal convinced her that men are illogical, improvident, and easily imposed upon.

(6) Clauses

Any group of words which makes a statement—that is, which contains a subject and a predicate—is called a CLAUSE. Except for elliptical questions and answers, every sentence must contain at least one clause.

Independent and Dependent Clauses

Though all sentences must contain a clause, not all clauses are sentences. Some clauses, instead of making an independent statement, serve only as a subordinate part of the main sentence. Such clauses, called DEPENDENT or SUBORDINATE, perform a function like that of adjectives, adverbs, or nouns. INDEPENDENT CLAUSES, on the other hand, are capable of standing alone as complete sentences. They provide the framework to which modifiers, phrases, and dependent clauses are attached in each sentence. Any piece of connected discourse is made up of a series of independent clauses.

"While I was sitting on the steps" is a clause, since it contains a subject, *I*, and a verb, *was sitting*. But it is a dependent clause; in meaning it is incomplete (what happened?) and it would normally be used as a modifier. Its purpose is to tell *when* something happened, and the complete sentence should state what did happen.

dependent clause	*independent clause*
While I was sitting on the steps,	I heard a siren.

A dependent clause is usually connected to the rest of the sentence by a relative pronoun (*who, which,* or *that*) or by conjunctions like *while, although, as, because, if, since, when,* or *where.* These are called SUBORDINATING CONJUNCTIONS because they introduce clauses which are elements of a sentence rather than independent statements. Notice how the addition of a subordinating conjunction to an independent clause makes the clause dependent. Here are two independent clauses, each a complete sentence:

independent clause	*independent clause*
We stayed home.	It was beginning to snow.

Adding the subordinating conjunction *because* makes the second clause dependent; written as a separate sentence, "because it was beginning to snow" would be a fragment. If joined to the preceding clause, however, it modifies the verb *stayed,* giving the reason for our staying.

independent clause	*conj. & dependent clause*
We stayed home	***because*** it was beginning to snow.

In sentences dependent clauses are used like nouns (as subjects or objects) or as modifiers, like adverbs and adjectives.

Noun Clauses

A NOUN CLAUSE functions as a noun in a sentence. It may be a subject or a complement in the main clause, the object of a preposition or of a gerund.

NOUN CLAUSE ***That he couldn't jump twenty-two feet*** was obvious.
The noun clause is used as the subject of the sentence.

NOUN CLAUSE He said ***that he could jump only twenty feet.***
The noun clause is used as the direct object of the verb "said."

NOUN CLAUSE Sell it to ***whoever will buy it.***
The noun clause is used as the object of the preposition "to."

NOUN CLAUSE Keep out of trouble by doing ***what comes naturally.***
The noun clause is used as the object of the gerund "doing."

Adverb Clauses

An ADVERB CLAUSE is a dependent clause used to modify a verb or an adjective or an adverb in the main clause.

ADVERB CLAUSE We ate ***whenever we felt like it.***
"Whenever we felt like it" modifies the verb "ate."

ADVERB CLAUSE The trip was as pleasant ***as we had hoped.***
The clause "as we had hoped" modifies the adjective "pleasant."

ADVERB CLAUSE The train arrived sooner ***than we had expected.***
The clause "than we had expected" modifies the adverb "sooner."

Adjective Clauses and Relative Pronouns

A dependent clause used to modify a noun or pronoun is called an ADJECTIVE CLAUSE.

ADJECTIVE CLAUSE The salesman ***we met yesterday*** showed us his library, ***which includes all the first editions of Dorothy Sayers.***
The adjective clause "we met yesterday" modifies the noun "salesman"; the adjective clause "which includes all the first editions of Dorothy Sayers" modifies the noun "library."

Adjective clauses are usually introduced by a RELATIVE PRONOUN, which serves both as a pronoun and as a subordinating conjunction. Its function can be seen by some examples.

Ken was a leader; Ken never failed us.

This sentence consists of two independent clauses, but it would be more idiomatic to substitute a pronoun for the second "Ken."

Ken was a leader; ***he*** never failed us.

If, instead of using the personal pronoun *he,* we substitute the relative pronoun *who,* the second clause becomes dependent.

Ken was a leader ***who*** never failed us.

"Who never failed us" no longer will stand as an independent sentence; but when it is joined to the first clause, it functions as an adjective, modifying *leader.*

The relative pronouns *who* (and *whom*), *which,* and *that* always have two functions: they serve as subordinating conjunctions, connecting dependent clauses to independent ones, but they also function like nouns, as subject or complement in the dependent clause. Often the relative pronouns can be omitted: "I received the book [*which, that*] I ordered."

Exercise 4

Find the simple subject and verb of each clause in the following sentences. Point out the main clauses and the dependent clauses, and be prepared to state the function in each sentence of each dependent clause.

1. The movie director who did much to perfect the one-reel Western as a distinct genre was D. W. Griffith.
2. Shortly after he had entered movies in New York, Griffith achieved immediate success with his first film, which he directed in 1908.
3. Between 1908 and 1913, while he was directing Westerns, Griffith continually worked with techniques which, though they had been introduced by others, were developed and refined by him.
4. Griffith was delighted by the Western because it offered opportunities for spectacle and scope.
5. He found that the Western was an ideal genre in which to experiment with close-ups and with cross-cutting, the techniques he employed to build narrative suspense.
6. Some critics have pointed out that Griffith was more interested in dramatic situations which lent themselves to lively visual treatment than he was in the details of plot or conventional justice.
7. He would willingly let the villains go free whenever he felt the dramatic situation warranted it.
8. The close-up of the outnumbered settlers grimly hanging on and the panoramic view of the battle seen from afar were characteristic Griffith shots.
9. In 1915, Griffith produced *The Birth of a Nation,* the first great spectacle movie.
10. It made use of many of the techniques he had developed while he was making one-reel Westerns.

1b Types of Sentences

Sentences are traditionally classified, according to their structure, as simple, complex, compound, and compound-complex.

(1) Simple Sentences

A SIMPLE SENTENCE consists of one independent clause, with *no* dependent clauses attached, although it may have modifying phrases.

SIMPLE The *[subject]* children hurriedly *[verb]* left for school.

SIMPLE *[mod. phrase]* Slumped in the bottom of a skiff, *[subj.]* I *[verb]* floated peacefully along.

Simple sentences are not necessarily short and jerky, but their overuse is apt to make one's writing seem both choppy and childish. So-called "primer" style is caused by a succession of short simple sentences. The remedy is to combine some of them into complex sentences.

(2) Complex Sentences

The COMPLEX SENTENCE contains one independent clause and one or more dependent clauses, which express subordinate ideas.

COMPLEX *[independent clause]* We lost touch with the Carters *[dependent clause]* after they moved.

COMPLEX *[ind. clause]* He was a man *[dependent clause]* who had many close friends.

COMPLEX *[dependent clause]* Although the spray contained endrin, *[dependent clause]* which may harm people, *[independent clause]* she used the poison on tomato plants.

The complex sentence has the advantage of flexibility; it can be arranged to produce a variety of sentence patterns. It also provides selective emphasis, since the subordination of dependent clauses throws the weight of the sentence on the main clause.

(3) Compound Sentences

The COMPOUND SENTENCE consists of two or more independent clauses.

	ind. clause		*ind. clause*
COMPOUND	He notified the office,	and	the manager corrected the error.

	ind. clause		*ind. clause*
COMPOUND	This sentence is compound	;	it has two main clauses.

(4) Compound-complex Sentences

When a compound sentence contains dependent clauses, the whole is sometimes described as a COMPOUND-COMPLEX SENTENCE.

COMPOUND-COMPLEX

dependent clause
Although the critics gave it good reviews,

independent clause
the play never attracted the public, and

independent clause
the producers closed it reluctantly after two weeks

dependent clause
because they could not afford the losses.

Exercise 5

Classify the following sentences as simple, compound, complex, or compound-complex. Identify the subject, verb, and complement, if any, of each clause. Describe the function of each dependent clause.

1. When Renaissance physicians began to study human anatomy by means of actual dissection, they concluded that the human body had changed since the days of antiquity.
2. Galen, an ancient Greek physician, was generally accepted as the authority on anatomy and physiology.
3. His theory of the four humors, blood, phlegm, bile, and black bile, was neat and logical, and authorities had accepted it for centuries.
4. Similarly, his account of the structure of the human body, revised by generations of scholars and appearing in many printed editions, was generally accepted.
5. If dissection showed a difference from Galen's account, the obvious explanation was that human structure had changed since Galen's time.

6. One man who refused to accept this explanation was Andreas Vesalius, a young Belgian physician who was studying in Italy.
7. Asked to edit the anatomical section of Galen's works, Vesalius found many errors in it.
8. Galen's statement that the lower jaw consisted of two parts seemed wrong to Vesalius, who had never found such a structure in his own dissections.
9. He finally concluded that Galen was describing the anatomy of lower animals—pigs, monkeys, and goats—and that he had never dissected a human body.
10. When he realized that Galen could be wrong, Vesalius began a study which came to be recognized as his major work: a fully illustrated treatise on the human body based on actual observation.

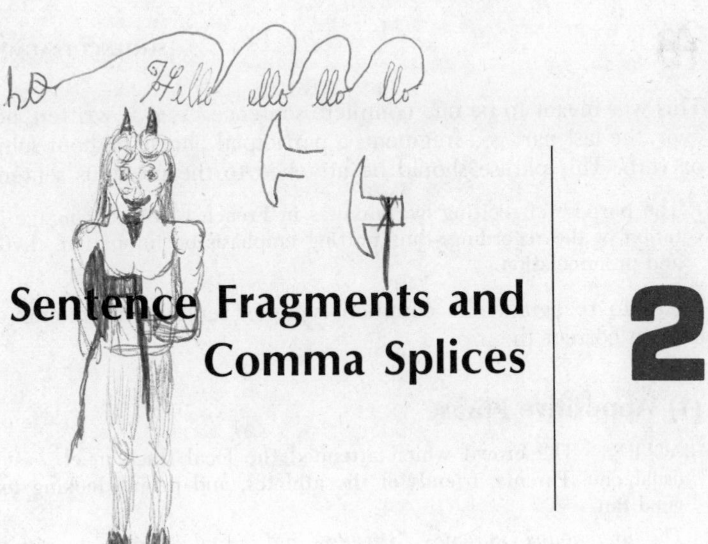

Sentence Fragments and Comma Splices 2

To correct fragments and comma splices, you must be able to recognize them, either by their sound, or "feel", when the sentence is read aloud, or by analysis of sentence structure. For the latter method, study Chapter 1 carefully. To get the feel for complete sentences, read your sentences aloud, listening to their accents, pitch, and rhythm. For example, say this sentence aloud. Notice that you pause after *example* and that you end the sentence by lowering the pitch of the last syllable of *aloud.* Try it on other sentences in this paragraph, making yourself notice how you say them.

2a Types of Sentence Fragments

A careless writer, putting the period in too soon, may seriously mislead the reader by cutting off a piece of the full sentence. If the piece does not contain an independent clause, a clause which can stand by itself as a complete sentence, the result is a *sentence fragment.* For example:

> The purpose of reciting five minutes in French was to encourage imitation of the recording. **Thus putting emphasis on intonation, rhythm, and pronunciation.**

This was meant to be one complete sentence. As it is written, however, the last part is a fragment, a participial phrase without subject or verb. This phrase should be attached to the previous sentence:

> The purpose of reciting five minutes in French was to encourage imitation of the recording, thus putting emphasis on intonation, rhythm, and pronunciation.

Learn to recognize the common types of sentence fragments and how to correct them.

(1) Appositive Phrase

FRAGMENT The crowd which attended the local track meet was the usual one. **Parents, friends of the athletes, and people looking for a good tan.**

The three nouns "parents," "friends," and "people" are in apposition to "one," and the appositive phrase should be attached to the rest of the sentence.

CORRECTED The crowd which attended the local track meet was the usual one—parents, friends of the athletes, and people looking for a good tan.

(2) Prepositional Phrase

FRAGMENT The receptionist was expected to appear efficient and serene, but it was impossible. **With the telephone ringing constantly and clients arriving every half hour for appointments.**

CORRECTED The receptionist was expected to appear efficient and serene, but it was impossible with the telephone ringing constantly and clients arriving every half hour for appointments.

The prepositional phrase beginning with "With" *modifies* "impossible" *and should be attached to it. Or the phrase might be made into an independent clause and written as a separate sentence.*

CORRECTED The receptionist was expected to appear efficient and serene, but it was impossible. The telephone rang constantly and clients arrived every half hour for appointments.

(3) Participial Phrase

FRAGMENT I was surprised at the commotion in the magazine's office. Reporters, copywriters, and secretaries were rushing all over the place.

Running up and down the aisles, conferring with the editors, and talking in little groups.

Running, conferring, *and* talking *are participles parallel in structure with* rushing; *that is, they are part of the first sentence and should be attached to it.*

CORRECTED I was surprised at the commotion in the magazine's office. Reporters, copywriters, and secretaries were rushing all over the place, running up and down the aisles, conferring with the editors, and talking in little groups.

FRAGMENT She had good reason for coming to college and choosing the one she did, unlike some of her classmates. **Having planned for several years to become a doctor.**

CORRECTED Unlike some of her classmates, she had good reason for coming to college and choosing the one she did, having planned for several years to become a doctor.

(4) Infinitive Phrase

FRAGMENT After a good deal of arguing, I finally received permission from my parents. **To work for Project Head Start that summer and perhaps even during the fall semester.**

CORRECTED After a good deal of arguing, I finally received permission from my parents to work for Project Head Start that summer and perhaps even during the fall semester.

(5) Dependent Clause

FRAGMENT The first car was trying to get far enough ahead to pull off safely. **While the second car kept close in an effort to pass.**

CORRECTED The first car was trying to get far enough ahead to pull off safely, while the second car kept close in an effort to pass.

Note that the fragment could have been corrected by omitting the conjunction "while" and making two complete sentences.

FRAGMENT After so many weeks of worrying, I was grateful to learn of the college's loan funds. **Because I didn't know where I could turn for help or see how I could take a part-time job.**

CORRECTED After so many weeks of worrying, I was grateful to learn of the college's loan funds because I didn't know where I could turn for help or see how I could take a part-time job.

Usually the best way to correct a sentence fragment is to join it to the sentence of which it is logically a part. Sometimes, however, it is better to change the fragment into a full sentence, by adding a verb, a subject, or whatever else is lacking.

2b Permissible Incomplete Sentences

Certain elliptical expressions are equivalent to sentences because the missing words are clearly understood. Such permissible incomplete sentences include the following:

(1) Questions and Answers in Conversation

Why not?	Because it's late.
How much?	Two dollars.

(2) Exclamations and Requests

At last!
This way, please.

(3) Transitions

So much for the first point.
Now to consider the next question.

In addition, fragments are sometimes deliberately used for particular effects, especially in narrative or descriptive writing. In most expository writing, however, there is seldom occasion or excuse for writing fragmentary sentences.

ACCEPTABLE He watched the needle swing rhythmically from one side of the dial to the other. Back and forth. Over and over. Beginning to get sleepy.

Exercise 1

For each of the following sentences, identify the cause of the fragment and correct it in whatever way seems most effective.

1. When you really get down to it, homework is more likely to be assigned in the academic subjects. Whether they are English, math, science, or some language.
2. One thing which I dislike very much is a person with a mean streak. A person who will go out of his way to do harm to others.
3. During the day the eel lies buried in the mud or concealed under rocks or in seaweed. But at night begins its prowling for food.
4. As this summary indicates, the first part of the story is deceiving. So far, just another tale about a college boy—maybe the all-American ideal—who gets his girl and job and is living on easy street.
5. For some people, life is only boring or painful. Especially if the person has no purpose, no goal in life.
6. The number of the very rich and the very poor having been reduced, leaving most Americans in one large middle class.
7. I now think that my high school was too progressive in some ways. Meaning that it didn't teach how to read and write correctly.
8. The head librarian threatened to close the stacks to all students. Because the cost of replacing stolen books was mounting each year.
9. Tyrone Guthrie's movie production of *Oedipus Rex* was very impressive. Although it took me a while to get used to the masked actors.
10. The City Council's decision to limit speed on a road in the campus but not on a street near an elementary school seemed ridiculous. Since small children are less able to cross streets responsibly.
11. Long hours of practice after classes, the weekends usually taken up with games, and most evenings spent in study. Athletes have little time for working their way through college.
12. Historians are interested only in the more civilized societies that have existed in the past. The ones that have produced great works of art, science, or technology.
13. Every month, the entire research staff spends a full day together in informal conference. To discuss at length current problems and propose and criticize new ideas.
14. A description of being lost in the Grand Canyon when Schuyler's life was saved by a discarded semi-rotten orange.
15. The distance between the stars is immense. So immense that it is difficult to find a unit of measurement which will help one grasp it imaginatively.

2c Correcting Comma Splices

Do not join two main clauses with only a comma between them (comma splice).

COMMA SPLICE I'm sure that the teen-agers of today didn't invent cheating, it must have been going on for quite a long time.

A comma splice (sometimes called a "comma fault") is two or more independent clauses separated *only* by a comma. The result can be either a misreading, as in

I wonder if he is thinking, he probably won't tell.

or a failure to show clear sequence and relationship, as in

There was an extremely heavy rain on Monday night, after the storm was over, the streams were overflowing.

You can catch many comma splices in revision by reading your paper aloud: if you drop your voice or pause conspicuously at a comma, check the sentence to see if it is two separate statements.

To correct a comma splice, you have several alternatives. Some illustrations follow.

(1) Subordination of One Main Clause

Correct the comma splice by subordinating one of the main clauses. The commonest subordinating conjunctions include *because, which, since.*

COMMA SPLICE The banks were closed, John couldn't get the necessary money.

SUBORDINATION ***Since*** the banks were closed, John couldn't get the necessary money.

COMMA SPLICE There are many good reasons for working in the summer, only a few of them can be discussed.

SUBORDINATION There are many good reasons for working in the summer, only a few ***of which*** can be discussed.

or

SUBORDINATION ***Of*** the many good reasons for working in the summer, only a few can be discussed.

(2) Coordination of Clauses by Conjunction

Correct the comma splice by using a coordinating conjunction to join the two main clauses if you want to give them equal emphasis.

COMMA SPLICE We will add another room to the house this summer**,** painting will have to wait until next year.

COORDINATION We will add another room to the house this summer, ***but*** painting will have to wait until next year.

COMMA SPLICE Reading is partly a matter of personal taste**,** every reviewer ought to keep this fact in mind.

COORDINATION Reading is partly a matter of personal taste, ***and*** every reviewer ought to keep this fact in mind.

The most usual pattern is the coordinating conjunction (*and, but, for, nor, or*) preceded by a comma. When long, complex clauses punctuated internally by commas are joined, a semicolon along with a coordinating conjunction may be needed to show the main division of the sentence.

COMMA SPLICE As the development of the atomic bomb, the computer systems, and guided missiles shows, technology, indeed basic scientific research itself, is often determined by political and military considerations**,** many people do not recognize this interdependence and instead regard changes in technology as changes which simply "happen."

COORDINATION As the development of the atomic bomb, the computer systems, and guided missiles shows, technology, indeed basic scientific research itself, is often determined by political and military considerations**;** ***but*** many people do not recognize this interdependence and instead regard changes in technology as changes which simply "happen."

(3) Coordination of Clauses by Semicolon

Correct the comma splice by using a semicolon to join the two main clauses. This method is appropriate when the relationship between the two statements is to be implied, rather than stated explicitly.

COMMA SPLICE Gambling is like a drug**,** after a while the gambler finds it impossible to stop.

CORRECTED BY SEMICOLON Gambling is like a drug**;** after a while the gambler finds it impossible to stop.

(4) Separation of Clauses into Sentences

Correct the comma splice by making each main clause into a sentence. Use this method if you want to emphasize the separation between the two statements.

COMMA SPLICE There was an extremely heavy rain on Monday night, after the storm had passed, the streams were overflowing.

TWO SENTENCES There was an extremely heavy rain on Monday night. After the storm had passed, the streams were overflowing.

(5) Commas with Short Independent Clauses

Commas without conjunctions may be used between short independent clauses for special effects or emphasis. Short, closely related independent clauses in a series are occasionally joined only by commas. Such punctuation is often used in narratives, more sparingly in expository writing.

ACCEPTABLE The wind blew, the shutters banged, the children trembled.

(6) Semicolon with Conjunctive Adverbs

Two main clauses linked by a conjunctive adverb require a semicolon or a period between them. One of the commonest forms of the comma splice is the use of the comma between two main clauses linked by a conjunctive adverb. Such conjunctive adverbs as *also, besides, hence, however, instead, moreover, then,* and *therefore* should be preceded by a semicolon or period when they introduce a second independent clause.

COMMA SPLICE I hadn't read the test very carefully, therefore I was surprised that I had done so well on it.

CORRECTED I hadn't read the test very carefully; therefore I was surprised that I had done so well on it.

COMMA SPLICE To a majority of the economists a gloomy forecast seemed inevitable, however three of the experts were unfashionably cheerful.

CORRECTED To a majority of the economists a gloomy forecast seemed inevitable; however, three of the experts were unfashionably cheerful.

Omitting the semicolon or period before the conjunctive adverb can result in grotesque misreading.

The sergeant had command of his temper and his men, also the general who was reviewing that day was in a good mood.

One way to tell a conjunctive adverb from a pure conjunction is to try to change its position in the sentence. A conjunctive adverb need not stand first in its clause:

We had been told to stay at home; **moreover,** we knew that we were not allowed to play outside after dark.

We had been told to stay at home; we knew, **moreover,** that we were not . . .

A pure conjunction will fit into the sentence only at the beginning of its clause:

We had been told to stay at home, **and** we knew . . .

2d Fused Sentences

Do not fuse two main clauses by omitting all punctuation between them.

FUSED SENTENCE He took the job he was offered otherwise he would have had to borrow more money.

The fused sentence is a more blatant error than the comma splice since it often results in serious misreadings. To correct a fused sentence, use any of the means for correcting the comma splice.

REWRITTEN To avoid borrowing money, he took the job he was offered.

CORRECTED He took the job he was offered**;** otherwise he would have had to borrow more money.

FUSED SENTENCE Congress passed the bill only after long hours of debate there was strong feeling on both sides.

CORRECTED Congress passed the bill only after long hours of debate. There was strong feeling on both sides.

Exercise 2

In the following sentences, revise the comma splices or fused sentences by whatever means seems most effective. Be prepared to explain the reasons for the means you choose.

2d

EXERCISE

1. On most report cards there is a special place for marking effort, this is put there so that the teacher can show how hard a student has tried.
2. I obeyed my elders, but I always weighed the facts and formed my own judgments, apparently this independence of mine made some adults angry.
3. But why shouldn't carols be played in shops and stores, it's all in the spirit of Christmas.
4. But Huck doesn't pray, instead he thinks of all the times that Jim has been good to him.
5. Once in her room she did a few dance steps, looked at her unmade bed, and shrugged unconcernedly, then she glanced out the window in hopes of catching sight of her little brother.
6. But with the first of September the warm days were over, cold winds began to blow, stirring up freshly turned dirt in the graveyard and causing old Charles to cast apprehensive glances at the sky.
7. Ironically, the population migration has been especially great to places like Arizona, New Mexico, and Southern California, these are places with a limited water supply.
8. There was a long string of gas stations outside the city, any driver could fill up easily.
9. We found the sea too choppy for sailing or swimming, we stayed on shore.
10. Permission was not granted for the interview, however the reporters never gave up hope.
11. The new dictionary was more than a revision of the old one, the compilers had redefined each entry and included many more examples of usage.
12. The critic wrote that as the commercials became longer and more offensive, the shows became shorter and more innocuous, also she felt advertisers ought to be forced to watch the commericals.
13. In speech class he announced he would give a demonstration-lecture on how not to pack a suitcase, after he was finished, the other students clapped reluctantly.
14. The counselor gathered the paddles, came down to the pier, and untied the canoe then he waited while the campers climbed in.
15. The medical insurance was cheap and comprehensive, according to its advertisers, the people who bought it soon claimed otherwise.

3 Coherent Sentences

A sentence is coherent when its various parts are properly connected and when the relationships between the parts are clear to a reader. To the writer, who knows what is being said, the parts of a sentence always seem to be connected. To the reader, however, implied connections may not always be clear. Lacking the writer's advantage of knowing the meaning in advance, the reader may be baffled by ambiguous reference of pronouns, by misplaced or dangling modifiers, by needless shifts in tense, and by faulty parallel construction. At the very least, he will be irritated by incoherent sentences; at worst, he will misunderstand them.

The time to check sentences for coherence is in revision. Ask yourself, "Could this sentence be misread or misunderstood?" instead of just hoping that someone will understand it. If there is any doubt, revise the sentence.

3a Parallel Structure

When the parts of a sentence are properly connected, any native speaker of the language will recognize the pattern as acceptable. We are used to having nouns connected by *and:* "bacon and eggs" or "bacon, eggs, and a waffle," where the *and* is implied between the first two elements of the series. Likewise, three prepositional phrases in a series is a normal pattern: "of the people, by the people, and for the people."

Elements in this kind of series pattern or any two elements properly connected by *and* have the same grammatical function and are said to be in parallel construction. A noun phrase can be parallel with another noun phrase; a subordinate clause can parallel another subordinate clause, but not a participle. John Ruskin lists the qualities required of great art in four subordinate clauses:

> For as
>
> (1) the choice of the high subject involves all conditions of right moral choice, and as
> (2) the love of beauty involves all conditions of right admiration, and as
> (3) the grasp of truth involves all strength of sense, evenness of judgment, and honesty of purpose, and as
> (4) the poetical power involves all swiftness of invention, and accuracy of the historical memory,
>
> the sum of all these powers is the sum of the human soul.

We use parallel structure constantly in our speech, joining two or more compound (that is, parallel) verbs or adjectives or phrases or clauses by one of the coordinating conjunctions, most often *and.* A single sentence can contain many kinds of parallel structure; note the parallel noun phrases within clauses (3) and (4) of Ruskin's statement.

(1) Coordinating Conjunctions

Sentence elements jointed by the coordinating conjunctions *and, or, nor, but* should be in parallel grammatical structure.

FAULTY He likes to swim in the summer and skiing in the winter.

Here an infinitive is incorrectly paralleled with a gerund.

PARALLEL He likes ***to swim*** in the summer and ***to ski*** in the winter. *Or* He likes ***swimming*** in the summer and ***skiing*** in the winter.

FAULTY Every player is taught to work with the team and that good sportsmanship must be shown.

Here and *joins an infinitive phrase and a subordinate clause beginning with* that.

PARALLEL Every player is taught ***to work*** with the team and ***to show*** good sportsmanship.

(2) Elements in a Series

Faulty parallelism of elements in a series is one of the commonest faults in coherence.

FAULTY I concluded that she was intelligent, witty, and liked to make people uncomfortable.

The first two elements are adjectives: the second is a predicate—a verb with an infinitive phrase as a complement.

The faulty parallelism can be corrected by making all three elements adjectives:

PARALLEL I concluded that she was intelligent, witty, and malicious.

Or the sentence can be corrected by inserting another "and" to make clear which elements parallel which.

PARALLEL I concluded that she was intelligent ***and*** witty and liked to make people uncomfortable.

FAULTY Harrison signed up as the camp counselor in charge of evening programs, swimming, sailing, and to lead occasional overnight hikes.

PARALLEL Harrison signed up as the camp counselor in charge of evening programs, swimming, sailing, and occasional overnight hikes.

(3) Repetition of Words

To make a parallel construction clear, you may need to repeat a conjunction, preposition, or other preceding word.

FAULTY The advisor told the girl that she spent far too much time in useless fretting and she needed confidence in herself.

The omission of "that" to introduce the second subordinate clause causes misreading.

PARALLEL The advisor told the girl ***that*** she spent far too much time in useless fretting ***and that*** she needed confidence in herself.

FAULTY Frank needed Elaine because she was his reminder of his past glory and she would also help get him into the right circles through her family.

PARALLEL Frank needed Elaine ***because*** she was his reminder of his past glory ***and because*** she would also help him get into the right circles through her family.

FAULTY The vineyard is often visited by tourists who sample the grapes and connoisseurs of wine.

PARALLEL The vineyard is often visited ***by*** tourists who sample the grapes ***and by*** connoisseurs of wine.

(4) Correlatives

Some conjunctions, called correlatives, occur in pairs: *either . . . or, neither . . . nor, not only . . . but also, both . . . and.* Be sure to place the first correlative so that the construction which follows will parallel the construction following the second correlative. That is, if you write "James is not only ......*a*...... but also ......*b*......," be sure that *a* and *b* are in parallel structure.

FAULTY Blake is not only famous for his poetry but also for his illustrations.

"Not only" is followed by the adjective "famous" with a prepositional phrase modifying it. "But also" is followed by a prepositional phrase. Correct this by moving "not only."

PARALLEL Blake is famous ***not only*** for his poetry ***but also*** for his illustrations.

FAULTY He either is a liar or a remarkably naive person.

PARALLEL He is either a liar or a remarkably naive person.

FAULTY The Legislature hoped both to raise taxes and stimulate business.

Placing "both" after "to" would make the two verbs parallel but it would produce an awkward split construction: "to both raise . . ." A smoother sentence would result from adding another "to."

IMPROVED The Legislature hoped both to raise taxes and to stimulate business.

(5) Subordinate Clauses

A subordinate clause should not be connected to its main clause by *and* or *but.*

FAULTY She is a woman of strong convictions and who always says what she thinks.

This error can be corrected either by omitting the coordinating conjunction:

CORRECT She is a woman of strong convictions, who always says what she thinks.

or by writing two subordinate clauses:

PARALLEL She is a woman who has strong convictions and who always says what she thinks.

FAULTY In the middle of the sleepy village is a statue dating from 1870 ***and which*** shows General Lee on horseback.

PARALLEL In the middle of the sleepy village is a statue ***which*** dates from 1870 ***and which*** shows General Lee on horseback.

FAULTY ***He*** appeared before the committee with a long written statement, ***but which*** he was not allowed to read.

CORRECT ***He*** appeared before the committee with a long written statement, ***but he*** was not allowed to read it.
Fault corrected by changing relative clause to a main clause.

(6) Sequence of Ideas

To be effective, elements in parallel structure should be parallel in sense. Used carelessly, parallel structure can lead to an illogical series or an awkward sequence of ideas.

INCOHERENT His slumping business, his friends, and even his wife Mary could in no way offer him a chance to find the happiness he had known while in college.
The three items are not parallel in meaning. A man might reasonably be expected to find a chance for happiness in those closest to him, his friends and his wife. But he would hardly be expected to find happiness in a "slumping business."

REVISED His friends and even his wife Mary could in no way offer him a chance to find the happiness he had known while in college.

MISLEADING During her last year in law school, she rose to the top of her class, worked on the legal review, and married the day after graduation.

REVISED During her last year in law school, she rose to the top of her class and worked on the legal review. She married the day after graduation.

Exercise 1

Revise the following sentences by giving parallel structure to coordinate ideas.

1. The bandleader told us to wear our uniforms next time and that we should expect a long rehearsal.
2. Among the primitive uses of fire were protection from wild animals and for preparing food.

3. When I was in grade school, my parents spent a lot of time on my homework with me, and then when I got to high school letting me do it myself.
4. The columnist argued that sports stars should be well paid because of their relatively short period of greatness and that they must achieve security for later on.
5. The congressman said we need comprehensive federal pollution laws to make enforcement easier and also for standardizing the regulations passed by individual states.

Exercise 2

Identify the cause of faulty parallelism in each of the following sentences and make the needed correction.

1. Applicants for the position must be United States citizens, willing to work abroad, and qualify under security regulations.
2. In the remedial reading clinic he learned how to coordinate his eye movements, how to scan for information, and how frequent reviewing for key ideas helps.
3. The opera's opening performance was spirited, colorful, and with many people attending.
4. During the summer, they planned to hitchhike along Route 40, to stop at interesting places, and take sidetrips whenever they felt like it.
5. John Brown was either regarded as a patriotic martyr or a crazed fanatic.
6. The flasks were difficult to fill, not only because their necks were narrow but also they were slippery and hard to hold.
7. The bumper crop of rice neither helped the farmer nor were the customers helped.
8. At the campground we met a Mr. Osborn from somewhere near San Francisco and who had his whole family with him.
9. And on these hunting trips, Sam teaches the boy when to kill and when not to, ability, patience, and endurance.
10. If you get ambitious, you might even shoot nine holes of golf from your new four-cylinder golf cart, or with your neighbor go bowling at that new air-conditioned alley, or you might even go and play miniature golf.

3b Faulty Reference of Pronouns

The antecedent of every pronoun—the person or thing to which the pronoun refers—should be immediately clear to the reader. Try to put yourself in the position of the person reading your sentences. If the pronoun is too far away from its antecedent, or if there are two possible antecedents, a reader may be uncertain of your meaning. Reading the first draft of a paper aloud may help you to catch pronouns with doubtful antecedents.

(1) Ambiguous Reference

Do not use a pronoun in such a way that it might refer to either of two antecedents. If there is any possibility of doubt, revise the sentence to remove the ambiguity.

AMBIGUOUS Virginia told her sister that she was unforgiving.
Who was unforgiving—Virginia or her sister?

CLEAR Virginia confessed to her sister, "I am unforgiving."

CLEAR Virginia said to her sister, "You are unforgiving."

AMBIGUOUS In *Nostromo* Conrad's style is ironic and his setting is highly symbolic, so that it sometimes confuses the reader.
Does "it" refer loosely to Nostromo, *Conrad's style, his setting, or a combination of these?*

CLEAR Conrad's ironic style and highly symbolic setting in *Nostromo* sometimes confuse the reader.

CLEAR In *Nostromo,* Conrad's style is ironic, and his highly symbolic setting sometimes confuses the reader.

(2) Remote Reference

A pronoun too far away from its antecedent may cause misreading. Either repeat the antecedent or revise the sentence.

REMOTE Two major highways converge at the sign, each lined with huge, ugly billboards rising above the corn stalks and obscuring the gently rolling hills. It is a convenient location for hitching rides.
The pronoun "it" is too far removed from its antecedent, "sign."

CLEAR Two major highways converge at the sign, each lined with huge . . . . The ***sign*** is a convenient location for hitching rides.
Antecedent repeated.

CLEAR Two major highways converge at the sign, a convenient location for hitching rides. Each highway is lined . . . .
The sentences have been recast.

REMOTE The waitress locked the door, slapped at the flies, and then sat down wearily to rest for a minute before cleaning up the litter. But they gave her no peace.
The antecedent, "flies," is too remote.

CLEAR The waitress locked the door, slapped at the flies . . . . ***But*** the ***flies*** gave her no peace.

CONFUSING The Tzotzil Indians are only nominal Catholics, using its symbols and adapting them to the traditional Mayan religion.
Antecedent of "its" has to be inferred from the noun "Catholics."

CLEAR The Tzotzil Indians are only nominal Catholics, using the symbols and names ***of the Church*** and adapting them . . . .

MISLEADING The botanist told us the plants' names which were all around us.

CLEAR The botanist told us the names of the ***plants which*** were all around us.

(3) Awkward Use of *his or her*

A problem arises from the fact that English has no singular pronoun to refer generically to both male and female persons. Strictly speaking, one would logically follow a noun like "student" with "his or her" or even "his/her," to indicate that the term "student" includes members of both sexes. But to write "Each student is responsible for his/her books," is awkward, and many people feel that even "his or her books" is repetitious.

In the past it has been accepted that the masculine pronoun can stand for both sexes: "Each student is responsible for his books," just as *man* has been understood to mean the human race, including both men and women. Recently, however, writers and publishers have begun to eliminate discriminatory language practices–words or constructions that may reflect the dominance of the male in western society. Women argue, with justice, that they are being ignored when a writer uses *his* to refer to both men and women, and many feel that terms like *congressman* or *policeman* help to perpetuate the false assumption that these positions are occupied only by men.

To avoid this, substitute alternative terms with no indication of gender, like *member of congress, representative* or *senator, police officer.* The plural pronouns *they, their, them* and neutral terms like *one, person, people* may also be used.

ACCEPTABLE Students are responsible for their books.
People in England like unchilled beer. (Instead of "The Englishman likes his beer unchilled.")
In England one usually drinks unchilled beer.

However, in order to avoid strained circumlocutions or awkward plurals, it may at times be preferable to use *his* to mean both his and hers, as it has done for centuries.

(4) Loose Use of *this, that,* or *which*

In informal usage, the relative pronouns *this, that,* and *which* are frequently used to refer to the whole idea of a preceding clause or sentence. In formal usage, these pronouns are usually expected to have a particular word as their antecedent. No hard and fast rules can be given here. Sometimes the broad reference is clear and a change would be awkward.

ACCEPTABLE BROAD REFERENCE The game ended a little before ten, which gave us plenty of time to catch our train home.

ACCEPTABLE BROAD REFERENCE At first glance, the desert seems completely barren of animal life, but this is an illusion.

Frequently, however, broad reference makes a sentence sound awkward. It may also be ambiguous if the preceding clause contains a noun which might be mistaken for the antecedent. If you are in doubt, recast the sentence to eliminate the pronoun or give the pronoun a definite antecedent.

LOOSE The beginning of the book is more interesting than the conclusion, which is very unfortunate.
On the first reading, the pronoun "which" seems to refer to "conclusion," although it is intended to refer to the whole main clause.

CLEAR Unfortunately, the beginning of the book is more interesting than the conclusion.
The misleading pronoun has been eliminated.

LOOSE In the eighteenth century, more and more land was converted into pasture, which had been going on to some extent for several centuries.

CLEAR In the eighteenth century, more and more land was converted into pasture, ***a process which*** had been going on to some extent for several centuries.

The vague reference has been corrected by the inclusion of the summarizing noun "process" to give the pronoun "which" an antecedent.

(5) Indefinite Use of *it, they,* and *you*

English contains a number of idiomatic expressions in which the impersonal use of the pronoun *it* is correct: "It is hot," "it rained all day," "it is late." The pronoun *it* is also used correctly in sentences like "It seems best to go home at once," in which *it* anticipates the real subject, *to go home at once.* Avoid, however, the unexplained *it,* the *it* that needs a clear antecedent and has none.

VAGUE Our neighbor was a semiprofessional golfer who took every spare moment he could get to practice ***it.***

CLEAR Our neighbor was a semiprofessional golfer who took every spare moment he could get to practice ***his game.***

The indefinite use of *they* is always vague and usually sounds childish.

VAGUE If intercollegiate sports were banned, they would have to develop an elaborate intramural program.

CLEAR If intercollegiate sports were banned, ***each college*** would have to develop an elaborate intramural program.

VAGUE They are finally beginning to pave the street outside our house.

CLEAR The street outside our house is finally being paved.

CLEAR The city is finally beginning to pave the street outside our house.

The indefinite use of the pronoun *you* to refer to people in general is widespread: "In Sparta you had to be strong to survive." Formal usage, however, still prefers the impersonal pronoun *one* or a passive verb unless the context clearly implies a definite audience or person addressed.

INFORMAL You shouldn't take sulfa drugs without a doctor's prescription.

FORMAL One should not take sulfa drugs without a doctor's prescription.

STANDARD Sulfa drugs should not be taken without a doctor's prescription.

Exercise 3

Revise the following sentences to correct the ambiguous reference of pronouns.

1. The runner lunged towards the tape, threw out his chest, and snapped it.
2. In the course of the argument, Jack told his father that he needed a new car.
3. It wouldn't hurt people to read about criminals because they live in a different kind of world and they don't have to follow their example.
4. Both parents were there when the twin brothers graduated together, and we couldn't help noticing how happy they were.
5. Under Roosevelt's leadership, the Democratic party, which had not really been united under one president for some years, came together effectively for a time. Historians tend to agree that this was a case of the right man at the right moment.
6. The hives buzzed with activity, and the beekeeper covered himself with netting before going after the honey and then motioned for us to follow at a distance. It was about fifty feet away.
7. In Joyce's novel, he delights in complex puns and in playing with words.
8. The spider gently shook the strands of his web as he scurried towards the fly and the moth. Although they were barely visible, they were obviously strong.
9. Engineering is the profession that applies scientific knowlege to the building of such things as bridges, harbors, and communication systems. This is my ambition.
10. Ethics must not be understood to be the same thing as honor because this is not the case.
11. When there is no harmony in the home, the child is the first to feel it.
12. Most of the students at the work camp were inexperienced, and many of them had never seen raw poverty before, but on the whole they were up to it.
13. It says in the brochure that in England they drink tea instead of coffee.

14. Fielding's *Shamela* successfully used farcical incident and character development as tools for his satire in the novel.
15. Since the white settlers held the Indians to be of no significant value, they regarded their rights as equally nonexistent. This is exemplified by several incidents in Kroeber's account.

3c Dangling Modifiers

A modifier is "dangling" when there is no word in the sentence for it to modify.

In the sentence "Swimming out into the lake, the water felt cold," the writer took it for granted that the reader would assume someone was swimming. But the only noun in the main clause is *water,* and the participial phrase cannot logically modify *water*—the *water* was not *swimming out into the lake.*

Note the position of the dangling modifier: almost all dangling modifiers occur at the beginning of a sentence. They can be corrected in either of two ways:

(1) By supplying the noun or the pronoun which the phrase logically modifies:

modifier *word modified*
Swimming out into the lake, ***I*** felt the water grow colder.

(2) Or by changing the dangling construction into a complete clause:

As I swam out into the lake, the water felt colder.

(1) Dangling Participial Phrases

modifier *word modified*
DANGLING ***Walking*** along the trestle, a ***train*** suddenly appeared.
The sentence is grammatically illogical: do trains walk?

IMPROVED ***Walking*** along the trestle, ***I*** suddenly saw a train.

IMPROVED ***As I*** walked along the trestle, a train suddenly appeared.
In this sentence the introductory clause modifies the verb appeared.

DANGLING The mountains were snow-covered and cloudless, ***flying*** over the Rockies.

Dangling modifiers at the end of a sentence are less frequent than those at the beginning, but they are often confusing and always awkward.

IMPROVED When ***I*** flew over the Rockies, the mountains were snow-covered and cloudless.

IMPROVED ***Flying*** over the Rockies, we saw snow-covered, cloudless mountains.

DANGLING Having followed directions carefully, my ***cake*** was a great success.

IMPROVED Since ***I*** had followed directions carefully, my cake was a great success.

(2) Dangling Gerunds

DANGLING After ***explaining*** my errand to the guard, an automatic ***gate*** swung open to let me in.

The gate can't explain; one must infer the subject of "explaining."

IMPROVED After ***I*** had explained my errand to the guard, an automatic gate swung open to let me in.

DANGLING Before ***climbing*** the mountain, our ***lunches*** were packed in bags.

Note that a change from the active to the passive voice will often correct the dangling modifier.

IMPROVED Before ***climbing*** the mountain, ***we*** packed our lunches in bags.

(3) Dangling Infinitives

DANGLING ***To be considered*** for college, the aptitude ***test*** must be taken.

IMPROVED To be considered for college, a ***student*** must take the aptitude test.

DANGLING In order to become a top entertainer, all types of audiences must be pleased.

"All types of audiences" are not going to become "a top entertainer."

IMPROVED In order to become a top entertainer, an ***actor*** must please all types of audiences.

The agent capable of the act is specified.

(4) Dangling Elliptical Clauses

Subject and main verb are sometimes omitted from a dependent clause (*while going* instead of *while I was going*, or *when a child* instead of *when he was a child*). If the subject of such an elliptical clause is not stated in the rest of the sentence, the construction may dangle.

DANGLING When six years old, my grandmother died.

DANGLING At the age of six, my grandmother died.

In both examples, the implied subject of the elliptical clause, "I," is omitted. Correct the dangling modifier by including subject and verb.

IMPROVED When ***I was*** six, my grandmother died.

DANGLING While sleeping, the covers were kicked off her bed.

The implied subject of the elliptical clause is "she." Make it the subject of the main clause.

IMPROVED While sleeping, ***she kicked*** the covers off her bed.

An alternative method is to make the implied subject of the elliptical clause the subject of a dependent clause:

IMPROVED While ***she*** was asleep, ***she kicked*** the covers off her bed.

DANGLING Do not apply the paint until thoroughly stirred.

IMPROVED Do not apply the paint until ***it*** has been thoroughly stirred.

(5) Permissible Introductory Expressions

Some verbal phrases, like *in the first place, judging from past experience, considering the situation, granted the results,* or *to sum up,* have become well-established as introductory phrases and need not be attached to any particular noun.

ACCEPTABLE Judging from past experience, he is not to be trusted.

ACCEPTABLE Granted the results, what do they prove?

ACCEPTABLE To sum up, all evidence suggests the decision was a fair one.

An absolute phrase consists of a participle with a subject (and sometimes a complement) grammatically unconnected with the rest of the sentence and usually telling when, why, or how something happened. It is not a dangling modifier.

CORRECT The floodwater having receded, people began returning to their homes.

CORRECT The weather being warm, we took light sleeping bags with us.

Exercise 4

Revise the following sentences to eliminate the dangling modifiers.

1. When waiting for the dentist, every sound from the office is nerve-wracking.
2. After correcting my original calculations, the problem was finally solved.
3. Having seen Beckett's *Waiting for Godot,* my attitude toward modern drama has changed completely.
4. The directions were clear, and my trouble could have been prevented, if followed correctly.
5. After hurrying to answer the phone, the operator told the woman the other party had hung up.
6. In order to see the comet in detail, a small telescope was set up in the backyard.
7. The zoning petition was widely supported, after having canvassed many people in the neighborhood and stirred up concern about the proposed high-rise apartment building.
8. Being covered with plastic, I did not expect the car seats would be cool, having sat in the hot parking lot for several hours.
9. At last able to earn my car insurance, my parents allowed me to buy my own car.
10. Although tired and out of practice, the last set of the tennis match was too much of a personal challenge for me to resist.

3d Misplaced Modifiers

Since word order is often crucial to meaning in English, try to place modifiers as close as possible to the words they are intended to modify. Consider, for example, what happens in the following sentence when the adverb *only* is moved about in it:

The notice said *only* [said *merely*] that clients were invited to see the exhibit on the third floor.

The notice said that *only* clients [clients *alone*] were invited to see the exhibit on the third floor.

The notice said that clients were invited ***only*** [invited for the one purpose] to see the exhibit on the third floor.

The notice said that clients were invited to see the exhibit on the third floor ***only*** [third floor ***alone***].

Most modifying phrases and clauses can be moved around to various positions in the sentence. An introductory clause, for example, can be shifted from the beginning of a sentence to the middle or the end.

Whatever the public may think, I am sure that Picasso will be remembered as one of the greatest artists of our times.

I am sure, ***whatever the public may think,*** that Picasso will be remembered as one of the greatest artists of our times.

I am sure that Picasso will be remembered as one of the greatest artists of our times, ***whatever the public may think.***

This freedom, however, has its dangers. Movable modifiers may be placed so as to produce misreadings or real ambiguities. Unlike the dangling modifier, which cannot logically modify any word in the sentence, the misplaced modifier may seem to modify the wrong word or phrase in the sentence:

AMBIGUOUS He sent us the full story of his rescue from the Ozarks.

The phrase "from the Ozarks" should be placed closer to the word it is meant to modify, "sent."

CLEAR He sent us from the Ozarks the full story of his rescue.

AMBIGUOUS Peacefully nibbling on the lawn, Jim finally found his pet rabbit.

To prevent an image of Jim grazing on the lawn, put the modifying phrase as close as possible to "rabbit."

CLEAR Jim finally found his pet rabbit peacefully nibbling on the lawn.

(1) Misplaced Adverbs

AMBIGUOUS I have followed the advice ***faithfully*** given by the manual.

REVISED I have ***faithfully*** followed the advice given by the manual.

The adverb has been placed nearer the word it is intended to modify.

AMBIGUOUS The woman scolded the boy for playing with matches ***severely.***

REVISED The woman ***severely*** scolded the boy for playing with matches.

(2) Misplaced Phrases and Clauses

MISPLACED PHRASE He lost the chance to make large profits ***through the work of imitators and plagiarists.***

CLEAR ***Through the work of imitators and plagiarists,*** he lost a chance to make large profits.

MISPLACED PHRASE Hamlet stabs Laertes with a poisoned sword ***in the last act.***

CLEAR ***In the last act*** Hamlet stabs Laertes with a poisoned sword.

MISPLACED CLAUSE He searched around and found an old bus schedule in the drawer ***that was out of date.***

CLEAR He searched around and found in the drawer an old bus schedule ***that was out of date.***

(3) Squinting Modifiers

Avoid placing a modifier in such a position that it may refer to either a preceding word or a following word.

SQUINTING The child who lies ***in nine cases out of ten*** is frightened.

CLEAR ***In nine cases out of ten,*** the child who lies is frightened.

SQUINTING The tailback who injured his knee ***recently*** returned to regular practice.

CLEAR The tailback who ***recently*** injured his knee returned to regular practice.

CLEAR The tailback who injured his knee returned ***recently*** to regular practice.

(4) Split Constructions and Infinitives

Avoid separating the parts of tight grammatical constructions. Separating the parts of a verb phrase or an infinitive by an inserted modifier can give the reader an awkward jolt.

AWKWARD The operator told him that he **should,** *if he expected to get his call through,* **place** it soon.

The verb phrase is needlessly broken up by the modifier.

IMPROVED The operator told him that he **should place** his call soon *if he expected to get it through.*

AWKWARD ***I**, more than the rest of my family,* **have been losing** sleep since we got a color television set.

Try reading this sentence aloud to see why a single pronoun subject should not be separated from its verb and complement.

IMPROVED *More than the rest of my family,* **I have been losing** sleep since we got a color television set.

Split infinitives—that is, infinitives with a modifier between the *to* and the verb (*to personally supervise*)—may be awkward, especially if the modifier is long.

AWKWARD I should like ***to**, if I ever get the chance,* **take** a trip to Mexico.

IMPROVED I should like ***to take*** a trip to Mexico *if I ever get the chance.*

Frequently, however, an adverb fits naturally between the two parts of an infinitive:

ACCEPTABLE Some young couples regard children as a nuisance, but as they grow older they begin ***to actually look*** forward to having a family.

If the modifier is moved, the emphasis is slightly changed: ". . . but as they grow older they actually begin to look forward. . . ."

ACCEPTABLE We expect in the coming year ***to more than double*** our assets.

Exercise 5

Revise the following sentences to correct misplaced words, phrases, and clauses.

1. She wore a ribbon in her hair which was a light pink.
2. The film about the life of the sea otter which I saw downtown was very interesting.
3. He wrote his book on gambling in Iowa.
4. We camped in a small shelter near the edge of the cliff which had not been used for months.
5. Bread which rises rapidly too often will have a coarse texture.
6. The dean told me I could return to school in a high rage.
7. He was hit by a rotten egg walking back to his apartment one night.
8. Wild and primitive, with hidden snags and rapids on one side, jungle and savage natives on the other, danger is ever present.
9. I promised during the evening to call her.
10. Often she would spend hours on the edge of the beach watching her small son build a sand castle with half-closed eyes.

Exercise 6

Revise the following sentences to correct the split constructions.

1. At the end of the period we were told to promptly hand in our bluebooks.
2. The pharmacist told her she should, since she needed the medicine in such a hurry, have the doctor phone in the prescription.
3. The term *reactionary* can be applied to political, social, or economic (or a combination of the three) beliefs.
4. After nicking a submerged rock, the canoe began to slowly but steadily leak and to gradually settle deeper in the water.
5. She told him to for Heaven's sake shut up.

3e Confusing Shifts

Consistency of structure makes sentences easier to read. If the first clause of a sentence is in the active voice, do not shift to the passive voice in the second clause unless there is good reason for the change. Similarly, avoid shifts in tense, mood, or person within a sentence unless they reflect an intentional shift in focus.

(1) Confusing Shifts of Voice or Subject

Shifting from the active to the passive voice almost always involves a change in subject; thus a shift in voice may make a sentence doubly awkward.

SHIFT IN SUBJECT AND VOICE After ***I*** finally ***discovered*** an unsoldered wire, the ***dismantling*** of the motor ***was begun.***

The subject shifts from "I" to "dismantling." The voice shifts from the active "discovered" to the passive "was begun."

CONSISTENT After I finally discovered an unsoldered wire, ***I dismantled*** the motor.

The sentence would be logically consistent if both verbs were in the passive voice: "After an unsoldered wire was found, the motor was dismantled." But the passive voice is unnecessary here.

SHIFT IN VOICE ***He left*** the examination after his answer ***had been proofread.***

Who proofread the answer?

CONSISTENT He left the examination after ***he had proofread*** his answer.

CONFUSING SHIFT IN SUBJECT As the guests entered the church, appropriate seats were assigned by the ushers conducting them.

IMPROVED As the guests entered the church, they were conducted to appropriate seats by the ushers.

(2) Confusing Shifts of Person or Number

A common shift in student writing is from the third person (*he, she, they, one*) to the second person (*you*); another is from a singular number (*a person, one, he*) to a plural (*they*). These errors usually occur when the writer has no particular individual in mind but is thinking of anybody or everybody and is stating some vague general truth applicable to all.

CONFUSING SHIFT IN PERSON When ***you*** try hard enough, ***one*** can do almost anything.
Confusing shift from the second to the third person.

CONSISTENT When ***you*** try hard enough, ***you*** can do almost anything.

CONSISTENT When ***one*** tries hard enough, ***one*** [or ***he***] can do almost anything.

CONFUSING SHIFT IN PERSON ***I*** could find only one fault with my new gun. When ***you*** fired it, gas would leak through the action.
Confusing shift from first to second person.

CONSISTENT ***I*** could find only one fault with my new gun. When ***I*** fired it, gas leaked through the action.

CONFUSING SHIFT IN NUMBER When ***a person*** gets an early start, ***they*** can work more efficiently.
Confusing shift from singular to plural number.

CONSISTENT When ***a person*** gets an early start, ***he*** can work more efficiently.

(3) Confusing Shifts of Mood or Tense

If you begin a sentence with an order or command (*imperative* mood), do not shift without reason to a statement (*indicative* mood).

CONFUSING SHIFT IN MOOD First stir in the flour; then you should add the butter and salt.

The first clause is an order, the imperative mood; the second clause is a statement giving advice, the indicative mood.

CONSISTENT First stir in the flour; then add the butter and salt.
Both clauses in the imperative mood.

ACCEPTABLE After you have stirred in the flour, add the butter and salt.
First clause modifies the imperative verb "add."

If you begin a sentence in the past tense, do not switch to the present unless you have good reason to do so.

CONFUSING SHIFT IN TENSE I ***stood*** on the starting block and ***looked*** tensely at the water below; for the first time in my life I ***am*** about to swim the 50-yard freestyle in competition.
Confusing shift from past to present.

CONSISTENT I ***stood*** on the starting block and ***looked*** . . . I ***was*** about to swim . . . .

CONSISTENT I ***stand*** on the starting block and ***look*** . . . I ***am*** about to swim . . . .

CONFUSING SHIFT IN TENSE At the beginning of the *Divine Comedy,* Dante ***finds*** that he has strayed from the True Way into the Dark Wood of Error. As soon as he ***realized*** this, Dante ***lifted*** his eyes in hope to the rising sun.
When you use the historical present, the tense normally used for summarizing plots of narratives, take special care not to lapse into the past tense.

CONSISTENT At the beginning of the *Divine Comedy,* Dante ***finds*** that he has strayed from the True Way into the Dark Wood of Error. As soon as he ***has realized*** this, Dante ***lifts*** his eyes in hope to the rising sun.

Exercise 7

Correct shifts in voice, person, number, mood, or tense in the following sentences.

1. After I finished planting my garden, the seeds were watered daily.
2. The matinee was enjoyed by all the children because they saw two monster films.
3. A person can always find something to criticize if they look hard enough.
4. In the school I attended, you had just five minutes between

classes, and that was not enough time for most of us.
5. Don't ride the clutch; you should keep your left foot off the pedal.
6. Because he was so naive, Candide listens to almost anybody he meets.
7. Parson Adams went to London to try to sell his sermons and finds out that people are neither kind nor generous; he does not worry about taking money with him because he thought that people would be hospitable to him.
8. Thus, in *The Way of All Flesh,* Butler is telling his readers to look ahead; he tells them not to be caught without knowing what is going on around you.
9. Of course, knowing how to use one's leisure is also important, but I do not think that it is up to the college to more or less arrange your social life, as many colleges do.
10. Fifty years ago, your house was the center of your everyday life; today, we Americans practically live in our cars.

3f Mixed Constructions

Do not begin a sentence with one construction and conclude it with another. English is full of alternative constructions, and it is easy to confuse them in a first draft and to produce a monster with the head of one sentence and the tail of another.

MIXED By requiring citizens to install pollution controls in their cars is one way to protect the air we breathe.

As it stands, the sentence begins with a modifying phrase which is then used as the subject of the verb is.

CORRECT By requiring citizens to install pollution controls in their cars, we can protect the air we breathe.

CORRECT Requiring citizens to install pollution controls in their cars is one way to protect the air we breathe.

(1) Dependent Clauses Used as Subjects or Complements

Using a dependent clause as subject or complement of a verb can produce a badly mixed construction.

MIXED Because he ran out of gas made him late for work.

CORRECT Because he ran out of gas, he was late for work.

CORRECT Running out of gas made him late for work.

(2) Adverbial Clauses Used as Nouns

A frequent cause of mixed construction is the illogical use of "when" or "where" as part of the complement of "is"—the "is when" or "is where" habit:

MIXED One thing which keeps me from enlisting ***is when*** I think of kitchen police.

The clause "when I think of kitchen police" is a modifier, not a thing. What is needed to complete the sentence is some kind of substantive.

CORRECT One thing which keeps me from enlisting ***is the thought*** of kitchen police.

MIXED A fanfare ***is where*** trumpets are sounded.

An adverb clause is misused as a noun; the verb "is" needs a substantive here.

CORRECT A fanfare ***is a flourish*** of trumpets.

Though widely used, "the reason . . . is because . . ." construction is both redundant and wordy. Instead of writing "*The reason* American teams perform well at the Olympics *is because* they have been well trained," drop either "the reason" or "is because."

CORRECT American teams perform well at the Olympics because they have been well trained.

CORRECT The reason American teams perform well at the Olympics is that they have been well trained.

(3) Idiomatic Comparisons

English has idiomatic ways of making comparisons, and these do not contain interchangeable parts. In making comparisons, use the same idiom throughout the sentence.

MIXED The amateur mechanic will find plastic easier to work with than with metal.

What is easier than working with metal? Working with plastic. Write it that way.

CORRECT The amateur mechanic will find plastic easier to work with than metal.

CORRECT The amateur mechanic will find it easier to work with plastic than [to work] with metal.

Exercise 8

In the following student sentences, analyze the constructions that have been mixed and revise the sentences.

1. Since cheating in schools instigates distrust on so a large scale that I think all people caught cheating should be punished as a lesson to all.
2. Because Joyce's stories are written with the greatest skill makes each and every character come alive before the reader's eyes.
3. In the container is where the experiment takes place.
4. For college students, I feel that teaching assistants who read papers for the professors are really a disadvantage to the student.
5. It would be hard for me to say what the outlook on life a person with this disease would have.
6. In choosing the class play, we found small reading groups much easier to work with than with the whole committee together.
7. In my high school, which is rated as one of the best in the state, it is my opinion that it was much too easy.
8. As the volume of sound increases in the earphones, the nearer the submarine is approaching.
9. In my study of campus slang, to get an A on a test or in a course is where you "ace" it.
10. Of course, if I decide to become an engineering major doesn't mean that it is too late to change later on.
11. By defining the term "socialism" accurately will save us argument.
12. When waiting for the mail on the day a check from home is expected is very frustrating.

3g Incomplete Constructions

Do not omit words and expressions necessary for grammatical completeness.

INCOMPLETE Worse still, he had a seven-day journey$_\wedge$the fort.
"To" is needed to complete the meaning of the predicate.

INCOMPLETE The very sound of the poem gives the feeling^fleeting light and life.

"Of" completes and clarifies the predicate's meaning.

(1) Incomplete Verb Forms

When the two parts of a compound construction are in *different tenses,* the auxiliary verbs should usually be fully written in so that their meanings will be clear.

INCOMPLETE Fishing ***has*** and always ***will be*** a profitable industry in Alaska.

"Be" is the proper auxiliary for "will" but not for "has." One cannot say "Fishing has be and always will be . . . ."

COMPLETE Fishing ***has been*** and always ***will be*** a profitable industry in Alaska.

When there is *no change* in tense, part of a compound verb can be omitted:

ACCEPTABLE Tickets will be sent to all students who have signed up for the trip and [who have] paid the fee.

In sentences whose predicate is the linking verb *to be,* make certain that the verb agrees with its subject in number.

INCOMPLETE He ***was lecturing*** and the students ***taking*** notes.

The singular "was" cannot be used with the plural "students."

COMPLETE He ***was lecturing*** and the students ***were taking*** notes.

(2) Idiomatic Prepositions

English idiom requires that certain prepositions be used with certain adjectives and verbs: we say, for example, "interested *in,*" "aware *of,*" "devoted *to.*" We expect others "to agree *with,*" or "to object *to,*" or even "to protest *against,*" our plans. Be sure to use the proper idiomatic preposition with each part of a compound construction. Your dictionary will often help here.

INCOMPLETE He was ***oblivious*** and ***undisturbed by*** the noise around him.

COMPLETE He was ***oblivious to*** and ***undisturbed by*** the noise around him.

INCOMPLETE No one could have been more ***interested*** or ***devoted to*** his students than Mr. Beattes.

COMPLETE No one could have been more ***interested in*** or ***devoted to*** his students than Mr. Beattes.

(3) Incomplete and Inexact Comparisons

In comparisons do not omit words necessary to make a complete idiomatic statement.

INCOMPLETE He is as tall, if not taller, than his brother.

As it stands, the sentence says that he is "as tall . . . than his brother."

COMPLETE He is ***as*** tall ***as*** his brother, if not taller.

INCOMPLETE Leonardo had one of the greatest, if not the greatest, minds of all times.

Two idioms: "one of the greatest minds" and "the greatest mind."

COMPLETE Leonardo had one of the greatest ***minds,*** if not the greatest ***mind,*** of all time.

Comparisons should be complete, logical, and unambiguous.

INCOMPLETE Her salary was lower than a typist.

Is a typist low?

COMPLETE Her salary was lower than ***that of*** a typist.

COMPLETE Her salary was lower than a ***typist's*** [salary].

INCOMPLETE The food here costs no more than any other restaurant.

Can one buy the food and a restaurant at the same low price?

COMPLETE The food here costs no more than [it does] ***at*** any other restaurant.

Avoid the illogical use of *than* and *any*.

ILLOGICAL For many years the Empire State Building was taller than any building in New York.

"Any building in New York" includes *the Empire State Building. Can it be taller than itself?*

REVISED For many years the Empire State Building was taller than ***any other*** building in New York.

Make sure that the reader can tell what is being compared with what.

INEXACT Claremont is farther from Los Angeles than Pomona.

CLEAR Claremont is farther from Los Angeles than Pomona ***is.***

CLEAR Claremont is farther from Los Angeles than ***it is*** from Pomona.

In the two revisions, both terms of the comparison are completely filled in.

INEXACT Philsoc Gas gives more and better mileage for the dollar.

More than what? Mule teams? Many commercials and advertisements only pretend to give information: by conveniently omitting any standard of comparison, they do not commit themselves to any real claims.

If clearly indicated by the context, the standard of comparison need not be specified:

CLEAR Boulder Dam is big, but the Grand Coulee Dam is bigger.

Note that the words *so, such,* and *too* when used as comparatives are completed by a phrase or clause indicating the standard of comparison.

CLEAR I'm ***so*** tired ***that I could drop.*** I had ***such*** a small breakfast ***that I was starving by noon,*** and when we stopped for lunch, I was ***too*** tired ***to eat.***

Exercise 9

Revise the following sentences by filling out the incomplete or illogical constructions.

1. The Japanese are at least as inventive as the United States or Germany.
2. Disneyland is as large, if not larger, than any other amusement park in the country.
3. The Hondas and Yamahas weigh less and are cheaper.
4. My father complained that his income tax was higher than last year.
5. The distributor was cleaned and the points adjusted.
6. Vale did some of her best work and learned a great deal from her high school history teacher.
7. Because of their climate and soil, Florida and Texas raise more citrus than all the states put together.
8. According to our map of Arkansas, Fort Smith is farther from Little Rock than Pine Bluff.
9. As your Class Secretary, I have and will continue to send you all the news that I receive about the class of '71.

10. Trying to analyze my good points and weaknesses made me a happier and secure person.

Exercise 10

The following student sentences contain faults discussed in the preceding chapter on coherence—faulty parallelism, faulty reference of pronouns, dangling and misplaced modifiers, confusing shifts, and mixed and incomplete constructions. Identify the cause or causes of faulty coherence in each sentence, and then revise the sentence.

1. Entering the door, after walking up several steps made of concrete, there is a policeman sitting behind his desk, who will gladly give you any needed information.
2. The politician has dinners given, circulars printed, and attends rallies.
3. If someone knows that a certain person is a "cheat," they wouldn't want to be around them and they wouldn't trust him.
4. By the way she tells the story is indication enough of how Mansfield feels.
5. I found Charlie Macklin to be the closest thing to perfection, but at the same time still being human, than any other I have either read about or known in real life.
6. Pulled through a broken window with pieces of glass scattered about, a passing motorist rescued a woman in her home early this morning, which was blazing.
7. One advertisement shows a washing machine "growing" before our eyes to be ten feet tall, and in a different commercial for soap portrays a giant in your washer who labors to clean your clothes.
8. Some occupations in which following directions might not be important are where a person is an artist, a potter, a novelist, or some other creative artist.
9. Although surprising to students, this writer feels that in most questionable cases, the uncertainty of science should be presented for what it is.
10. While personally finding nothing to recommend Marx's system, it is fitting to examine him in order to see how and why so many people have believed in it.
11. He certainly didn't look like a man of my father's age and he certainly didn't have a particle of dignity that I so commonly associated with my father of having.

12. Paul has different ideas about schooling than the school principal.
13. Just because our campus radio station plays so much popular music is no reason for the college to cut its funds.
14. The Lilliputians are much more like the human race than the giants.
15. After being locked in the cabin about two hours, our first roll call of the evening took place.

Grammatical Usage 4

4a Agreement

In standard English a verb agrees with its subject in person and number. That is, if the subject is first person (*I*), the verb is first person (*am*); if the subject is plural, (*they*), the verb is plural (*are*). The rule is simple enough in theory, but in practice we occasionally make agreement errors for a number of reasons.

In the first place, the third person singular of many verbs is formed by the addition of *s* (he/she/it walk*s*), while *s* added to a noun forms the plural (noun*s*). We have to live with this inconsistency in the language, but we should be aware that it can be a source of confusion. Another difficulty is that some writers speak a dialect which does not observe the agreement convention. Furthermore, all of us from time to time violate the principle in conversation, either in haste or carelessness or in sheer forgetfulness of how we began the sentence. It is easy to understand why agreement is a troublesome rule for some writers. Perhaps the pronoun is so far away from its antecedent (the word it refers to) that the writer forgets what the antecedent is. Or a writer may be uncertain whether a compound subject, like "Either Angela or Carol," should be considered singular or plural. Such questions will be discussed in following sections.

Another problem, sociological rather than grammatical, arises from the lack in English of a singular pronoun which refers to either sex.

For centuries it has been a convention to use the masculine third-person singular pronoun to refer to a noun of which the gender is either unknown or irrelevant.

> A *child* should be taught to take care of ***his*** teeth.

This convention, however, has led to some bizarre constructions:

> At her strongest and most characteristic, she [Edith Wharton] is a brilliant example of the writer who relieves an emotional strain by denouncing his generation.
>
> —EDMUND WILSON

To avoid such a logical inconsistency, don't hesitate to use the feminine pronoun where its antecedent is clearly female, as in the example above. You can avoid the problem entirely by casting general statements about human beings in the plural: "*Children* should be taught to take care of *their* teeth."

Avoid the "everyone . . . his" construction when possible, in consideration of those women in your audience who might feel uncomfortable with a pronoun which sometimes refers to them, sometimes not. Some writers in published books use first "he," then "she" to refer to the sexually neutral *person, artist, student;* others frown on this practice as confusing and inconsistent. A number of new pronouns have been suggested to replace "his or her": *tes, shis, vis.* Experimenting with these forms will teach you, if nothing else, how difficult it is to break ourselves of old language patterns and introduce new words into our grammar.

(1) Agreement of Subject and Verb

Everyone knows that a pet *requires* care, whereas pets *require* care. Violations of this principle usually occur when (1) it is not clear which word is the simple subject or (2) when there is doubt whether the subject is singular or plural.

1. Which word is the subject?

Modifying phrases do not change the number of the subject.

NONSTANDARD A program of two Bergman films were shown last night.

It is easy to become confused here, since the pattern "films were shown" is a familiar one. But the simple subject in this sentence is "program," and the verb must agree with it.

STANDARD A *program* of two Bergman films *was* shown last night.

Although phrases like "accompanied by," "as well as," and "together with" suggest a plural idea, they do not change the number of the subject.

STANDARD The ***prisoner,*** accompanied by guards and her lawyer, ***was*** in the courtroom.

STANDARD The ***property,*** as well as the guest house and the extra garage, ***is*** up for rent.

When two nouns are connected by some form of the verb *to be,* the first noun is the grammatical subject, and the verb agrees with it.

STANDARD The first ***thing*** we noticed ***was*** the tuna boats.

STANDARD The tuna ***boats were*** the first thing we noticed.

When the subject follows the verb, a common error is to make the verb agree with the word which precedes it.

NONSTANDARD Beyond the old mud fort was the endless sands of the desert.

What was beyond the fort? The "sands," and they "were."

In sentences beginning with *there is* or *there are,* you will always find the subject following the verb.

There ***are*** a million ***laughs*** in this bouncy little comedy.
There ***is*** only one correct ***solution*** to the problem.
There ***is*** a long ***list*** of jobs to be done before we leave.
There ***are*** many ***jobs*** to be done before we leave.

2. Is the subject singular or plural?

When compound subjects are joined by *and* they are usually considered to be plural.

STANDARD ***Mathematics*** and ***science are*** my best subjects.

STANDARD The ***evaluating, hiring,*** and ***training*** of the applicant ***are*** left to the Personnel Department.

There are, however, some exceptions to this principle. If the two nouns of a compound subject refer to the same person, the verb should be singular.

STANDARD This young bachelor and man-about-town ***was*** finally discovered to be an imposter.

Sometimes two compound nouns are needed to indicate one thing.

STANDARD Bacon and eggs ***is*** the typical American breakfast.

In informal English, a singular verb is occasionally used when a compound subject follows the verb.

FORMAL In the office there ***are*** a ***desk,*** a ***chair,*** and a filing ***cabinet.***

INFORMAL In the office there ***is*** a desk, a chair, and a filing cabinet.

When *each* or *every* is used to modify the compound subject, a singular form of the verb is used.

STANDARD Each soldier and sailor ***was*** given a complete examination.

STANDARD Every camera and light meter ***has*** been reduced in price.

Two or more subjects joined by *or* or *nor* usually take a singular verb form.

STANDARD Local information or a good road map ***is*** needed to get you to the camp.

STANDARD Neither the producer nor the consumer ***was*** treated fairly.

When one subject is singular and one is plural, the verb agrees with the subject nearer it.

STANDARD Neither my brother nor my sisters ***have*** ever been there.

In informal English, a plural verb is occasionally used when a *neither . . . nor . . .* construction expresses a plural idea.

STANDARD Neither the union nor the company ***seem*** to like the plan.

Collective Nouns

Collective nouns, like *class, committee, team, family, number,* are considered singular when they refer to the group as a unit. If you want to emphasize the individual members of the group, you may use the plural form of the verb.

STANDARD The ***committee was*** unanimous in its recommendations.

STANDARD The ***class were*** unable to agree on a day for the party.

Many writers would feel this sentence to be awkward, even though correct, and would rephrase it: "The members of the class were unable. . . ."

STANDARD A large ***number*** of votes ***is*** required.

STANDARD A large ***number*** of notes in his journal ***are*** inaccurate.

STANDARD The ***number*** of correct answers ***was*** small.

Indefinite Pronouns

Indefinite pronouns, like *each, every, either, neither, any, some,* and their compounds with *–one* or *–body,* are singular in number and should be followed by singular verb forms.

STANDARD ***Each*** of the boys ***was*** tested.

STANDARD ***Either*** of them ***is*** qualified for the job.

STANDARD ***Neither*** of the speakers ***was*** willing to answer questions.

In speech and in informal writing, especially in questions, a plural verb is common.

INFORMAL ***Are either*** of the boys qualified for the job?

COLLOQUIAL ***Each*** of the children ***have*** their own room.

None, some, more, most, and *all* may be either singular or plural, depending on the context and the intended meaning.

STANDARD ***None*** of the money ***was*** wasted.

STANDARD ***None*** of the dresses ***are*** paid for.

STANDARD ***Most*** of the pie ***has been*** eaten.

STANDARD ***Most*** of the students ***have read*** that play.

Relative Pronouns

The relative pronouns *who, which,* and *that* take a singular verb form when the antecedent is singular, a plural verb form when the antecedent is plural.

STANDARD Betsy is the kind of ***woman who prefers*** to earn her living.
The antecedent of who *is* woman.

STANDARD This is one of those ***motors that were*** imported from Japan.
The antecedent of "that" is "motors." The sentence is about one of a group of motors–those that were imported from Japan.

Nouns Ending in s

Some abstract nouns which are plural in form are grammatically singular—e.g., *aesthetics, economics, linguistics, mathematics, news, physics, semantics.*

STANDARD Physics ***was*** the hardest course I had in high school.

Note that certain nouns ending in *s* have no singular form and are always plural: *trousers, scissors, measles, forceps.* Some nouns ending in *ics* (*athletics, politics, statistics*) may be either singular or plural, often with a distinction in meaning.

STANDARD Athletics [the collective activity] ***builds*** the physique.

STANDARD Athletics [particular sports and teams] ***are*** his favorite pastime.

STANDARD Statistics ***is*** my most difficult course.

STANDARD Statistics ***show*** that . . . .

Latin Plurals

Words like *data* and *strata* are Latin plurals, but there is a strong tendency in current English to treat them as collective nouns, which may be either singular or plural.

FORMAL We must classify all the data that ***have*** been collected.

ACCEPTABLE This data ***was*** collected in a survey.

STANDARD These ***strata go*** back to the Miocene period.

Exercise 1

Give reasons for using the singular or the plural verb form in the following sentences.

1. Every one of the nine men on the team (is, are) important.
2. The close relationship with professors and fellow students (makes, make) the small college the choice of many entering freshmen.
3. Doug sprawled in the chair and knocked over one of the lamps which (was, were) on display.
4. There (has, have) never been hard feelings between the families on this street.

5. The symptoms of lead poisoning (varies, vary) with each individual case.
6. Next in the waiting line (was, were) an elderly lady and her grandson.
7. He believes that athletics (improves, improve) school morale.
8. Up goes the starter's gun, and each of the runners (becomes, become) tense.
9. The doctor said that there is always a possibility the infection will return but that so far there (has, have) been no signs of its recurrence.
10. The family (takes, take) its annual vacation during August.
11. A majority of the hospital's patients (has, have) some kind of medical insurance.
12. Either the *Times* or the *Tribune* (is, are) a reliable source of news.
13. The catcher, as well as the pitcher and the coach, (was, were) arguing furiously with the umpire.
14. Her chief interest in life (was, were) horses.
15. Slater is one of those legislators who (has, have) always opposed spending.

Exercise 2

In the following sentences, determine the cause of the faulty agreement and supply the correct form of the verb.

1. In addition, there is the students who cheat because they have never been taught differently.
2. The author's portrayal of the guests and the games add up to an extremely vivid picture of that particular society, with its petty concerns and rituals.
3. Another of the unpopular activities that take place during freshman week are the roll calls.
4. The theme of suffering, its causes and its consequences, are treated by Shakespeare, Tolstoy, and Conrad.
5. The first thing which catches your eye are the headlines.
6. The fact that the children are so beautiful and so intelligent add to their goodness and make ghosts appear even more evil.
7. Everyone else in the story have readjusted to their roles, and Pam is the only one who is injured by the experience.
8. But their way of expressing themselves are totally different.

9. These products of automation may have made life more pleasant but has reduced the population from hardworking pioneers to button-pushing time-servers.
10. She is one of the women who has made this country what it is.

(2) Agreement of Pronoun and Antecedent

Pronouns should agree in number with the words they refer to—their antecedents.

STANDARD Many ***people*** pay a genealogist to look up ***their*** ancestry.
"People," the antecedent, is plural, and so the correct pronoun is "their."

STANDARD My ***uncle*** paid a genealogist to look up ***his*** ancestry.
"His" agrees with "uncle."

Such indefinite antecedents as *each, either, neither, everyone, everybody, someone, somebody, anyone, anybody* are followed in Edited English by a singular pronoun.

STANDARD ***Everyone*** at times finds ***himself*** facing failure.

STANDARD ***Anybody*** can eat ***his*** meals at the Club.

The terms *everyone* and *anybody* include my sister, and she never finds "himself facing failure" nor eating "his meals at the Club." Many women object to this illogical construction, but to fill it out—"eats his or her meals"—is awkward and wordy. Such a sentence, however, can often be improved by rewriting.

REVISED Everyone at times faces failure.

REVISED Anybody can eat meals at the Club.

Compound antecedents are usually considered plural when joined by *and*, singular when joined by *or* or *nor.*

STANDARD My father encouraged ***Henry*** and ***me*** not to postpone ***our*** trip.

STANDARD Neither the senator nor his press secretary would admit that ***he*** was responsible.

If a singular pronoun, even though correct, produces an awkward or clumsy sentence, the plural pronoun is often acceptable in informal writing.

ACCEPTABLE Almost everybody eats some fruit as a part of ***their*** basic diet.

When the antecedent is a collective noun, the singular pronoun is used to emphasize the cohesiveness of the group, the plural to emphasize the separate individuals.

STANDARD The ***audience*** showed ***its*** approval by applause.

STANDARD The ***audience*** were cheering, booing, whistling and stamping ***their*** feet.

Note in the sentence above that the verb "were" also is in the plural form. Be consistent. If the verb form shows the antecedent to be singular, the pronoun should be singular. If the verb is plural, the pronoun should be plural.

INCONSISTENT The ***jury is*** about to return and give ***their*** verdict.

CONSISTENT The ***jury is*** about to return and give ***its*** verdict.

Demonstrative pronouns (*this, these; that, those*) are sometimes used as adjectives and should then agree in number with the words they modify.

NONSTANDARD ***These kind*** of vegetables are grown in the Valley.

STANDARD ***This kind*** of vegetable is grown in the Valley.

STANDARD ***These kinds*** of vegetables are grown in the Valley.

Exercise 3

Give reasons for using the singular or plural form of the pronoun in the following sentences. Be prepared to say which pronoun forms would be acceptable in speech and informal writing but would be discouraged in college writing.

1. Maybe some day each person will have (his, their) own helicopter for commuting to the city.
2. Nobody needs servants because nobody has more housework than (he, they) can manage.
3. The school was preparing to put on (its, their) annual May Day Dance.
4. Any parent hopes to get the best education for (his, their) children.
5. The congregation were divided in (its, their) feelings about the new minister.

6. Neither Faulkner nor T. S. Eliot won the Nobel Prize in literature until well after (he, they) had written (his, their) most important works.
7. Each man and woman must make (his, their) own decision.
8. The United States has to look out for the rights of (its, their) citizens.
9. Neither Macbeth nor the Emperor Jones cared how (he, they) got what (he, they) wanted.
10. I believe that a person should never ask someone else for advice on (his, their) problems.

Exercise 4

In the following sentences, determine the cause of the faulty agreement and supply the correct form of the pronoun.

1. Either the members or the secretary may submit their objections.
2. The family was quite frank in stating their opinions.
3. These kind of scrimmages can be very bruising.
4. Each camper was supposed to bring their own bedding.
5. Now that everything was perfect, he was going to make sure they stayed that way.
6. Dorm meetings are always a spectacle because someone always loses their temper.
7. The prisoner's attitude toward society is largely determined by the treatment they receive in prison.
8. Every new proposal was vetoed by the chairman because he thought they weren't practical.

4b Case of Pronouns and Nouns

Case means the changes in the form of a noun or pronoun that show how it is used in a sentence: *man, man's, he, his, her, them,* etc. English nouns used to have many case forms, but over the centuries the forms have been reduced to those which indicate possession. Most pronouns, however, have three case forms: NOMINATIVE (or subjective) when the pronoun is the subject of a verb, the POSSESSIVE (or genitive) case to show possession, and the OBJECTIVE case when the pronoun functions as a complement—the object of a verb or preposition.

NOMINATIVE	I	we	he	she	it	they	who
POSSESSIVE	my	our	his	her	its	their	whose
OBJECTIVE	me	us	him	her	it	them	whom

As with agreement, people usually get case right without consciously thinking about it. But a few constructions can cause writers trouble.

(1) Compound Constructions

A noun and a pronoun used in a compound construction should be in the same case; the same principle applies to constructions like *we boys* and to appositives.

My father and ***I*** often hunt together.
"I" is a subject of the verb "hunt."

The professor invited my father and ***me*** to his house.
Because a construction like "my father and I" is so familiar, it is easy to slip into using it even when, as here, the objective case is needed. He invited my father and he invited "me," not "I."

Between you and ***me,*** Porter doesn't have a chance to win.
The compound construction "you and me" is the object of the preposition "between."

My father always spanked ***us boys*** for staying out late.

We boys always tried to avoid being seen coming in.
In the first sentence, "us boys" is the object of "spanked." In the second, "we boys" is the subject of "tried."

Most of the float was designed by two members of the class, Howard and ***me.***
Since "two members" is the object of the preposition "by," the appositive should also be in the objective case. However, in speech, "Howard and I" would be fairly common. After all, Howard and I did it.

(2) *Who* in Dependent Clauses

When in doubt about the case of the relative pronoun *who,* try a personal pronoun in its place. If *he* or *they* sounds right, use *who;* if *him* or *them* fits the grammatical context, use *whom.*

Here is a man ***who*** can explain eclipses.
Would you say of this man that "him can explain eclipses"?

Prentice is the man ***whom*** I told you about.
The preposition "about" needs an object, like "him" or "whom."

Note that a parenthetical expression like *I think* or *he says* does not change the case of the pronoun.

The woman ***who*** I thought would accept the nomination changed her mind.
I thought "she" would accept the nomination, and so the relative pronoun should be the nominative "who."

Here are extra bluebooks for ***whoever*** needs them.
The relative pronoun is the subject of "needs." "Whomever" would be correct in a sentence like "Give the tickets to whomever you choose." But most speakers and many writers would find the construction too formal and would rephrase the sentence: "Give the tickets to anyone you choose."

In formal writing, the interrogative pronouns *who* and *whom* are used exactly like the relative pronouns.

Who is coming to the party?

Whom are you expecting at the party?
"Whom" is the object of "are expecting."

In speech and in much informal writing, there is a decided tendency to use *who* as the interrogative form whenever it begins a sentence, no matter what its construction in the sentence. *Whom* is usually avoided unless it directly follows a preposition. Since the use of *who* and *whom* is often picked on as a crucial test of literacy, it is safer to use the formal case form in Edited English.

INFORMAL ***Who*** are you expecting for dessert?

FORMAL ***Whom*** are you expecting for dessert?

INFORMAL ***Who*** are you driving with?

FORMAL With ***whom*** are you driving?

(3) Complement of *to be*

In formal writing, the complement of the linking verb *to be* is in the nominative case.

The members of the delegation are ***you***, your ***sister***, and ***I***.

We hoped the speaker would be President Markson, but it was not ***she***.

A voice on the telephone asked for Professor Poynter, and I said, "This is ***he***."

In speech and informal writing, the form "It is me" and analogous forms like "I thought it was her" and "It wasn't us" are commonly used. In college writing, such forms usually occur in dialogue, where informality is appropriate.

When the infinitive form of *to be* is used, its complement is always in the objective case.

I wouldn't want to be ***him***.

(4) Pronoun after *than, as,* or *but*

After *than* or *as*, the case of a pronoun is determined by its use in the shortened clause of which it is a part.

My cousin is taller than ***I*** [am].

They take more photographs than ***we*** [do].

I can type as well as ***he*** [can].

He chooses you more often than [he chooses] ***me***.

I thought her as guilty as [I thought] ***him***.

But is sometimes used as a preposition meaning "except." In such constructions, the object of *but* should be in the objective case.

By morning everyone had left but ***them***.

At Judy's party all the children had a good time but Judy and ***me***.

(5) Possessives with Gerund

A noun or pronoun modifying a gerund should be in the possessive case.

Julie's giggling disturbed those around her.

Alan's father and mother approved of ***his*** joining the Navy.

The subject of a gerund, however, should be in the objective case.

We could hear ***John*** snoring.

We saw ***them*** washing the dishes.

Exercise 5

In each sentence, choose the proper case form and be prepared to explain your choice.

1. My brother is a better skier than (I, me).
2. If Harvey hadn't finished college, my parents would never have permitted Betty and (he, him) to get married.
3. There was no comment from the two members (who, whom) I thought were sure to protest.
4. All the students (who, whom) I talked to seemed to like the new coach.
5. My father used to nag us—my sister and (I, me)—about using his pipe cleaners to make bracelets.
6. All the family went to the funeral but (I, me).
7. The new dictator won't be sure of (who, whom) he can trust.
8. His father objects to (him, his) watching sports every spare minute he can.
9. The reward was divided between my older brother and (I, me).
10. The Holes have not lived here as long as (we, us).
11. That year we finally had a teacher (who, whom) won the respect of all of (we, us) students (whom, whom) she had in class.
12. Only two members of the family are double-jointed in the thumb, my mother and (I, me).
13. Another good reason for (him, his) joining the Coast Guard is the chance for special training.
14. The ten remaining tickets will be given to (whoever, whomever) applies first.
15. I would hate to be (he, him).

4c Correct Use of Adjectives, Adverbs, and Verbs

Most adverbs are formed by adding *ly* to the adjective: *clear, clearly; immediate, immediately,* etc. But note that some adjectives also end in *ly:* a *friendly* gesture, a *manly* appearance, *monthly* payments. A few adverbs have the same form as the adjective: *far* out, *much* pleased, I *little* thought, do it *right,* run *fast,* go *slow.* The dictionary will tell you whether a word functions as an adjective or an adverb, or both.

The car stopped **suddenly.**
The adverb modifies the verb "stopped."

The car came to a **sudden** stop.
The adjective modifies the noun "stop."

(1) Adjectives with Linking Verbs

Verbs like *be, become, seem, appear,* as well as verbs indicating the use of the five senses (*look, feel, taste, sound, smell*) are often used to link an adjective to the subject of a sentence. Do not use the adverbial form as the complement of a linking verb.

The swimmer { looked / seemed / felt / sounded / became / was } **cold.**

I felt **terrible** about my mistake.

I knew I had played **terribly.**

The melon tasted **sweet,** and my aunt smiled **happily.**

Though the surgeon looked **tired,** he felt my ankle **carefully.**

I smelled the fish **cautiously,** but it smelled **fresh.**

Watching him, Betty felt **uneasy.** (*tells something about Betty*)

Betty watched him **uneasily.** (*tells how she watched him*)

I felt **bad** about her illness. (*adjective complement of* "felt")

I felt **badly** bruised. (*adverb modifying* "bruised")

In speech, the following adjectives are often used to modify a verb or an adjective:

COLLOQUIAL He looks **real** good in blue.

COLLOQUIAL I slept **good** last night.

COLLOQUIAL Today I feel **some** better.

COLLOQUIAL We were **sure** glad to see them again.

In writing, use the corresponding adverbs: *really* good, slept *well*, *somewhat* better, *surely* (or *certainly*) glad.

(2) Comparatives and Superlatives

Formal writing distinguishes between the comparative and superlative in making comparisons. The comparative is used in speaking of two persons: "He was the *taller* of the two." The superlative is used when three or more are being compared: "He was the *tallest* man on the team." In speech and informal writing this distinction is not always observed, and the superlative is often used in comparing two persons or things.

FORMAL He was the **more** influential of the two vice-presidents and the **most** powerful of all the stockholders.

INFORMAL Of the two styles offered, the first was the **most** popular.

According to logic, adjectives like *perfect* or *unique* should not have comparative or superlative forms; a thing is either perfect or not perfect, and since *unique* means "the only one of its kind", no object can be more unique than another. Consequently, formal writing tends to avoid expressions like *most perfect* or *more unique*, even though it regularly uses modifiers indicating an approach to the absolute, like *nearly perfect* playing, or an *almost unique* diamond. Informal writing often uses the superlative form, *most perfect*, but *rather unique* and *the most unique* were considered unacceptable by 94% of the Usage Panel of *The American Heritage Dictionary.*

FORMAL Holmes is the **most nearly perfect** actor we have seen this season.

INFORMAL Holmes is the **most perfect** actor we have. . . .

ACCEPTABLE We, the people of the United States, in order to form a **more perfect** union. . . .

Exercise 6

Correct the use of adjectives and adverbs as may be necessary to bring the following sentences up to the level of standard *written* English.

1. If you listen close, you should be able to hear it quite distinct.
2. The colors in the living room contrasted harshly and looked shockingly.

3. People today live more secure because of new drugs and antibiotics.
4. I am sure I didn't do too good on the objective part of the final.
5. The sky was clear and the air smelled freshly.
6. In the laboratory we were shown a seemingly impossibility.
7. An exciting documentary affects me quite different from a dramatized story about the same thing.
8. We were real pleased that so many people were willing to help.
9. That disastrous Thursday started out quite normal.
10. The sunset was beautiful that evening, but the sky looked threateningly the next morning.
11. During the whole time that Blaisdel was chairman, business went along very smooth.
12. The trick worked as perfect as we had hoped.
13. By looking real close at the ballot, I could see somebody had changed it.
14. A small minority of students have given this university a real bad image.
15. At the end of the play, he finds that defeat tastes bitterly.

4d Tense and Mood of Verbs

Tense means variations in the form of a verb to indicate time differences. There are six principal tenses in English.

PRESENT
I believe this is the right thing to do.

PAST
I mowed the lawn, and my sister **pruned** the bushes.

FUTURE
I will fly to Denver next month.

PRESENT PERFECT
I have tried to encourage him, but he **has** never **dared** to dive.

PAST PERFECT
She **had finished** the assignment by the time I arrived.

FUTURE PERFECT
He **will have arrived** before we get to the station.

(1) Sequence of Tenses

Every native speaker of English knows the following tense patterns:

When I **press** this button, the motor **begins** to run.

The instant he **pressed** the button, the motor **began** to run.

If you **press** (or **will press**) the button, the motor **will start.**

Now that he **has pressed** the button, he **expects** the motor to start.

Since he **had pressed** the button, he **expected** the motor to start.

Ignoring these patterns occasionally produces a monstrosity like "When he died, his fellow citizens realized how much he contributed to the community, and since then they collected funds for a memorial."

CORRECT SEQUENCE OF TENSES When he **died** [a particular time in the past], his fellow citizens **realized** [from that time on] how much he **had contributed** [up to the time of his death] to the community, and since then they **have been collecting** [from that time to the present] funds for a memorial.

An infinitive should be in the present tense unless it represents an action earlier than that of the main verb.

July 14, 1789, must have been a great day **to be alive** [not **to have been alive**].

I realized later that it was a mistake **to have chosen** [not **to choose**] the life of an artist two years earlier.

Statements that are permanently true should be put in the present tense (sometimes called the "timeless present") even though the main verb is in the past.

Copernicus **found** that the Sun **is** the center of our planetary system. [Not **was**; it still **is**.]

I **insisted** that the Amazon River **is** longer than the Nile.

The present tense is often used in book reviews and criticism for describing a novel, play, or movie. But statements about the facts of a dead author's life are normally in the past tense.

Oliver La Farge's novel **is** the story of a young Navajo whose wife **seeks** revenge for her mistreatment by a white man.

The setting of Hawthorne's short stories **is** the New England village that Hawthorne **knew** so well. [The setting of the stories is still the same; Hawthorne knew them in the past.]

(2) Principal Parts of Irregular Verbs

Irregular verbs are a small group which, instead of forming their past tenses by adding *ed* (*start, started*), change the vowel to indicate the past tense and the past participle (*begin, began, begun*). The principal parts consist of (1) the present infinitive (*begin*); (2) the past tense (*began*); (3) the past participle (*begun*). All tense forms can be derived from the three principal parts. The first principal part is the basis for all present and future tenses, including the present participle; the second principal part is used for the simple past tense—"I began the job yesterday." The third principal part is used in all the compound tenses: "I have begun," "he had begun," "the job was begun," etc.

In the speech of children, errors in the use of principal parts of the irregular verbs are common: "I throwed the ball," "We brung it home," "He has went home." The following list gives the principal parts of some irregular verbs which are apt to be confused.

present	*simple past*	*past participle*
begin	began	begun
bid **(*offer*)**	bid	bid
bid **(*command*)**	bade	bidden
bite	bit	bitten
blow	blew	blown
break	broke	broken
bring	brought	brought
burst	burst	burst
choose	chose	chosen
come	came	come
dive	dived (dove)	dived
do	did	done
draw	drew	drawn
drink	drank	drunk
eat	ate	eaten
fall	fell	fallen
fly	flew	flown
forget	forgot	forgotten (forgot)
freeze	froze	frozen

get	got	got (gotten)
go	went	gone
grow	grew	grown
know	knew	known
lie	lay	lain
ride	rode	ridden
ring	rang	rung
rise	rose	risen
run	ran	run
see	saw	seen
shrink	shrank (shrunk)	shrunk
sing	sang	sung
speak	spoke	spoken
spring	sprang (sprung)	sprung
steal	stole	stolen
swim	swam	swum
swing	swung	swung
take	took	taken
throw	threw	thrown
wear	wore	worn
write	wrote	written

(3) *Shall* and *will*

More space may be spent on the distinctions between the verbs *shall* and *will* than the topic warrants. But since very formal writing preserves the traditional distinction, it deserves an explanation. To express the simple future (the tense which indicates an event yet to occur), Formal English demands *shall* in the first person and *will* in the second and third persons. To express determination, promise, or prophecy, *will* is used in the first person and *shall* is used in the second and third person.

Simple Future:
- If you don't mind, I ***shall join*** you and we ***shall go*** together.
- If you don't hurry, you ***will be*** late.
- When he arrives, he ***will*** probably ***be*** tired.

Determination etc.:
- Despite the inconvenience, we ***will pay*** the bill.
- He ***shall do*** as I tell him.
- Thou ***shalt*** not ***kill.***
- You ***shall*** not ***escape*** the consequences of your crime.

In most speech and writing these distinctions are ignored. To express the simple future, *will* is used for all three persons. *Shall* is rarely used at all in informal speech and writing, except in questions, as a polite substitute for *let's*, or to find out what the person addressed wants.

Shall we go now? (Meaning "Let's go.")

Shall I leave the window open? (Meaning "What would you like?")

(4) Subjunctive Mood

Subjunctive forms of the verb are used much less than formerly. In speech, the subjunctive is retained only in formulas like "If I were you. . . ." Informal writing, however, often uses, and formal writing demands, the subjunctive on a few occasions:

Condition Contrary to Fact	I wish I ***were*** younger. If this ***were*** Saturday, we would be at the lake. Though the dog has just had his supper, he acts as if he ***were*** still hungry.
Indirect Imperative	The terms of the will require that the funds ***be spent*** on education. Her lawyer insists that she ***open*** a savings account.
Motions and Resolutions	I move that the minutes ***be approved.*** Resolved, that this question **be submitted** to arbitration.

Exercise 7

Correct any errors in the use of verbs in the following sentences.

1. She wore a faded blue dress, and her dusty gray shoes were once white.
2. The astronomer said that the moon was approximately 239,000 miles from the earth.
3. For a reader who had never run across advertising of this kind, a further explanation may be necessary.
4. Zephyr, our cat, would lay on the floor for hours and played with a ball of string.
5. He would have liked to have told her what he thought of her.
6. If I had chose physics as my major, I wouldn't have to write all these papers.

7. It was a serious mistake to have been so candid.
8. The book had laid right where I had put it.
9. The water level began to raise, and by noon it had rose ten feet.
10. She recognized the boy who had spoke to her at the dance.

Exercise 8

For each of the following sentences choose the proper verb form and be prepared to justify your choice.

1. I wouldn't tolerate such noise if I (*were, was*) you.
2. He moved that the motion (*is, be*) approved.
3. His mother insists that he (*come, comes*) in right now.
4. If Alaska (*was, were*) a warmer state, its population would be larger.
5. He acts as if he (*was, were*) drunk, and he probably is.
6. (*Shall, Will*) the play begin promptly at eight?
7. I am determined that he (*shall, will*) not escape punishment.
8. That bell sounds as though it (*was, were*) cracked.

Exercise 9

Correct all grammatical errors in the following sentences.

1. Most ski accidents are the results of someone being careless or thinking they are more skillful than they really are.
2. But along with increased speed comes many new problems in jet design.
3. Their bird was setting right on the perch, right where they left him three hours earlier.
4. The adolescent feels that if they do not conform, they will be unpopular.
5. Intercollegiate sports, even though the whole student body does not participate in it, provides amusement for most of the students.
6. Certain basic traits in humans, such as love of power, is a real obstacle to a peaceful world.
7. I know several people in my class whom I'm convinced scarcely opened a book in four years.
8. Criminals receive very fair trials in our country in that he is considered innocent until proved guilty.
9. Her favorite reading matter are novels, preferably science fiction.

10. According to the report, the company will give a bonus to whomever discovers the source of leakage.
11. Extra work was assigned to we students who came in late.
12. Every time any of us open a newspaper, we read of new trouble abroad.
13. The foreman of the lumber gang told Stan and I to report early the next morning.
14. Anyone with a little practice can learn to drive, can't they?
15. Within the broad limits of the assignment there are a great variety of topics for students to choose from.
16. He says he always feels bad after he had worked hard.

5 The Dictionary and Levels of Usage

5a Use of the Dictionary

Like all languages, English is continually changing. New words are added as names are required for new inventions, discoveries, and ideas: *laser, meson, transistor, cybernetics, apartheid.* Old words acquire new meanings as they are used in new ways: *half-life* (physics), *snow* (television), *software* (computers), *cartridge* (high-fidelity recording). Some old words disappear as the need for them vanishes; a whole vocabulary dealing with horse-drawn vehicles is on its way out. Words gain or lose prestige: *strenuous* and *mob* are now standard words, although they were once considered slang. *Negro,* once considered a neutral word, has taken on bad connotations and is now widely replaced by *Black.*

A dictionary is an attempt to record the current uses and meanings of words. Though many people believe that a dictionary tells them what a word *ought to* mean, or how it *should be* used, a modern dictionary tries to be an accurate and objective record of what is actually being said and written. It discriminates among the current meanings of a word and tries to indicate the ways in which each is used. Since words and constructions differ in prestige value, a conscientious lexicographer will also try to record the current status of words, usually by labels such as Dialectal or Regional, Obsolete or Archaic, Informal, Colloquial, Nonstandard, or Slang.

Large, unabridged dictionaries include a history of the past meanings of words, biographical and geographical data, guides for pronunciation, spelling, and punctuation, and a variety of other useful information. The large dictionaries in established widespread use in most college libraries include:

The Oxford English Dictionary, 12 volumes and Supplement, Clarendon Press, Oxford, 1933. Supplement A–G, 1972. (This is the standard historical dictionary of the language; it traces and illustrates the development of each word from its earliest appearance to the present.)

Webster's New International Dictionary of the English Language, Second Edition, G. & C. Merriam Co., Springfield, Mass., 1954.

Webster's Third New International Dictionary of the English Language, G. & C. Merriam Co., 1961. (This dictionary gives few usage labels.)

The Random House Dictionary of the English Language, New York, 1966.

Webster's New Twentieth Century Dictionary of the English Language, Second Edition, New York, 1958.

Unabridged dictionaries are invaluable for occasional reference, but more practical for the student are the following abridged desk dictionaries. All are reliable, but some instructors may have preferences, which they will indicate.

The American Heritage Dictionary of the English Language, Houghton Mifflin Company, Boston

Funk and Wagnalls Standard College Dictionary, Harcourt, Brace & World, Inc., New York.

The Random House College Dictionary, New York.

Webster's New Collegiate Dictionary, G. & C. Merriam Co., Springfield, Mass.

Webster's New World Dictionary, Collins, William & World Publishing Co., Inc., Cleveland, Ohio.

(1) Abbreviations and Symbols

To use a dictionary effectively, you must understand the abbreviations and symbols it uses. These are explained in its introductory section. Here are entries from four collegiate dictionaries.

spelling & syllabication ↓ *etymology* ↓

[1]**im•ply** (im plī′) *vt.* **-plied′, -ply′ing** [ME. *implien* < OFr. *emplier* < L. *implicare,* to involve, entangle < *in-,* in + *plicare,* to fold < IE. base °*plek-,* to plait, wrap together, whence Gr. *plekein,* to braid: cf. FLAX] **1.** to have as a necessary part, condition, or effect; contain, include, or involve naturally or necessarily [drama *implies* conflict] **2.** to indicate indirectly or by allusion; hint; suggest; intimate [an attitude *implying* boredom] **3.** [Obs.] to enfold; entangle **—*SYN.*** see SUGGEST

↑ *usage label*

[1]With permission. From *Websters New World Dictionary of the American Language,* Second College Edition. Copyright © 1976 by William Collins + World Publishing Co., Inc.

pronunciation ↓ *part of speech* ↓ *meanings*

[2]**im•ply** (im•plī′) *v.t.* **•plied, •ply•ing** **1.** To involve necessarily as a circumstance, condition, effect, etc.: An action *implies* an agent. **2.** To indicate or suggest without stating; hint at; intimate. **3.** To have the meaning of; signify. **4.** *Obs.* To entangle; infold. **—Syn.** See INFER. [< OF *emplier* < L *implicare* to involve < *in-* in + *plicare* to fold. Doublet of *EMPLOY.*]

—Syn. 1. *Imply* and *involve* mean to have some necessary connection. *Imply* states that the connection is causal or inherent, while *involve* is vaguer, and does not define the connection. 2. *Imply, hint, intimate, insinuate* mean to convey a meaning indirectly or covertly. *Imply* is the general term for signifying something beyond what the words obviously say; his advice *implied* confidence in the stock market. *Hint* suggests indirection in speech or action: our host's repeated glances at his watch *hinted* that it was time to go. *Intimate* suggests a process more elaborate and veiled than hint: she *intimated* that his attentions were unwelcome. *Insinuate* suggests slyness and a derogatory import: in his remarks, he *insinuated* that the Senator was a fool.

full discussion of synonyms

[2]From *Funk & Wagnalls Standard College Dictionary.* Copyright © 1963, 1966, 1968, 1973 by Funk & Wagnalls Publishing Company, Inc. Used by permission of the publisher.

inflected forms

[3]**im•ply** ĭm-plī′) *tr.v.* **-plied, -plying, -plies.** **1.** To involve or suggest by logical necessity; entail: *His aims imply a good deal of energy.* **2.** To say or express indirectly; to hint; suggest: *His tone implied a malicious purpose.* **3.** *Obsolete.* To entangle. —See Synonyms at **suggest.** —See Usage note at **infer.** [Middle English *implien, emplien,* from Old French *emplier,* from Latin *implicāre,* infold, involve, IMPLICATE.]

[3]Reprinted by permission from *The American Heritage Dictionary of the English Language.* © 1969, 1970, 1971, 1973, 1975, 1976, Houghton Mifflin Company.

[4]**im•ply** im-′plī *vt* **im•plied; im•ply•ing** [**ME** *emplien,* fr. **MF** *emplier,* fr. L *implicare*] **1** *obs* **:** ENFOLD, ENTWINE **2 :** to involve or indicate by inference, association, or necessary consequence rather than by direct statement <rights ~ obligations> **3 :** to contain potentially **4 :** to express indirectly <his silence *implied* consent> ***syn*** see SUGGEST ***ant*** express

↑ *illustration of use* ↑ *synonyms* ↑ *antonyms*

[4]By permission. From *Webster's New Collegiate Dictionary* © 1976 by G. & C. Merriam Co., Publishers of the Merriam-Webster Dictionaries.

(2) Information Found in a Dictionary

Spelling and Syllabication When more than one spelling is given, the one printed first is usually to be preferred. Division of the word into syllables follows the conventions accepted by printers.

Pronunciation A key to the symbols used to indicate pronunciation of words is usually printed on the front or back inside cover of the dictionary. Some dictionaries also run an abbreviated key to pronunciation at the bottom of each page or every other page. Word accent is shown by the symbol (′) after the stressed syllable or by (ˈ) before it.

Parts of Speech Abbreviations (explained in the introductory section of the dictionary) are used to indicate the various grammatical uses of a word: e.g., *imply, v.t.* means that *imply* is a transitive verb. Note that some words can be used as several different parts of speech. *Forfeit,* for example, is listed first as a noun, and its various meanings in this use are defined. Then its meaning when used as an adjective is given, and finally its meaning as a transitive verb.

Inflected Forms Forms of the past tense and past and present participles of verbs, the comparative or superlative degree of adjectives, and the plurals of nouns are given whenever there might be doubt as to the correct form or spelling.

Etymology The history of each word is indicated by the forms in use in Middle or Old English, or in the language from which the word was borrowed. Earlier meanings are often given.

Meanings Different meanings of a word are numbered and defined, sometimes with illustrative examples. Some dictionaries give the oldest meanings first; others list the common meanings of the word first.

Usage Labels Descriptive labels, often abbreviated, indicate the level of usage: Archaic, Obsolete, Colloquial, Slang, Dialectal, Regional, Substandard, Nonstandard, etc. Look up the meanings of these words in the dictionary you use. Sometimes usage labels indicate a special field, rather than a level of usage: e.g., *Poetic, Irish, Chemistry.* If a word has no usage label, it may be assumed that, in the opinion of the editors, the word is in common use on all levels; that is, it is *standard* English. Usage labels are often defined and illustrated in the explanatory notes in the front of a dictionary. Check yours; it is important to understand how the labels are used.

Synonyms Words that have nearly identical or closely related meanings often need careful discrimination to indicate the precise connotation of each. A full account of the distinctions in meaning between synonyms (for example, *suggest, imply, hint, intimate,* and *insinuate*) may be given at the end of the entry for the basic word, or cross references to its synonyms may be provided.

Exercise 1

In looking up the meanings of words, try to discover within what limits of meaning the word may be used. Read the definition as a whole; do not pick out a single synonym and suppose that this and the word defined are interchangeable. After looking up the following words in your dictionary, write sentences which will unmistakably illustrate the meaning of each word.

anachronism	innocuous	precocious
eminent	materiel	sinecure
fetish	misanthropy	sophistication
hedonist	nepotism	taboo
imminent	philanthropy	travesty

Exercise 2

Look up each of the following words both in an unabridged dictionary and in an abridged one, and write a report showing how the larger volume explains the use of each word more discriminatingly and clearly than the smaller one does. State the exact title, the publisher, and the date of both dictionaries.

Bible	Christian	court	idealism
catholic	color	evolution	liberal

Exercise 3

How may the etymologies given by the dictionary help one to remember the meaning or the spelling of the following words? (Note that when a series of words has the same etymology, the etymology is usually given only with the basic word of the series.)

alibi	insidious	privilege
capitol	isosceles	sacrilegious
cohort	magnanimous	sarcasm
concave	malapropism	subterfuge
denouement	peer (noun)	thrifty

Exercise 4

Most dictionaries put abbreviations in the main alphabetical arrangement. Look up the following abbreviations and be ready to state in class what they mean:

at. wt.	colloq.	E.T.A.	K.C.B.	LL.D.	PBX
CAB	e.g.	ff.	l.c.	OAS	QKtP

Exercise 5

Consult the dictionary for the distinction in meaning between the members of each of the following pairs of words:

neglect–negligence	instinct–intuition
ingenuous–ingenious	nauseous–nauseated
fewer–less	eminent–famous
admit–confess	criticize–censure
infer–imply	increment–addition

Exercise 6

In each sentence, choose the more precise of the two italicized words. Be able to justify your choice.

1. Many in the class were *disinterested, uninterested* and went to sleep.
2. His charming innocence is *childlike, childish.*
3. The problem is to assure the farm workers *continuous, continual* employment.
4. She is *continuously, continually* in trouble with the police.
5. I am quite *jealous, envious* of your opportunity to study in Europe.
6. She is so *decided, decisive* in her manner that people always give in to her.
7. If we give your class all of these privileges, we may establish *precedents, precedence* which are unwise.
8. She always makes her health her *alibi, excuse* for her failures.

Exercise 7

Find the precise meaning of each word in the following groups, and write sentences to illustrate that meaning.

1. abandon, desert, forsake	4. meager, scanty, sparse
2. ludicrous, droll, comic	5. knack, talent, genius
3. silent, reserved, taciturn	6. anxious, eager, avid

5b Levels of Usage

(1) Standard English

STANDARD ENGLISH includes the great majority of words and constructions that native speakers would recognize as acceptable in any situation or context. All words in a dictionary that are not specifically labeled are, in the judgment of the editors, Standard English and acceptable for general use. However, a good many words and constructions have, for various reasons, a more limited use and these are commonly labeled in dictionaries. For example, words used in some sections of the country but not in all, like *carry* in the sense of "escort to a dance or party," will be labeled REGIONAL or DIALECTAL. If the usage is more localized, like *arroyo* (a dry gully), the word will be labeled *Southwestern U.S.*, or *New England*, or whatever. Other labels explain words still found in books but no longer in common use, like OBSOLETE (for example, *deer* used in the sense of "any animal," as in Shakespeare's "Rats and mice and such small deer") or ARCHAIC (very old but preserved for historical or poetic reasons, like *olden*).

In addition to such geographic or temporal limitations on word use, most people feel that certain kinds of language, or certain dialects, have more or less prestige because of the people who use them. In the past, the language of the educated upper class was thought of as Good English, and all other dialects or levels were ignored or condemned as incorrect, ungrammatical, or illiterate. To the modern linguist, all the dialects spoken by different groups in American society are equally valid varieties of English, but they are not always appropriate in serious public writing.

In a country where many people are trying to improve their position in an open society, differences in prestige among dialects need to be pointed out. The usual way to do this in a handbook is to attach Usage Labels to words which are limited in some way. This handbook, in addition to regional and temporal labels, tries to indicate levels of acceptability by using the following labels: STANDARD (acceptable in formal and informal use), FORMAL, INFORMAL, (or general), COLLO-

QUIAL, SLANG, and NONSTANDARD. The overlapping of various levels and labels (in capital letters) can be seen in the following diagram.

Levels of Usage

Edited English	FORMAL	Not Labeled
	INFORMAL (General)	
Spoken English	COLLOQUIAL	Labeled
	SLANG	
	NONSTANDARD	

Notice that Edited English, the main concern of this handbook, is not labeled in most dictionaries. Accordingly, any word that *is* labeled in your dictionary should be used sparingly, if at all, in public writing.

Sharp lines cannot always be drawn between the levels indicated by these labels, but relative differences are clear. *Fatigued* and *exhausted* are more formal than *tired,* which in turn is more formal than *bushed* (Colloquial) or *pooped* (Slang). *Fatigued* seldom occurs in speech and is usually found only in technical or poetic writing. *Tired* is acceptable in any spoken or written context. *Bushed* would be used mainly in familiar conversation or in writing among friends. The slang term *pooped* would seldom appear in serious writing, and then only for its shock value or its slightly comic effect.

As we have seen, levels of usage, like the language itself, undergo changes from generation to generation. Such changes have been especially rapid in recent decades. During the past fifty years, the center of Edited usage has moved away from the Formal level toward the Informal. Especially in magazines and newspapers, good writers are more apt to use colloquialisms and even slang rather than risk the stilted pomposity of Formal English in a commonplace context. Many once-forbidden words are coming up in the world, too. *Ain't* used to be universally regarded as Nonstandard; today, though it is generally disapproved even in informal writing, some dictionaries label it Nonstandard only when it is used to mean "has not" or "have not," as in "I ain't got any." As a result of a campaign by the advertising industry, *like* is now widely used as a conjunction ("like a cigarette should"; "tell it like it is"), though recent dictionaries continue to label this usage Nonstandard or Colloquial. It seems likely that, eventually, this use of *like* will be generally acceptable, despite the distaste of purists. Meanwhile, if your dictionary indicates by a usage label that a word is limited in its use, you will do well to keep that word out of your serious writing—that is, an article for a college magazine (unless you are trying for some special effect), a term paper, or a letter of application.

The basic principle of good usage is to fit the level of your language to the situation and to the expected reader. Formal English is for formal occasions, like Commencement or a funeral, or for official personages, like college presidents in their public speech and writings. You would not be apt to use the noun *gripe* in a Commencement address, an obituary or a letter to the President. Conversely, language suitable for a letter of application might be inappropriate in the locker room or a poker game. In making such discriminations, your own sense of the language (your Grammar 1), aided in doubtful cases by the dictionary, will have to serve you. But before your dictionary can help you with such problems, you must study the meaning of the labels it uses. The labels used in this handbook are explained below.

(2) Formal English

FORMAL ENGLISH appears in scholarly or scientific articles, formal speeches, official documents, and any context calling for scrupulous propriety. It makes use of words and phrases like "scrupulous propriety," which nobody would use in speech and which would seldom appear in ordinary writing. As another example, consider the word *scrutinize.* This is a perfectly good word that everyone knows, but its use is almost entirely limited to formal written English, and even there it is not common. It is apt to give a bookish flavor to ordinary writing, and it is almost never used in speech. (Try to imagine yourself handing a friend a piece of writing with the request "Scrutinize this.") Formal English also includes technical language—the specialized vocabularies used in such professions as law, medicine, and the sciences. Technical language can be very precise and economical, but it is Greek to the ordinary reader and out of place in most Edited English. A good general rule is to use formal or technical language, like best clothes, only on special occasions.

(3) Edited English

EDITED ENGLISH is the written language of books from reputable publishers, good magazines, and many newspapers. It is defined, not merely by choice of words, but by generally accepted conventions of spelling, punctuation, grammatical patterns, and sentence structure. In this section, we are considering Edited English primarily as it is reflected in choice of words. But the general purpose of all the rules laid down in this handbook is to enable you to write Edited English, the normal means of official communication in the professions and in the upper levels of business and industry.

Authorities, it must be admitted, often differ among themselves. Many handbooks, including this one, deplore the use of *contact* as a verb meaning "to get in touch with." Theodore Bernstein of the *New York Times*, though he dislikes the usage, admits in *The Careful Writer* that it is a useful verb and "will undoubtedly push its way into standard usage sometime." The most recent editions of three leading dictionaries differ widely: one accepts the usage, with no label, as standard English; one gently reproves it as an "Americanism"; the third labels it *Informal* and disapproves its use in Edited English.

Faced with such disagreement, what practical conclusion can we draw? If you use *contact* as a verb and someone challenges it, you can of course defend yourself by citing *Webster's New Collegiate Dictionary*, which makes no objection to it. But being challenged is a nuisance, and your defensive explanations are seldom convincing. If the main purpose of your writing is to get something said, don't use words that are likely to be challenged or that need lengthy defense.

(4) Colloquial English

COLLOQUIAL ENGLISH means, literally, conversational English. Everyone's language is more casual and relaxed among friends than in public speech or writing. Colloquial expressions are part of Standard English, since everyone uses them, but they may be jarringly out of place in formal contexts or in serious writing. Examples are words like *rock hound*, to *get away with* something, *sure* in the sense of "certainly" (I sure would like . . .), or a *square deal*. When words and constructions are labeled *Colloquial* (some dictionaries use *Informal* for the same purpose), you should consider their possible effects on a reader before writing them. If in doubt, look for an accepted synonym.

(5) Nonstandard English

The label NONSTANDARD indicates the wide variety of usages not generally accepted in writing: misspellings, unconventional punctuation, illiterate grammatical constructions, and certain widely heard expressions that educated people have qualms about writing. Examples are words like *nowheres, hain't,* especially in double negative constructions like "I hain't got none," and constructions like *he don't,* or *of* for *have* in sentences like "I would of gone. . . ." Expressions labeled *Nonstandard* have no place in serious Edited English, except in direct quotation.

(6) Dialect

A DIALECT is a form of the native language spoken in a particular region of the country or in a large geographical area by a particular group of persons. Its vocabulary and grammatical structures often differ from Standard English, which is the dialect of prestige and power in the United States. Within the region or among the group, however, the dialect may be more prestigious than Standard English. Dialect words are often colorful and vigorous: *varmint, poke, blood, polecat, da kine, foxy, streak-o-lean, talk story, branch water.* Some dialects, such as that in the Southeast, retain words from the early settlers—*reckon, yonder*—and echo grammar that was in use before Latin rules were imposed on English syntax. There's no question about what the dialect phrase "it don't bother me none" means, even though double negatives were banished from Standard English in the eighteenth century. Black dialect retains the "be" verb in its aspectual sense, as a state of being, a form now lost to Standard English. "I be working when he be bothering me" is not the same sentence as "I am working when he bothers me," its standard English approximation. An important distinction is lost in translation.

Often people create dialects in order to speak to one another. Black Dialect began as a means of communicating among slave traders (who were not always English), English slave owners, and persons sold into slavery who spoke a number of African languages. The pidgin dialect of Hawaii came about when persons from radically differing language families—the Tagalogs of the Philippines, Portuguese, Hawaiians, Japanese, Chinese—needed to communicate as they worked under English overseers side by side in the cane fields. The dialect is characterized by the absence of features which give English speakers difficulty: prepositions, tenses of verbs, articles. Because the dialects are spoken, the many inflections of English are not needed. Neither Black Dialect nor Hawaiian Pidgin consistently obeys the agreement rule. Students who are bi-dialectal, that is, fluent in Standard English and a dialect, are wise to be aware of those areas where their spoken and written voices conflict; they should proofread scrupulously to make sure they have followed the conventions of Edited English.

(7) Regional English

The label REGIONAL refers to a usage which is considered reputable in certain areas of the country, but which has not gained nationwide acceptance. These words are not necessarily nonstandard in the regions where they are found, and sometimes they are useful additions to the local vocabulary. But for general college writing, they should not be used when equivalent words in national currency are available. Some examples of regional words are *crack grass* for *crab grass*, *monkeychop* for *chipmunk*, *you all* to refer to one person, *eastworm* or *angle dog* for *angleworm*.

(8) Slang

SLANG is the label given to words with a forced, exaggerated, or humorous meaning used in extremely informal contexts, particularly by persons who wish to set themselves off from the average, respectable citizen.

To call a man whose ideas and behavior are unpredictable and unconventional "a kook" and to describe his ideas as "for the birds" or "way out" apparently satisfies some obscure human urge toward irreverent, novel, and vehement expression. Some slang terms remain in fairly wide use because they are vivid ways of expressing an idea which has no exact standard equivalent: *stooge, lame duck, shot* of whiskey, a card *shark*. Such words have a good chance of becoming accepted as Standard English. *Mob, banter, sham,* and *lynch* were all once slang terms. It is quite likely that, eventually, useful slang words, like *honkytonk* or *snitch* will be accepted as standard colloquial English.

A good deal of slang, however, reflects nothing more than the user's desire to be different, and such slang has little chance of being accepted into the language. Newspaper columnists and sports writers often use a flamboyant jargon intended to show off their ingenuity or cleverness. For centuries criminals have used a special, semisecret language, and many modern slang terms originated in the argot of the underworld: *gat, scram, squeal,* or *sing* (confess), *push* (peddle). Hippies and rock musicians have developed a constantly changing slang which seems intended to distinguish the user as a member of a select group or inner circle.

Whatever the motive behind it, slang should be used with discretion. Its incongruity in a sober, practical context makes it an effective way of achieving force and emphasis.

ACCEPTABLE SLANG His book is so intelligently constructed, so beautifully written, so really acute at moments—and so *phony*.

But most slang terms are too violent to fit comfortably into everyday writing. Furthermore, slang goes out of fashion very quickly through overuse, and dated slang sounds more quaint and old-fashioned than Formal English. *Tight* has worn well, but *boiled, crocked, fried,* and *plastered* may soon be museum pieces.

The chief objection to the use of slang is that it so quickly loses any precise meaning. Calling a person a *fink,* a *square,* or a *creep* conveys little more than your feeling of dislike. *Cool* and *crummy* are the vaguest kind of terms, lumping all experience into two crude divisions, pleasing and unpleasing. Try to get several people to agree on the precise meaning of *square* and you will realize how vague and inexact a term it is. The remedy is to analyze your meaning and specify it. What exactly are the qualities which lead you to classify a person as a *square,* or as a *weirdo?*

If, despite these warnings, you must use slang in serious writing, do it deliberately and accept the responsibility for it. Do not attempt to excuse yourself by putting the slang term in quotation marks. If you are ashamed of a slang term, do not use it.

Exercise 8

With the aid of a dictionary and your own linguistic judgment (i.e., your ear for appropriateness), classify the following Standard English words as Formal, Informal, or Colloquial.

1. crank, eccentric, [a] character
2. hide, sequester, ditch
3. irascible, cranky, grouchy
4. increase, boost, jack [up the price]
5. decline, avoid, pass [up]
6. pass [out], faint, swoon
7. necessity, [a] must, requirement
8. inexpensive, [a] steal, cheap
9. snooty, pretentious, affected
10. room, domicile, pad

Exercise 9

For each of the following Standard English words supply one or more slang terms and, to the best of your ability, judge which are so widespread that they have already begun to creep into highly informal writing (e.g., letters to friends; college newspaper columns) or seem likely to do so in the near future.

Example: to become excited [to be turned on by, *slang*]

1. money
2. to relax
3. a skilled performer
4. to be going steady or in love
5. failure
6. to tell off
7. pleasant or enjoyable
8. to play a part
9. liquor
10. to ignore or disregard
11. complaint
12. a dull person
13. unconventional person
14. to be unfairly treated
15. puzzling

Exercise 10

Pick five or six slang terms widely used around campus and ask at least five people to define the meaning of each term in Standard English. Write the results and your conclusions.

6 Effective Diction

Diction, or choice of words, is the foundation of good style. The word *diction* is derived from the Latin *dicere,* to say, and ultimately from the Indo-European root *deik,* to show, or to point out, as its kinship with the Latin word for finger, *digitus,* and the English *digit* reveals. When we don't know the name for something we point to it. Written words are ways of pointing out things we do not always see to persons who are not there.

No word, of course, can ever duplicate what we touch and see or the turmoil that we feel. Recognizing this limitation of language, writers who are attentive to diction achieve precision by selecting words which most nearly approximate their thoughts. That even the most scrupulous stylists are occasionally misunderstood is evidence that no system of communication is perfect. But too often apprentice writers have the suspicion or hope that under, over, or behind what appears on the page lies a meaning that can be discovered, not by going through the words, but by brushing them aside. For the unskilled writer words seem barricades which obstruct understanding. "You *know* what I'm saying," such a writer insists, but no one knows what goes on in our heads until we choose the words that say precisely what we mean.

To do this we need a large, active vocabulary that we can use confidently in writing as well as passively in reading. Good writers own and use dictionaries. Look up both the meaning and pronunciation of the unfamiliar words you come across in reading and those which seem familiar but which you cannot define. Keep a vocabulary notebook and use these words frequently in conversation and writing. You may blunder in getting acquainted with a new word, for context often determines diction. But the awareness you will gain of a word's appropriateness is worth the risk of having a word circled on the returned manuscript.

6a Denotation and Connotation

Words resonate, and connotations are the echoes, the overtones. They have little to do with the denotations or literal meanings, but they often dictate what is suitable diction. *House, home,* and *domicile* all have the same denotation—a place of residence. But their connotations are quite different: *house* emphasizes the physical structure; *home* suggests family life, warmth, comfort, affection; *domicile* has strictly legal overtones.

The connotation of each word must be appropriate to the context. It would not be possible to write a sentimental song entitled "House, Sweet House," nor would it seem fitting to call the guest residence of the President of the United States "Blair Home." Similarly, the word *skull* is appropriate in a medical book or ghost story, but its connotations make it unsuitable in an advertisement for men's clothing: not "a hat to suit each type of *skull*" but "a hat to suit each type of *head*."

Colors connote a variety of associations beyond their literal definition as qualities which differ on the basis of absorbed or reflected light. A translator of the Spanish poet, García Lorca, for example, can count on English readers bringing the associations of youth, vigor, freshness, spring to the translation of "Verde que te quiero verde" as "Green, how much I want you green," even though the music of the Spanish line is lost. When Andrew Marvell three centuries ago praised "a green thought in a green shade," he knew very well that readers of English after his lifetime would bring to the phrase associations of grass, trees, growth, life, tranquility. Blue thoughts would be moody and troubled, yellow thoughts sprightly, brown thoughts pensive and melancholy, black thoughts foreboding.

Since English, along with some other languages, uses color words to designate racial groups, we should be alert to connotations which might result from unconscious or primitive reactions to the physical world. Our fears of the night, the absence of the sun's light and warmth, contribute to the negative overtones some speakers still associate with the word *black,* and which have produced the words *blackhearted, blackmail, blacklist.* The campaign of American Blacks to offset the negative connotations of the word with the positive ones of power and beauty and to strip the word *white* of its exclusive associations with purity, holiness and innocence represents a conscious effort by users of the language to alter the ways in which our minds respond to words.

Poets and children know that a similarity of sounds often prompts an association of words. "Sticks and stones may break my bones, but names will never hurt me," a taunted child chants with the grim bravado of the wounded. The magical power of the incantation, invoked in the midst of evidence which proves the contrary, is created by the alliteration of the words or the repetition of initial consonants —*st* and *st, b* and *b, n* and *n*—as well as by the true rhyme of *stones* and *bones.* The harmony of sound and syllable gives the authority of truth to what is a strategic falsehood. Besides sounding alike, *bones* and *stones* associate on the basis of shared qualities: they are gray-white in color, hard, dry. They can be used as weapons, lead to death, lie together in tombs, which is itself a slant rhyme for the words. The poet, Phyllis Thompson, concludes a poem: "When I die, I will turn to bone/like these. And dust of bone. And then, like God,/to stone," relying on the assonance or vowel repetition to give the lines the finality of a well fabricated design. *Rocks* and *bones* do not associate in the same way, neither do *stones* and *skin* even though they begin with the same letter.

Such word communities are not described in dictionaries or in a thesaurus, but we can recognize them by paying close attention to the sounds of words.

6b Abstract and Concrete

Words which name specific, tangible things are concrete; words which designate general qualities, categories, or relationships are abstract. A general term like *food* is a name for a whole group of specific things—from vegetable soup to T-bone steak to strawberry shortcake. If you want to make a statement about all foods, the general term is appropriate: "Food is becoming more and more expensive." But do not use the general term when concrete details and specific words are called for.

VAGUE AND GENERAL For dinner we had some really good food.

SPECIFIC For dinner we had barbecued steaks and sweet corn.

VAGUE AND GENERAL She liked to argue about controversial subjects.

SPECIFIC She liked to argue about politics and religion.

Note that specific *and* general *are relative, not absolute terms. In the following list, which runs from specific to more general, any of the four terms might be used to refer to a famous tree growing on campus:*

SPECIFIC Charter Oak (one particular tree)

LESS SPECIFIC oak (includes thousands of trees)

MORE GENERAL tree (includes oaks, pines, palms, etc.)

MORE GENERAL plant (includes trees, flowers, bushes, etc.)

Tree is more specific than *plant,* but more general than *oak.*

Many common nouns and adjectives were once the names of places and persons: *maudlin* (Mary Magdalen), *tawdry* (St. Audrey), *laconic* (Laconia), *romance* (Rome). Language begins in the concrete. We can trace most English words back to Indo-European roots which plunge into the firm soil of the tangible world. Indeed, the word *concrete* derives from the Latin prefix *com* (together) and the word *crescere* (to grow), which itself grows out of the name for the Roman earth goddess, *Ceres,* a curious beginning for a word which today denotes pavements and connotes the covering of growing things.

When we are learning a language we ask for the names of what we see, hear, smell, touch, taste: red, thunder, burning, smooth, salty. Later we begin to classify the particulars of our experience into categories which are abstract: color, sound, odor, texture, flavor. The word *abstract,* a combination of the prefix *ab* (away from) and *trahere* (to pull) means literally "to take away from." The process of abstraction takes the particularities away from things and arranges them in groups according to their sameness. It deals in generalities rather than in specifics.

Teachers of writing with good reason urge their students to be specific, to be concrete. Too often students write in vague generalities which seem to have no reference to the world of particular experience. We cannot, of course, avoid the abstract altogether. Nor should we, for we must organize the evidence gathered by our senses into summaries and concepts. The best writing moves gracefully from abstract to concrete and back from particular to general. Writing of the poet, William Wordsworth, Margaret Drabble ballasts abstract statement with vivid, concrete images:

> ***To people who do not know or do not like his poetry, he presents an image made up of all kinds of forbidding and unpleasant characteristics:*** he is a pious, grey-haired, elderly Victorian grandfather; a puritanical, humorless water-drinker; a lover of Nature, friend to butterflies, bees and little daisies; in fact, a sentimental, tedious old bore, with a moral reflection ready for any subject that should come up, from Alpine scenery to railways or his neighbour's spade.

The less skillful writer might have ended the sentence with the colorless abstraction, *characteristics,* but Drabble uses her keen eye for detail to fill out a portrait of the poet as he exists in the minds of his detractors.

6c Weak and Vigorous Verbs

Anemic writing often results when, rather than using a vigorous verb, we connect subject and complement with a form of the verb *to be.* Such forms, known as *linking* (or *copulative*) verbs, also include *become, seem, appear, remain,* etc. We cannot, of course, write without linking verbs, especially when indicating logical equivalents:

> "Yoruk doctors, with extremely rare exceptions, were women—all their great doctors were women." (Theodora Kroeber)

The linking verb were *functions as an equal sign in mathematics and is appropriate to Kroeber's sentence.*

Acceptable in speech, the phrase "the reason is because" weakens written assertions. Don't waste words: "The reason I like the play is because Nora walks out the door." Be assertive: "I like the play because Nora walks out the door."

Make your verbs work. Good writers enliven their observations by selecting sharp verbs and by using verbals as modifiers. Consider these sentences from an essay by the Black poet, Langston Hughes:

> Let the blare of Negro jazz bands and the bellowing voice of Bessie Smith singing Blues penetrate the closed ears of the colored near-intellectuals until they listen and perhaps understand. Let Paul Robeson singing Water Boy, and Rudolph Fisher writing about the streets of Harlem, and Jean Toomer holding the heart of

> Georgia in his hands, and Aaron Douglas drawing strange black fantasies cause the smug Negro middle class to turn from their white, respectable, ordinary books and papers to catch a glimmer of their own beauty.

The verbs which make the assertion of the statement, *let, penetrate, listen, understand, cause, to turn, to catch,* are reinforced by the continuous action of the participles, *bellowing, singing, writing, holding,* and *drawing.* Even the nouns *blare* and *glimmer* contribute energy, since they can function in other contexts as verbs.

Occur, took place, prevail, exist, happen, and other verbs expressing a state of affairs have legitimate uses, but they are often colorless, tossed in merely to complete a sentence.

WEAK In the afternoon a sharp drop in the temperature occurred.
STRONGER The temperature dropped sharply in the afternoon.

WEAK Throughout the meeting an atmosphere of increasing tension existed.
STRONGER As the meeting progressed, the tension increased.

Linking verbs completed by an adjective or participle are usually weaker than concrete verbs.

WEAK He was occasionally inclined to talk too much.
STRONGER Occasionally he talked too much.

WEAK In some high schools there is a very definite lack of emphasis on the development of a program in remedial English.
STRONGER Some high schools have failed to develop programs in remedial English.

Unnecessary use of the passive voice also produces weak sentences.

6d Jargon

There are two kinds of jargon: the technical language used by certain professionals and the empty generalities that are the bluff of the incompetent, unthinking writer. We should take pains to excise from our writing the jargon which obscures the obvious. Ponderous, wordy, vague, inflated writing is characteristic of those bureaucrats, publicists, government employees, college professors, and students who hope that the dense air of their prose will give depth and authority to commonplace ideas.

Our minds are numbed everyday by foggy phrases like *capability factors, career potential, culturally disadvantaged, socio-personal development, substantive social interaction, protective reaction strike, inoperative fiscal procedures*. It is not easy to escape from this widely publicized network of confused language, but if we learn to recognize the stylistic flavor of jargon, we may avoid it in our own writing. Jargon words are, by and large, abstract rather than concrete, and contain more than one syllable (as if the jargon writer assumed that the addition of a syllable would add weight to the word). Jargon words are often nouns masquerading as verbs: *concretize, minimize, finalize, interiorize*. Sometimes nouns are turned into adverbs or adjectives by the addition of the suffix *wise: languagewise, subjectwise, moneywise, weatherwise*. Jargon is best deflated by a translation into clear English:

> A corollary of reinforcement is that the consequences of responding may be represented exhaustively along a continuum ranging from those that substantially raise response likelihood, through those that have little or no effect on response likelihood, to those that substantially reduce response likelihood. An event is a positive reinforcer if its occurrence or presentation after a response strengthens the response. Sometimes good grades, words of praise, or salary checks act as positive reinforcers. An object or event is a negative reinforcer if its withdrawal or termination after a response strengthens the response. Often bad grades, shame, or worthless payments act as negative reinforcers. The above notion sounds complex and difficult to apply but is indeed extremely simple.

The relatively plain English of the third and fifth sentences contrasts vividly with the puffy syllables, the awkward constructions, the straining adverbs and unclear substantives which clutter the rest of the paragraph. What the writer wants to say is, as he notes, fairly simple, though abstract:

> The psychological principle of reinforcement means that the likelihood of a learned response is increased if a person is rewarded for responding correctly. Good grades, words of praise, or salary checks act as positive reinforcers. Bad grades, shame, or worthless payments are negative reinforcers in that a response is strengthened only if such consequences are eliminated.

In addition to being obscure and tiresome, jargon, when it conceals or distorts the reality it describes, can be dangerous, even deadly. The phrase *anti-personnel detonating devices* obscures the bitter reality of bombs which kill men, women, and children. Similarly, the deviousness of official statements like "The U.S. cannot foreclose any option for retaliation" distracts us from the protest we might register had the writer said what he meant: "The U.S. will use nuclear weapons if necessary."

6e Idiom

In English we rely on prepositions to indicate subtle but essential relationships between words. To take a stand *on* an issue, to be *in* a quandary, *out of* luck, *off* your rocker—these idiomatic expressions make a kind of spatial sense. But some verbs require prepositions which are arbitrary and cannot always be explained. How can persons who are learning English and know the words *take, in, up, down,* and *over,* deduce the meaning of *take in* (comprehend), *taken in* (fooled), *take up* (begin to do something), *take down* (humiliate), *take over* and *overtake?* They can't; they must learn each idiom separately. Here are some idiomatic uses of prepositions:

Abide *by* a decision
agree *with* a person; *to* a proposal; *on* a procedure
argue *with* a person; *for* or *against* or *about* a measure
angry *at* or *about* something; *with* a person
compatible *with*
correspond *to* or *with* a thing; *with* a person
differ *from* one another in appearance; differ *with* a person in opinion
independent *of*
interfere *with* a performance; *in* someone else's affairs
listen *to* a person, argument, or sound; listen *at* the door
with regard *to* or *as* regards
stand *by* a friend; *for* a cause; *on* an issue
superior *to;* better *than*
wait *on* a customer; *for* a person; *at* a place; *in* the rain; *by* the hour

Idiom demands that certain words be followed by infinitives, others by gerunds. For instance:

able to go	capable of going
like to go	enjoy going
eager to go	cannot help going
hesitate to go	privilege of going

If two idioms are used in a compound construction, each idiom must be complete.

INCOMPLETE He had no love or confidence in his employer.
COMPLETE BUT AWKWARD He had no *love for,* or *confidence in,* his employer.
IMPROVED He had no love for his employer and no confidence in him.
INCOMPLETE I shall always remember the town because of the good times and the friends I made there.
COMPLETE I shall always remember the town because of the *good times I had* and the *friends I made* there.

6f Pretentious Diction

Pretentious diction, like the pretentious person, is stiff, attitudinizing, phony—in short, a bore. Our diction becomes pretentious if we always choose the polysyllabic word over the word of one syllable, a Latinate word when an Anglo-Saxon one will do, flowery phrases in place of common nouns and verbs. Writing should be as honest and forthright as plain speech. And since we have the opportunity to revise and edit what we write, it should be even more economical, direct, and to the point.

Sometimes ordinary words seem inadequate to carry the weight we wish thoughts to have, so we encumber statements with ornate language:

> A perusal of the tomes penned by the ancient bards can influence our future life patterns.

The sentence is saying little more than "the study of ancient books can teach us how to live," but the pompous and wordy language is out of proportion to the statement it makes.

Occasionally we lapse into pretentious diction in an attempt to give our prose a lofty or poetic tone. To protect yourself against this, read your writing aloud to a classmate. If he or she looks uncomfortable or laughs at the wrong places or seems annoyed by the tone, examine the diction of your paper for phony phrases, for words that don't sound like you.

Be wary of words which swell hard facts into tepid air: *impecunious* for *poor, inebriated* for *drunk, interred* for *buried, expired* for *died, pulchritude* for *beauty, perambulate* for *walk, lacerate* for *cut, alleviate* for *relieve, utilize* for *use, attired* for *clothed, abandoned* for *left, verdant* for *green.* As you consult dictionaries and a thesaurus in order to develop your vocabulary, note the fine distinctions among synonyms and listen to the sounds of the words to judge whether they will strike your reader as false or genuine.

6g Wordiness and Euphemism

Writing which is needlessly repetitious has a strained, awkward tone. If handled carefully, repetition can be effective:

> A *people* that grows accustomed to sloppy writing is *a people* in process of losing grip *on its* empire and *on its*elf.
>
> Ezra Pound
>
> *Pound emphasizes his declaration by restating the subject and repeating the preposition* on *and the pronoun* its *as a reflexive.*

Often, however, repetition is cumbersome:

AWKWARD Probably the next problem that confronts parents is the problem of adequate schooling for their children.

There is no reason for emphasizing problem *and no excuse for clumsily echoing its sound in the cautious* probably.

IMPROVED The parents' next problem is finding adequate schooling for their children.

Read your writing aloud to catch offenses to the ear which are elusive to the eye. Alliteration and other repetition of sounds, functional in poetry, are rarely suited to expository prose.

UNSUITABLE Henderson set some kind of record by sliding farther on the slippery slope than anyone else had slid.

Intensives such as *really, very, so, much,* which may give emphasis to conversation, weaken written language. They are usually attempts to relieve the writer of finding a word that is emphatic in itself. Why settle for *really angry* when there are *enraged* and *furious,* with *so sad* when there are *desolate, doleful, crushed,* with *very bad* when there are *wicked, detestable, rotten, vile?*

Often when we want to avoid harsh facts we resort to a particular kind of circumlocution, the *euphemism.* The Greek word means "good speech," but euphemisms seldom are good for writers. Too often they are cosmetics to cover up painful realities. To avoid facing the cold finality of death people have always used euphemisms: *passed on* or *passed, gone west, met his Maker, gone to her reward.*

The *dear departed* rests in his casket in the *slumber room,* often having been *prepared* by the *funeral director* who today is likely to preside at a *memorial service* instead of a funeral. Ultimately, the *loved one* is not buried but *laid to rest,* not in a graveyard but in the *Valley of Memories.* Such sentimental wordiness is intended to comfort the bereaved by pretending that death is sleep, but its effect is one of stilted insincerity. There is no need, however, to go to the opposite extreme and speak ill of the subject. *Croak* and *kick the bucket,* while brisk and salty, are no closer to the fact of dying than *wrestled with the Angel of Death and was vanquished.*

6h Figurative Language

A statement which advises you to prune deadwood from your writing uses a metaphor which implicitly compares language to a growing tree and revising to the gardener's art of cutting out decayed and useless limbs. We speak in pictures all the time, calling them figures of speech. Words often contain images of the world around us. I *see* what you mean, we say; it is *as clear as day.* These are dead metaphors, the clichés of everyday speech which we rely on for quick communication, but which make for dull writing. The more we are aware of the pictures words make, the better we will be able to use them.

The word *metaphor,* the comparison of two different things on the basis of a shared quality, is itself a buried metaphor, since it means to transfer or carry across. When we compare, we are carrying a trait from one thing to another as if over a bridge or a road. Metaphor says one thing *is* another:

> "the prairie is an anvil's edge . . . the houses are sentinels" (Scott Momaday).

A *simile* uses the words *like* or *as* to state a comparison:

> "I sensed a wrongness around me, like an alarm clock that had gone off without being set." (Maya Angelou)

A comparison can be extended into an *analogy* which not only illustrates a point, but suggests an argument or point of view, as Mary Ellman does in her startling analogy between astronauts and pregnant women:

> The astronaut's body is as awkward and encumbered in the space suit as the body of a pregnant woman. It moves about with even more graceless difficulty. And being shot up into the air suggests submission too, rather than enterprise. Like a woman being carted to a delivery room, the astronaut must sit (or lie) still, and go where he is sent. Even the nerve, the genuine courage it takes simply not to run away, is much the same in both situations—to say nothing of the shared sense of having gone too far to be able to change one's mind.

In an *allusion* the comparison made is between some present event, situation, or person and an event or person from history or literature. Usually it is a brief reference to something which the reader is assumed to be familiar with, as when Adrienne Rich says of a woman who reads about women in books written by men:

> "She finds a terror and a dream, she finds a beautiful face, she finds La Belle Dame Sans Merci, she finds Juliet or Tess or Salome, but precisely what she does not find is that absorbed, drudging, puzzled, sometime inspired creature, herself, who sits at a desk trying to put words together."

A sense of audience should determine what allusions, if any, are appropriate. While you should expect intelligence in persons who read what you write, there is no point in throwing away allusions or in alienating your readers by appearing to be more knowledgeable than they.

Trite Metaphors

Figures of speech which may have been fresh when they were first coined become trite and stale in time. We call such worn out figures of speech dead metaphors or clichés. Writing filled with clichés is dull, banal, hackneyed. By and large, we are wise to the politician who claims that he is all for *mom and apple pie,* for *God's country* and *man's best friend,* for the *man on the street* and *the little woman,* whose *place is in the home,* which is a *man's castle* where the *apple of his eye* and *the chip off the old block* are lucky to live in the *land of opportunity* where *every boy can grow up to be president.* But you should also watch out for similar tired expressions in your own writing. Here is a modest list of clichés you would do well to *avoid like the plague:*

abreast of the times
acid test
agony of suspense
as luck would have it
beat a hasty retreat
bitter end
bolt from the blue
breathless silence
checkered career
cool as a cucumber
deep, dark secret
depths of despair
doomed to disappointment
few and far between
green with envy
heave a sigh of relief
hit the nail on the head
last but not least
live from hand to mouth
other side of the coin
poor but honest
proud possessor of
quick as a flash
reigns supreme
rotten to the core
slow but sure
straight from the shoulder
tempest in a teapot
undercurrent of excitement
walking on air
water under the bridge
wave of optimism
wended their way
worth its weight in gold

Mixed Metaphors

Create metaphors out of your own observations and with your own eyes, but be careful that your metaphors make logical and visual sense. Often the metaphors impressed like fossils into everyday words become so faint we have difficulty seeing them. Unless we pay close attention to what words mean, we can make some bizarre assertions:

> He was saddled with a sea of grass-roots opinion that his campaign workers had ferreted out for him.

Such a surrealistic image is a badly mixed metaphor. Combinations as confused as this one can often be caught by picturing what the words are saying.

> The administration jettisoned the groundwork laid by the student government.
>
> He penetrated the impervious gaze of his challenger.

Can we *jettison groundwork, penetrate* the *impervious?* Ask of your nouns and verbs: can it sensibly be done, even in the liberal world of metaphor?

A cheerful curiosity about words and their earthy origins, a respect for their resonances, and a pleasure in your own power to create new and striking images will instruct you in diction better than any language handbook. "Words must be shouted into, like wells, rather than joined in a series like pipelengths," the translator Ben Belitt writes in a compound simile which rings with associations of echos and water. Call down into words, squint at them against the light to see their changing colors, bite them like dimes to test their mintage and their savor. "Words," says the poet Yeats, "alone are certain good."

Exercise 1

With the help of a dictionary (and perhaps a dictionary of Roman and Greek mythology) discover the concrete particular in which each of these abstract words originated. Write a brief explanation of why and how you think some of these words came to mean what they mean today.

cereal	cupidity	hackneyed	panic
chapter	erotic	infant	paradise
comma	genius	language	surgery

Exercise 2

Analyze the following paragraph from a memo distributed by a Communications Department. Is it jargon and why? What clichés or submerged figures of speech can you find? Do they conflict with one another? Translate the paragraph into Standard English if you can, and if not, be prepared to say why.

> All courses (process or outcome) in the University system that are judged to contain written or oral communication goal statements should constitute a set of courses from which a student must select some number. This client-oriented marketplace approach to core requirements is a solution. Enrollment determines which courses will survive and which will not. However, academic tradition is rife with distrust of student judgment; and it can result in a self-fulfilling prophecy where faculty compete in playing to the "house" because they are convinced that ultimately only those who do will survive. This solution is usually condemned without trial.

Exercise 3

Analyze the diction of the following sentences for exactness, connotation, figures of speech. Be prepared to discuss what words would more effectively express what the writer was trying to say.

1. Thus the young athletes are the workhorses that made the ends of the budget meet to form a vicious circle.
2. Our balloons of egotism filled with the air of freshman knowledge were soon to be pricked by the pin-points of self-awakening.
3. As the town grew, the theatre obtained a foothold in the hearts of the citizens.
4. This is the Achilles' heel of their position. For once a set of ideas are ruled fair game for witch-hunters, Pandora's box has been opened, and there is no ending.
5. Drinking seems to have its claw in the economy of San Francisco.
6. Our tariff wall will continue to be an unsurmountable obstacle until we throw a span across the ebb to link the rest of the world to our industrial growth.
7. Poring through *Paradise Lost* was like wading in deep water.
8. A good education is the trunk for a good life for it is the origin of all the branches which are your later accomplishments.
9. His immaturity may improve with age.
10. The basic objective of the indoctrination program is to build strong class spirit and to weed out those who are leaders in the class.
11. Darwin's *Origin of Species* began an epic of materialism.
12. Margaret Mead's book had a great success because Americans are grossly interested in sex.
13. I flitted away my first three years in college.
14. Jefferson and Madison were two of the most prolific characters our nation produced at that time in history.
15. The reason I like Christina Rossetti's *Goblin Market* is because it shows how love between sisters triumphs over the prowess of darkness.

Exercise 4

On the basis of sound association and of your knowledge of words, make an educated guess as to the lexical meaning of the following archaic words. Then look up the words in Charles MacKay's *Lost*

Beauties of the English Language. If you arrived at a meaning different from that listed in MacKay, explain the reasons for your definition.

crambles (n)	roaky (adj)
flathers (n)	sculsh (n)
glunch (v)	skime (v)
jugbitten (adj)	slive (v)
mazle (v)	slodder (n)
mirkshade (n)	sloom (v)
overword (n)	snurl (v)
pleach (v)	suckets (n)
prog (v)	tartle (v)
quillet (n)	ugsome (adj)

Exercise 5

Write a short essay or prepare a class discussion using examples from your own experience in which you defend or deny the truth of this Confucian maxim: "If language is incorrect, then what is said is not meant. If what is said is not meant, then what ought to be done remains undone."

6

Glossary of Usage

This Glossary discusses only the more commonly misused words which crop up frequently in student prose. In recommending that you observe rules of usage, no one is suggesting that you abandon your natural speech for what may to your taste seem stilted. But remember that written language is selective. It is the cultivation of that which grows wild and natural in our speech. Teachers of language, like practiced gardeners, tend to be conservationists. Before becoming annoyed with what may seem to you petty complaints, consider that your teacher and the editors of handbooks and dictionaries are attempting to preserve distinctions which you may not know exist. Roger Sales devotes a number of pages in his book *On Writing* to a concept that will be lost should the distinction between *disinterested* and *uninterested* not be preserved. Rather than decide that the difference in prefixes is inconsequential, read the entry in this chapter and then read his argument. The choice of whether or not to observe standards of usage is yours, but the choice should be an informed and prudent one.

a, an Indefinite articles. *A* is used before words beginning with a consonant sound, *an* before words beginning with a vowel sound. Before words beginning with *h*, use *an* when the *h* is silent, as in *hour*, but *a* when the *h* is pronounced, as in *history*.

above Colloquially used as an adjective: "The above remarks." In writing, this usage should be confined to legal documents.

accept, except Different verbs which sound alike. *Accept* means "to receive," *except* "to leave out."

I *accepted* the diploma.

When assigning jobs, the dean *excepted* students who had already worked on a project.

adapt, adopt To *adapt* is to change or modify to suit some new need, purpose, or condition.

Man can *adapt* to many environments. The movie was *adapted* from a novel.

To *adopt* something is to make it one's own, to choose it.

The couple *adopted* a child. Our club *adopted* "Opportunity knocks" as its motto.

adverse, averse Often confused, but important to distinguish. *Adverse* means "antagonistic" or "unfavorable."

Adverse weather forced postponement of the regatta.

Averse means "opposed to"; only sentient beings can be *averse.*

She *was averse* to sailing under such conditions.

affect, effect Words close in sound and therefore often confused. *Affect* as a verb means "to influence." *Effect* as a verb means "to bring about."

Smoking *affects* the heart.

How can we *effect* a change in the law?

As a noun *effect* means "result."

One *effect* of her treatment was a bad case of hives.

The noun *affect* is a technical term used in psychology.

aggravate Means "to intensify" or "to make worse."

The shock *aggravated* his misery.

Colloquially it means "to annoy," "irritate," "arouse the anger of."

ain't A nonstandard contraction of *am not, is not,* or *are not.* Not to be used in formal writing.

all ready, already Not synonyms. *All ready* refers to a state of readiness.

The twirlers were *all ready* for the half-time show.

Already means "by or before the present time."

Has the game *already* started?

all right Unlike the pairs of words in the preceding and following entries, *all right* stands alone. There is no word *alright,* although many people, misled by the existence of *altogether* and *already,* assume that there is.

all together, altogether *All together* refers to a group with no missing elements.

If we can get our members *all together,* we can begin the meeting.

Altogether means "completely."

You are *altogether* mistaken about that.

allude, refer To *allude* is to make an indirect reference.

Did her letter *allude* to Sam's difficulties?

To *refer* is to call attention specifically to something.

The instructor *referred* us to Baudelaire's translations of Poe.

allusion, illusion, delusion An *allusion* is a brief, indirect reference.

> Anyone who speaks of "cabbages and kings" is making an *allusion* to *Alice in Wonderland.*

An *illusion* is a deceptive impression.

> He enjoyed the *illusion* of luxury created by his imitation Oriental rugs.

A *delusion* is a mistaken belief, implying self-deception and often a disordered state of mind.

> She fell prey to the *delusion* that she was surrounded by enemy agents.

among, between *Among* always refers to more than two.

> He lived *among* a tribe of cannibals.

Between is used to refer to two objects or to more than two objects considered individually.

> The scenery is spectacular *between* Portland and Seattle.
>
> The governors signed the agreement *between* all three states.

amoral, immoral Anything *amoral* is outside morality, not to be judged by moral standards.

> The behavior of animals and the orbits of the planets are equally *amoral.*

Anything *immoral* is in direct violation of some moral standard.

> Snatching an old lady's purse is generally considered to be an *immoral* act.

amount, number *Amount* is used as a general indicator of quantity; *number* refers only to what can be counted.

> An immense *amount* of food was prepared for the picnic, but only a small *number* of people came.

but Often used colloquially in such idioms as *I can't help but think.* In writing *I can't help thinking* is preferred. If the nonstandard expression *I don't know but what he wants to do it* leads to confusion (does he or doesn't he?), it should be avoided in speech, too.

can, may In formal speech and in writing, *can* is used to indicate ability, *may* to indicate permission.

> If you *can* open that box, you *may* have whatever is in it.

In informal questions, *can* is often used even though permission is meant.

> *Can* I try it next? Why *can't* I?

censor, censure To *censor* something (such as a book, letter, or film) is to evaluate it on the basis of certain arbitrary standards to determine whether it may be made public.

All announcements for the bulletin board are *censored* by the department secretary.

Censor is often used as the equivalent of "delete."

References in the report to secret activities have been *censored.*

Censure means "to find fault with," "to criticize as blameworthy."

Several officers were *censured* for their participation in the affair.

compare to, compare with, contrast with *Compare to* is used to show similarities between different kinds of things.

Sir James Jeans *compared* the universe *to* a corrugated soap bubble.

Compare with means to examine in order to note either similarities or differences.

Compare this example *with* the preceding one.

Contrast with is used to show differences only.

Contrast the life of a student today *with* that of a student in the middle ages.

concur in, concur with *Concur in* refers to agreement with a principle or policy.

She *concurred in* their judgment that the manager should be given a raise.

Concur with refers to agreement with a person.

She *concurred with* him in his decision to give the manager a raise.

contact The use of *contact* as a verb meaning "to get in touch with" has gained wide acceptance, but a more exact term such as *ask, consult, inform, meet, see, telephone,* or *write* is generally preferable.

continual, continuous The first is widely used to indicate an action which is repeated frequently, the second to indicate uninterrupted action.

We heard the *continual* howling of the dog.

The dog kept a *continuous* vigil beside the body of his dead master.

data, phenomena, criteria Latin plural, not singular forms, and so used in formal writing. But the use of *data* (rather than *datum*) with a singular form is widespread.

These *data* have been taken from the last Census Report.

Criteria and *phenomena* are always plural. The singular forms are *criterion* and *phenomenon.*

Scientists encountered a *phenomenon* that could not be evaluated under existing *criteria.*

different from, different than *Different from* is always acceptable usage.

College is *different from* what I had expected.

Different than, when used to avoid wordiness or awkwardness, is also acceptable.

College is *different* now *than* it was twenty years ago.

disinterested, uninterested *Disinterested* means "unbiased," "impartial." *Uninterested* means "without any interest in," or "lacking in interest."

Though we were *uninterested* in her general topic, we had to admire her *disinterested* treatment of its controversial aspects.

due to In writing *due to* should not be used adverbially to mean *because of.*

COLLOQUIAL	He made many mistakes, *due to* carelessness.
PREFERRED IN WRITING	He made many mistakes *because of* carelessness.

Due to is an adjective and usually follows the verb *to be: His illness was due to exhaustion.*

either, neither As subjects, both words are singular. When referring to more than two, use *none* rather than *neither.*

Either red or pink is appropriate.

I asked Leahy, Mahoney, and another Irishman, but *none* of them was willing.

enthused Either as a verb (he *enthused*) or adjective (he was *enthused*), the word is strictly colloquial. In writing use "showed enthusiasm" or "was enthusiastic."

equally as good A confusion of two phrases: *equally good* and *just as good.* Use either of the two phrases in place of *equally as good.*

Their TV set cost much more than ours, but ours is *equally good.*

Our TV set is *just as good* as theirs.

-ess Feminine ending acceptable in such traditional words as *waitress, actress, hostess.* But many persons object to *poetess, authoress, sculptress* as patronizing and demeaning. Unless an *-ess* word has a long history and you are sure there are no objections to its use, it is best to avoid it.

etc. Avoid the vague use of *etc.;* use it only to prevent useless repetition or informally to represent terms entirely obvious from the context.

VAGUE The judge was honorable, upright, dependable, *etc.*"
PREFERRED The judge was honorable, upright, and dependable.
STANDARD Use even numbers like four, eight, ten, *etc.*

Avoid *and etc.,* which is redundant.

expect Colloquial when used to mean "suppose," "presume": I *expect* it's time for us to go.

PREFERRED I *suppose* it's time for us to go.

factor Means "something which contributes to a result."

Industry and perseverance were *factors* in her success.

Avoid using *factor* to mean vaguely any thing, item, or event.

VAGUE Ambition was a *factor* which contributed to the downfall of Macbeth.

Since factor includes the notion of "contributing to," such usage is redundant as well as vague and wordy.

PREFERRED Ambition contributed to the downfall of Macbeth.

farther, further In careful usage *farther* indicates distance; *further* indicates degree and may also mean "additional." Both are used as adjectives and as adverbs: *a mile farther, further disintegration, further details.*

faze, phase *Faze* is a colloquial verb meaning "to perturb," "to disconcert." *Phase* as a noun means "stage of development" (a passing *phase*); as a verb it means "to carry out in stages." Be wary of *phase in* and *phase out,* which have the ring of jargon.

fewer, less *Fewer* refers to number, *less* to amount. Use *fewer* in speaking of things which can be counted and *less* for amounts which are measured.

Fewer persons enrolled in medical schools this year than last.

Less studying was required to pass Chemistry than we had anticipated.

flaunt, flout Commonly misspelled, mispronounced and, therefore, confused. *Flaunt* means "to exhibit arrogantly," "show off."

He *flaunted* his photographic memory in class.

Flout means "to reject with contempt."

They *flouted* the tradition of wearing gowns at graduation by showing up in bluejeans.

flunk Colloquial for *fail.* In formal writing, I *failed* (not *flunked*) the test.

former, latter Preferably used to designate one of two persons or things. For designating one of three or more, write *first* or *last.*

get, got, gotten *Get to* (go), *get away with, get back at, get with* (something), and *got to* (for *must*) are widely used in speech but should be avoided in writing. Either *got* or *gotten* is acceptable as the past participle of *get.*

good An adjective. Should not be used in formal writing as an adverb meaning "well."

COLLOQUIAL She plays tennis *good.*
STANDARD She plays tennis *well.* She plays a *good* game of tennis.

had have, had of Nonstandard when used for *had.*

NONSTANDARD If he *had have* (or *had of*) tried, he would have succeeded.
STANDARD If he *had* tried, he would have succeeded.

had ought Nonstandard as a past tense of *ought.* The tense of this verb is indicated by the infinitive which follows.

He *ought to go;* she *ought to have gone.*

hanged, hung When *hang* means "to suspend," *hung* is its past tense.

The guards *hung* a black flag from the prison to signal the execution.

When *hang* means "to execute," *hanged* is the correct past tense.

After the flag was *hung,* the prisoner was *hanged.*

hardly, barely, scarcely Since these words convey the idea of negation, they should not be used with another negative.

NONSTANDARD We *couldn't hardly* see in the darkness.
We *hadn't barely* finished.
STANDARD We *could hardly* see. We *had barely* finished.

hopefully Though widely used in speech to mean "it is to be hoped," or "I hope" (*Hopefully,* a check will arrive tomorrow), the adverb *hopefully* is used in writing to mean "in a hopeful manner":

They spoke *hopefully* of world peace.

imply, infer *Imply* means "to suggest" or "hint"; *infer* means "to reach a conclusion from facts or premises."

His tone *implied* contempt; I *inferred* from his voice that he did not like me.

insupportable, unsupportable Often confused, but not synonymous. *Insupportable* means "unable to be endured."

The noise of the bulldozers during the lecture was *insupportable.*

Unsupportable means "not capable of support."

The building program, though imaginative, is financially *unsupportable.*

inter, intra As a prefix *inter* means "between" or "among": *international, intermarry; intra* means "within" or "inside of": *intramuscular, intramural.*

irregardless A nonstandard combination of *irrespective* and *regardless.*

Regardless (or *irrespective*) of the minority opinion, we included the platform in the campaign.

its, it's Often confused. *Its* is the possessive form of *it.*

My suitcase has lost one of *its* handles.

It's is the contracted form of *it is* or *it has.*

It's a good day for sailing.

It's been a month since I mailed the check.

kind, sort Colloquial when used with a plural modifier and verb: *These kind* (or *sort*) of books *are* trash.

STANDARD *This sort* of book *is* trash.
These kinds of books *are* classics.

In questions, the number of the verb depends on the noun which follows *kind* (or *sort*).

What kind of *book is* this?
What kind of *books are* these?

kind of, sort of Colloquial when used to mean "rather."

COLLOQUIAL I thought the lecture was *kind of* dull.
STANDARD I thought the lecture was *rather* dull.

Also colloquial when followed by *a* or *an:*

What *kind of a* house is it? It is *sort of a* castle.

PREFERRED IN WRITING What *kind of* house is it?
It is *a sort of* castle.

latest, last *Latest* means "most recent"; *last* means "final."

I doubt that their *latest* contract proposal represents their *last* offer.

lay, lie Often confused. *Lay* is a transitive verb meaning "to put" or "place" something. It always takes an object. Its principal parts are *lay, laid, laid. Lie* is intransitive; that is, it does not take an object, and means "to recline" or "to remain." Its principal parts are *lie, lay, lain.* When in doubt, try substituting the verb *place.* If it fits the context, use some form of *lay.*

PRESENT TENSE	I *lie* down every afternoon. Every morning I *lay* the paper by his plate.
PAST TENSE	I *lay* down yesterday after dinner. I *laid* the paper by his plate two hours ago.
PERFECT TENSE	I *have lain* here for several hours. I *have laid* the paper by his plate many times.

let's Contraction of *let us.* In writing, it should be used only where *let us* can be used.

COLLOQUIAL	*Let's don't* leave yet. *Let's us* go.
STANDARD	*Let's not* leave yet. *Let's* go.

liable, likely, apt In careful writing, the words are not interchangeable. *Likely* is used to indicate a mere probability.

They are *likely* to be chosen.

Liable is used when the probability is unpleasant.

We are *liable* to get a parking ticket.

Apt implies a natural tendency or ability.

She is *apt* to win the musical competition.

like The use of *like* to introduce a clause is widespread in informal English, especially that used by advertising agencies. In edited writing, *as, as if,* and *as though* are preferred.

COLLOQUIAL	This rose smells sweet, *like* a flower should.
STANDARD	This rose smells sweet, *as* a flower should. This perfume smells *like* roses.

However, don't always avoid *like* in favor of *as,* or you may end up in ambiguities.

As Lady Macbeth, she was disturbed by the sight of blood.

Does the writer mean "in the role of Lady Macbeth" or "similar to Lady Macbeth?"

literally Means "precisely," "without any figurative sense," "strictly." It is often inaccurately used as an intensive, to emphasize a figure of speech: "I was *literally* floating on air." This makes sense only if one is capable of levitation. Use the word *literally* with caution in writing.

loan, lend, Traditionally, *lend* is a verb, *loan* a noun, but *loan* is also used as a verb, especially in business contexts.

The company *loaned* us money for the down payment.

most As a noun or adjective, *most* means "more than half."

Most of us plan to go to the dance.

Most people admire her paintings.

As an adverb, *most* means "very."

His playing was *most* impressive.

Most is colloquial when used to mean "almost," "nearly."

COLLOQUIAL	*Most* everyone was invited.
PREFERRED IN WRITING	*Almost* everyone was invited.

myself Correctly used as a reflexive: I cut *myself*, sang to *myself*, give *myself* credit. Colloquial when used as an evasive substitute for *I* or *me*.

COLLOQUIAL	My brother and *myself* prefer coffee. She spoke to my brother and *myself*.
PREFERRED IN WRITING	My brother and *I* prefer coffee. She spoke to my brother and *me*.

of *Could of, may of, might of, must of, should of,* and *would of* are slurred pronunciations for *could have, may have, might have, must have, should have,* and *would have;* they are nonstandard in writing.

off of A colloquial usage in which *of* is superfluous.

COLLOQUIAL	Keep *off of* the grass.
PREFERRED IN WRITING	Keep *off* the grass.

outside of Correct as a noun: He painted the *outside of* the house. Colloquial as a preposition: He was waiting *outside of* the house. Omit the *of* in writing. Nonstandard as a substitute for *except for, aside from.*

part, portion A *part* is any piece of a whole; a *portion* is that part specifically allotted to some person, cause or use.

We planted beans in one *part* of our garden.

She left a *portion* of her estate to charity.

party Colloquial when used to mean "person," as in "The *party* who telephoned left no message." Write *person.*

percent In formal writing use *percent,* or *per cent,* only after a numeral—either the spelled-out word (six) or the numerical symbol (6). The sign (%) is used only in strictly commercial writing. The word *percentage,* meaning "a part or proportion of a whole," is used when the exact amount is not indicated.

A large *percentage* were Chinese.

Thirty-one *percent* were Chinese.

real Colloquial when used for "very." Write *very* hot, not *real* hot.

regarding, in regard to, with regard to, in relation to, in terms of These windy phrases are usually dispensable. Replace them with concrete terms.

WORDY *With regard to* grades, she was very good.
CONCRETE She *got* very good grades.

Reverend In formal writing should be preceded by *the* and followed by a title or full name, or both.

The Reverend Mr. (or *Dr.*) *Carter* preached.

The Reverend Amos Carter led the march.

The widely-used form *Reverend Amos Carter* is deplored by usage panels but accepted by the clergy. The use of *the reverend* as a noun, to mean "a clergyman," is strictly colloquial.

sarcasm Not interchangeable with *irony. Sarcastic* remarks, like *ironic* remarks, convey a message obliquely, but sarcasm contains the notion of ridicule, of an intention on the part of the writer to wound. Only persons can be *sarcastic,* while both persons and events can be *ironic.*

The sergeant inquired *sarcastically* whether any of us could tell time; it was *ironic* that his watch turned out to be ten minutes fast.

sensual, sensuous Both words refer to impressions made upon the senses. Their connotations, however, are widely different. *Sensual* most often carries unfavorable connotations. It is applied primarily to the gratification of appetite and lust.

Sensual delights are often considered inferior to spiritual pleasures.

Sensuous, on the other hand, is used literally or approvingly of an appeal to the senses (the *sensuous* delight of a swim on a hot day), and can even refer to such abstract appeals as those found in poetry.

Milton's *sensuous* imagery calls upon sight, touch, and even smell to form the reader's impression of Eden.

set A transitive verb meaning "to put" or "place" something. It should be distinguished from *sit,* an intransitive verb.

PRESENT TENSE	I *sit* in the chair.
	I *set* the book on the table.
PAST TENSE	I *sat* on the chair.
	I *set* the book on the table.
PERFECT TENSE	I *have sat* in the chair.
	I *have set* the book on the table.

shall, will The distinction is rapidly fading, although many grammarians still conjugate the verb as *I shall, you will, he will, we shall, you will, they will.* Most writers, however, now use *will* throughout. *Shall* may still be used for emphasis (He *shall* be heard); since it is less common than *will,* it has a formal tone. See page 77.

should, would Generally interchangeable in modern American usage, though they formerly followed the pattern of *shall* and *will.* Each word does, however, have some special uses. *Should* substitutes for "ought to" (He *should* go on a diet); *would* for "wanted to" (He could do it if he *would*). *Should* indicates probability (I *should* be finished in an hour); *would* indicates custom (He *would* always call when he got home).

so, such Avoid using *so* and *such* as vague intensifiers: I am *so* glad; I had *such* a good time. The full forms, which should always be used, are *so . . . that, such . . . as.*

I was *so* glad to find that print *that* I bought copies for all my friends.

Such a good time *as* that is worth repeating.

some Colloquial when used as an adverb meaning "somewhat" (I am *some* better today) or when used as an intensifying adjective (That was *some* dinner).

PREFERRED	I am *a little* (or *somewhat*) better today.
IN WRITING	That was *an excellent* dinner.

sure Colloquial when used for "certainly, "surely," as in "He *sure* can play poker."

that, which *That* is largely confined to introduce restrictive clauses, which limit or define the antecedent's meaning and are not set off by commas.

The law *that* gave women the right to vote was passed in 1920. *Which* is used to introduce non-restrictive clauses, which are not essential to the meaning of the sentence and are set off by commas.

The 19th Amendment, *which* gave women the right to vote, was passed in 1920.

toward, towards Interchangeable. *Toward* is more common in America, *towards* in Britain.

transpire In formal writing, where the word properly belongs, it means "to become known." It is colloquial in the sense of "happen," or "come to pass."

try and Often used for "try to," but should be avoided in writing. I must *try to* (not *try and*) find a job.

unique Adverbs such as *rather, more, most, very* are colloquial when used to modify *unique*. Since the word means "being the only one of its kind," no thing can be more (or less) unique than another.

This copy of the book is *unique*.

This copy of the book is *very rare*.

up Do not add a superfluous *up* to verbs: We opened *up* the box and divided the money *up*. Write: We opened the box and divided the money.

***very* and *much* with past participles** A past participle that is felt to be a part of a verb form, rather than an adjective, should not be immediately preceded by *very* but by *much, greatly*, or some other intensive. A past participle that can be used as an adjective may be preceded by *very*.

COLLOQUIAL	He was *very* disliked by other students. He was *very* influenced by the teacher.
PREFERRED IN WRITING	He was *very much* disliked by other students. He was *greatly* influenced by the teacher. He was a *very* tired boy.

wait on Colloquial for *wait for*.

ways Colloquial in such expressions as *a little ways*. In writing, the singular is preferred: *a little way*.

where . . . to, where . . . at Colloquialisms whose prepositions are redundant or dialectal.

COLLOQUIAL	*Where* are you going *to*? *Where* is he *at*?
PREFERRED IN WRITING	*Where* are you going? *Where* is he?

who, whom (For the choice between these forms see the section on Case, page 68.)

-wise Commercial jargon when attached to nouns in such combinations as *taxwise, languagewise, timewise, moneywise.* To be avoided in serious writing.

would have Colloquial when used in *if* clauses instead of *had.*

COLLOQUIAL	If he *would have stood* by us, we might have won.
PREFERRED IN WRITING	If he *had stood* by us, we might have won.

write-up Colloquial for a description, an account, as in "a *write-up* in the newspaper."

7 Punctuation

Punctuation is, at best, a minor aid to clarity of communication. A sentence which is badly constructed or poorly phrased cannot be saved by punctuation alone; it must be revised or phrased more accurately.

Some rules for the use of punctuation are intended to make communication easier, but many rules can be justified only on the grounds of accepted editorial practice. Moreover a good deal of punctuation is optional. A writer may use commas or not, depending on his taste or his intention, in such a sentence as the following:

> Eleven All-Americans would not in fact guarantee a good team.
>
> Eleven All-Americans would not, in fact, guarantee a good team.

Most readers would probably feel that setting off the *in fact* gives it a little more emphasis, but either sentence is correct.

The rules in the following sections specify where punctuation marks are needed and, occasionally, where they are acceptable. Beyond this, you must use your judgment. If you are in doubt and no positive rule covers the point, you will probably be safer to omit the punctuation mark.

7a End Punctuation

(1) The Period

Use a period to mark the end of a declarative or imperative sentence.

CORRECT This is an example of a declarative sentence.

CORRECT Use a period at the end of a sentence like this.

A period is also used after abbreviations, like *Dr., Mr., Ph.D., etc.,* A.D, *Calif., Inc.* For the proper use of abbreviations see Chapter 9.

Three spaced periods (. . .), called ellipsis marks, are used to indicate the omission of a word or words from a quoted passage. If the omitted words come at the end of a sentence, a fourth period is needed.

CORRECT We hold these truths to be self-evident: that all men . . . are endowed by their Creator with certain unalienable rights. . . .

Similarly, three (or four) periods are sometimes used in dialogue and interrupted narrative to indicate hesitation and pauses. Beginning writers should use these with caution.

CORRECT He inspired uneasiness. That was it! Uneasiness. Not a definite mistrust—just uneasiness—nothing more. You can have no idea how effective such a . . . a . . . faculty can be.

—JOSEPH CONRAD

(2) The Question Mark

Use a question mark after a direct question.

CORRECT Where did you find such information?

CORRECT How much of the White Sands is gypsum?

CORRECT Looking at me, the officer said, "Where do you live?"

An indirect question should be followed by a period, not a question mark.

CORRECT He asked what had caused the delay.

CORRECT I wonder how many Americans walk to work these days.

A request which is phrased as a question for politeness' sake is followed by a period.

CORRECT Will you please send me your latest catalog.

(3) The Exclamation Mark

Exclamation marks are appropriate only after statements which would be given unusual emphasis if spoken. This mark is seldom appropriate to expository writing. Do not use it to lend force to flat statements or ironic remarks.

INAPPROPRIATE The professor suggested that we take out our notebooks since he was going to give us a little (!) test.

7b The Comma

The comma is perhaps the most used and, consequently, the most abused punctuation mark. It separates coordinate elements within a sentence, and sets off certain subordinate constructions from the rest of the sentence. Since it represents the shortest breath pause and the least emphatic break, it cannot separate two complete sentences.

A primary function of the comma is to make a sentence clear. Always use commas to prevent misreading: to separate words which might be erroneously grouped together by the reader.

(1) To Separate Independent Clauses

Two independent clauses joined by a coordinating conjunction (*and, or, nor, but, for*) should be separated by a comma. Note that the comma is always placed before the conjunction.

CORRECT I failed German in my senior year of high school**, *and*** it took me a long time to regain any interest in foreign languages.

CORRECT She went through the motions of studying**, *but*** her mind was elsewhere.

Very short independent clauses need not be separated by a comma if they are closely connected in meaning.

CORRECT The bell rang and everyone left.

Coordinating conjunctions are often used to join the parts of a compound predicate: that is, two or more verbs with the same subject. In such a sentence a comma is not required to separate the predicates. However, if the two parts are long or imply a strong contrast, a comma may be used to separate them.

CORRECT We ***measured*** the potassium and ***weighed*** it on the scale.

CORRECT Mr. Fossum ***demonstrated*** the differences between preserving wood with oil and with shellac**, and** advised the use of oil for durable table tops.

CORRECT To our dismay, the suede could not be ***washed*** at home nor ***dry cleaned*** at an ordinary place**, but** ***had to be sent*** to a specialist.

When the clauses of a compound sentence are long and are also subdivided by commas, a stronger mark of punctuation than a comma may be needed to separate the clauses from each other. For this purpose a semicolon is regularly used.

CORRECT For purposes of discussion, we shall recognize two main varieties of English, Standard and Nonstandard**;** and we shall divide the first type into Formal, Informal, and Colloquial English.

(2) To Separate Elements in Series

Separate words, phrases, or clauses in a series by commas. The typical form of a series is *a, b,* and *c.* A series may contain more than three parallel elements, and any of the coordinating conjunctions may be used to connect the last two. If *all* the elements of a series are joined by coordinating conjunctions (*a and b and c*), no commas are necessary to separate them.

SERIES OF ADJECTIVES The shy devil-fish blushes in blue**,** red**,** green**,** or brown.

SERIES OF PHRASES Water flooded ***over the riverbed, over the culverts, and over the asphalt road.***

SERIES OF PREDICATES The bear ***jumped away from the garbage can, snarled at the camper, and raced up the tree.***

SERIES OF NOUNS ***Resistors, transistors, capacitors, and connectors*** are small electronic parts.

SERIES OF INDEPENDENT CLAUSES Stone was hauled twelve miles**,** casing was built as the hole deepened**,** and a well 109 feet deep was completed in Greensburg, Kansas.

The comma before the last item in a series is omitted by some writers, but its use is generally preferred since it can prevent misreading.

MISLEADING The three congressional priorities are nuclear disarmament, the curtailment of agricultural trade and aid to underdeveloped countries.

Without the comma before "and," "agricultural trade" and "aid to underdeveloped countries" can be read as compound objects of "curtailment of," and the reader reaches the end of the sentence still waiting for the third priority. No such misreading occurs if the comma is included.

(3) Uses with Coordinate Elements

Adjectives modifying the same noun should be separated by commas if they are coordinate in meaning. Coordinate adjectives are those which could be joined by *and* without distorting the meaning of a sentence.

CORRECT Bus lines provide inexpensive, efficient transportation.

The adjectives are coordinate: transportation which is "inexpensive" and "efficient."

Sometimes, however, an adjective is so closely linked with the noun that it is thought of as part of the noun. Such an adjective is not coordinate with a preceding adjective.

CORRECT Paynes bought a spacious summer cabin.

This does not mean "a cabin which is spacious and summer." "Summer" indicates the kind of cabin; "spacious" describes the summer cabin.

Note that numbers are not coordinate with other adjectives and are not separated by commas.

CORRECT They screened in two large, airy outdoor porches.

"Two" and "large" should not be separated by a comma. But since the two outdoor porches were "large" and "airy," a comma is used to separate these two coordinate adjectives.

Coordinate words or phrases which are sharply contrasted are separated by commas.

CORRECT He is ignorant, not stupid.

CORRECT Our aim is to encourage question and debate, not criticism and argument.

An idiomatic way of asking a question is to make a direct statement and add to it a coordinate elliptical question. Such a construction should be separated by a comma from the direct statement.

CORRECT You will come with us, won't you?

CORRECT He won't test on last semester's units, will he?

Another idiomatic construction which requires a comma is the coordinate use of adjectives, as in *the more . . . , the more . . . .*

CORRECT The faster the bird, the higher the metabolism.

CORRECT The more a candidate meets voters, the more he may learn about their concerns.

Exercise 1

Insert the proper punctuation marks where they are required in the following sentences, and give a reason for your choice.

1. Seven legislators from the southern part of the state changed their votes and with their aid the bill was passed.
2. During many periods of history men's clothing has been no less extravagant in cut color and richness of fabric than women's and there have been times when men's clothes have been the gaudier.
3. By the end of the twenty-mile hike we were all fairly tired and some of us were suffering from sore feet as well.
4. Three of the editors argued that the article was biased and malicious and voted to reject it in spite of the distinguished name of the author.
5. The teller at the bank looked dubiously at the check I offered him and even though I knew the check was good I could feel a guilty look freezing on my face as his doubts increased.
6. Painted surfaces should be washed with a detergent sanded lightly and covered with a thin coat of plastic varnish.
7. I painted the house a warm deep pearl gray.
8. His latest novel was marred by pretentious writing the absence of solid characterization and a hackneyed plot.
9. I believe that a state lottery can be useful because it can provide revenue for education increase employment and relieve the tax burden.
10. I judge people of any race by what they say and how they act not by the color of their skin.

(4) To Set Off Nonrestrictive Modifiers

A dependent clause, participial phrase, or appositive is nonrestrictive when it can be omitted without changing the main idea of the sentence. A nonrestrictive modifier gives additional information about the noun to which it refers. A restrictive modifier, on the other hand, restricts the meaning of the word to which it refers to one particular group or thing. If it is omitted, the main idea of the sentence is changed. One check is to read the sentence aloud: if the voice pauses and drops slightly before and after the modifier, the modifier is probably nonrestrictive; if the voice is sustained and unhesitant before and after the modifier, the modifier is probably restrictive and is *not* set off by commas.

Nonrestrictive Clauses and Phrases

Note that *two commas* are required to set off a nonrestrictive modifier in the middle of a sentence; one comma is sufficient if the modifier is at the beginning or end of the sentence.

NONRESTRICTIVE CLAUSE My faculty advisor***, who had to sign the program card,*** was very hard to find.

If the clause were omitted, some information would be lost, but the sentence would still make the same point: that my advisor was hard to find.

RESTRICTIVE CLAUSE A faculty advisor ***who is never in his office*** makes registration difficult.

Omitting the clause here changes the sense completely. The purpose of the clause is to limit the statement to a certain kind of faculty advisor—those who are never in their offices.

nonrestrictive clause

CORRECT I found the letter under the door***, where the postman had put it.***

restrictive clause

CORRECT The letter was still ***where the postman had put it.***

nonrestrictive phrase

CORRECT Uncle Jasper's letter***, lying unclaimed in the dead letter office,*** contained the missing document.

restrictive phrase

CORRECT We have had many complaints about letters ***undelivered because of careless addressing.***

Notice how the meaning of a sentence may be altered by the addition or the omission of commas:

CORRECT The board sent questionnaires to all members**,** who are on Social Security.

Nonrestrictive clause. The sentence implies that all members are on Social Security.

CORRECT The board sent questionnaires to all members who are on Social Security.

Restrictive clause. The questionnaire is sent only to some members, those on Social Security.

Nonrestrictive Appositives

Appositives are usually nonrestrictive and hence are set off by commas. If, however, an appositive puts a necessary limitation upon its noun, it is restrictive and no punctuation is necessary.

NONRESTRICTIVE APPOSITIVE Scientists working with cryogenics have produced temperatures within a thousandth of a degree of absolute zero***, approximately 459.7 below zero Fahrenheit.***

RESTRICTIVE APPOSITIVE The noun cryogenics comes from a Greek word meaning "icy cold."

Note that an appositive used to define a word is often introduced by the conjunction *or*. Such appositives are always set off by commas to distinguish them from the common construction in which *or* joins two coordinate nouns.

CORRECT The class found a fine specimen of pyrite***, or fool's gold.***

CORRECT We couldn't decide whether to plant phlox or coral bells.

Note that an abbreviated title or degree (K.C.B., USMC, M.D., Ph.D.) is treated as an appositive when it follows a proper name.

CORRECT He was introduced as Robert Harrison***, L.L.D.,*** and he added that he also held a Ph.D. from Cornell.

Exercise 2

Insert commas in the following sentences to set off nonrestrictive clauses and participial phrases. In doubtful cases, explain the difference in meaning produced by the insertion of commas.

1. King Leopold of Belgium who was Queen Victoria's uncle also gave her a great deal of advice.
2. Many people who have never been to the United States think of it as a country of wealth and luxury where everyone lives on the fat of the land.
3. Some years ago I lived in a section of town where almost everyone was a Republican.
4. With the advent of the jet engine which is more efficient at high than at low altitudes aircraft could attain greater heights.
5. The astronauts who had been trained for any circumstance were calm when launching was called off at the last minute.
6. The student hoping to get a C without too much work should stay out of Economics 152.
7. We shall have to hire a caretaker if you can't find time to keep the place neat and orderly.
8. The packing plant where I worked all summer is on the Aleutian Islands.
9. She has made a special study of the native women who are monogamous.
10. The average American tired of last year's models and seeking something new is an easy prey for the designers who capitalize on herd psychology and the craving for novelty.

(5) To Set Off Parenthetic Elements

Parenthetic is a general term describing explanatory words or phrases which are felt to be intrusive and subordinate. That is, they interrupt the normal sentence pattern to supply additional, supplementary information, and they are accordingly set off by commas or other punctuation marks. In the widest sense of the term, nonrestrictive modifiers are a kind of parenthetic element. Many other sentence elements may become parenthetic if they are removed from their regular place and inserted so that they interrupt the normal order of a sentence.

For example, adjectives normally are placed before the words they modify: *Two tired, hungry boys came into camp.* If the adjectives are inserted elsewhere in the sentence, they become parenthetic and should be set off: *Two boys, tired and hungry, came into camp.* Similarly, it is possible to rewrite a sentence like *I am certain that space science will bring some unexpected discoveries* so that one clause becomes parenthetic: *Space science, I am certain, will bring some unexpected discoveries.*

CORRECT The minutes, I regret to say, need several additions.

CORRECT The discovery that mammals can learn to breathe under water may, in the opinion of some experts, lead to a technique which will prevent drowning.

Transitional Words

Transitional words and phrases, like *however, moreover, indeed, consequently, of course, for example, on the other hand,* are usually set off by commas, especially when they serve to mark a contrast or the introduction of a new point. In short sentences where stress on the transitional word is not needed or desired, the commas are often omitted.

CORRECT The beginning violinist needs patience. For example, six lines of music can have 214 bowing variations.

CORRECT The best beef should be bright red and be marbled with pure white fat. However, a customer may be fooled by tinted lighting which, in fact, cheats the buyer.

CORRECT The court ruled, consequently, that no damages could be collected.

Notice that *however* is sometimes used as a regular adverb, to modify a particular word rather than as a sentence modifier, and that when so used it is not set off by a comma.

CORRECT However much he diets, he does not lose enough weight. *Since "however" modifies "much," it is not set off.*

Dates and Addresses

Multiple elements of dates, addresses, and references are set off by commas. If only one element (day of month, year, city, etc.) appears, no punctuation is needed.

CORRECT April 4 is her birthday.

CORRECT New York is her native state.

CORRECT Act IV moves toward the climax.

But if other elements are added, they are set off by commas.

CORRECT April 4, 1953, is the date of her birth.

CORRECT The return address was 15 South Main Street, Oxford, Ohio.

CORRECT The quotation is from ***King Lear***, II, ii, 2.

Direct Address, Interjections, yes *and* no

Nouns used as terms of direct address, interjections, and the words *yes* and *no* should be set off by commas.

CORRECT Miss Kuhn, would you like to be a teaching assistant?

CORRECT This preposterous charge, ladies and gentlemen, reveals my opponent's ignorance.

CORRECT Oh, yes, we have a more expensive rental.

Quotation Expressions

Quotation expressions such as *he said* are set off by commas when used with a direct quotation.

CORRECT "When I was young," he said, "seeing a monoplane was exciting."

Do not use a comma to set off an indirect quotation.

CORRECT The jeweler said that he could reset the sapphire.

CORRECT They told us that they had sent a wire.

When the quotation contains two independent clauses and the quotation expression comes between them, a semicolon may be required to prevent a comma fault (see section 2c).

CORRECT "Please try," he said; "you could win."

CORRECT "Please try," he said. "You could win."

CORRECT "I'd like you to try," he said, "but I won't insist."

For other rules regarding the punctuation of direct quotations, see section 7d.

Absolute Phrases

An absolute phrase should be set off by commas. An absolute phrase consists of a participle with a subject (and sometimes a complement) not part of the basic structure of the sentence but serving as a kind of sentence modifier. It usually tells when, why, or how something happened.

CORRECT The gale having quieted, highway workers began to clear fallen trees and signs from the roads.

CORRECT The marks on her transcript didn't annoy her, grades representing only part of her education.

Exercise 3

Insert commas where they are required to set off parenthetic elements or to follow conventional usage.

1. Money is not to be sure the only problem that people worry about.
2. Yes I have lived in Minnesota most of my life but I was born in Seattle Washington.
3. My uncle formerly one of the richest men in Woodstock promised to put me through college.
4. In the first place there is no evidence Mr. Jones that my client was driving a car on July 14 1965.
5. Teaching of course has certain disadvantages class size being what it is.
6. "From here" said Mr. Newman "you can see the car double-parked in the alley."
7. The study of Latin or of any other foreign language for that matter helps to clarify English grammar.
8. My cousins tired and wet returned from their fishing trip at sunset.
9. Stricter laws it is argued would be of no use without more machinery for their enforcement.
10. Portland Maine was not as I remember an unpleasant place for a boy to grow up in.

(6) To Set Off Introductory Elements

A dependent clause coming first in the sentence is usually set off by a comma. If a dependent clause follows the main clause, however, a comma is used only when the dependent clause is nonrestrictive.

CORRECT If you see him, tell him to write me soon.
Introductory adverbial clause, set off by a comma.

CORRECT Since the melting point of tallow is 127° Fahrenheit, slow-burning candles are made with beeswax.

CORRECT Tell him to write me as soon as he can.
Restrictive adverbial clause following main clause.

CORRECT Take a trip abroad now, even if you have to borrow some money.
Nonrestrictive adverbial clause following main clause.

An introductory verbal phrase (participial, gerund, or infinitive) is usually followed by a comma. A prepositional phrase of considerable length at the beginning of a sentence may be followed by a comma.

participial phrase

CORRECT ***Suffering from disease, overcrowding, and poverty,*** the people of Manchester were prime victims of the early Industrial Revolution in England.

gerund phrase

CORRECT ***After seeing the poverty and unfair treatment of the working class people,*** Mrs. Gaskell wrote several protest novels.

infinitive phrase

CORRECT ***To understand Hemingway's uneasy friendship with F. Scott Fitzgerald,*** one must know something of Hemingway's attitude toward Fitzgerald's wife, Zelda.

long prepositional phrase

CORRECT ***Soon after his first acquaintance with Fitzgerald,*** Hemingway took an intense dislike to Zelda.

(7) To Prevent Misreading

Use a comma to separate any sentence elements that might be incorrectly joined in reading and thus misunderstood. *This rule supersedes all others.*

MISLEADING Ever since he has devoted himself to athletics.

CLEAR Ever since, he has devoted himself to athletics.

MISLEADING Inside the house was brightly lighted.

CLEAR Inside, the house was brightly lighted.

CORRECT Soon after, the minister entered the chapel.

CORRECT To elaborate, the art of Japanese flower arranging begins with simplicity.

(8) Misuse of the Comma

Modern practice is to use less, rather than more, punctuation in narrative and expository prose. A good working rule for the beginner is to use no commas except those required by the preceding conventions. Here are some examples of serious errors caused by excessive punctuation. In all the following sentences, the commas should be omitted.

INCORRECT His ability to solve the most complicated problems on the spur of the moment, never failed to impress the class.

The comma erroneously separates subject and predicate.

INCORRECT The men who lived in the old wing of the dormitory, unanimously voted to approve the new rules.

If the clause is restrictive, no commas should be used; if the clause is nonrestrictive, two commas are required.

INCORRECT During chapel the minister announced, that the choir would sing Handel's *Messiah* for Easter.

The comma erroneously separates an indirect quotation from the rest of the sentence.

INCORRECT Gigi is so tall, that she may break the record for rebounds.

The comma erroneously splits an idiomatic construction, "so tall that."

Do not put a comma before the first member or after the last member of a series, unless the comma is required by some other rule.

INCORRECT For lunch I usually have, a sandwich, some fruit, and milk.

The comma after "have" separates the whole series from the rest of the sentence. It should be omitted.

INCORRECT Rhode Island, New Jersey, and Massachusetts, were the most densely populated states in 1960.

The comma after "Massachusetts" erroneously separates the whole series from the rest of the sentence.

CORRECT Rhode Island, New Jersey, and Massachusetts, in that order, were the most densely populated states in 1960.

The comma after "Massachusetts" is required to set off the parenthetic phrase "in that order."

Exercise 4

Some of the following sentences omit necessary commas, while others contain unnecessary and misleading ones. Punctuate the sentences correctly and be prepared to justify each comma you use and the eliminations you make.

1. The person who used to speak precisely and clearly, may now mumble and run words together the way a favorite television star does.
2. Some parents feel there should be a limit to the amount of homework which students are assigned but I feel most teachers are quite reasonable about the amount given.
3. When one cheats, he cheats no one, but himself.
4. This purity of spirit combined with the courage to stand up for what he believes, makes Huck the great character that he is.
5. Finally when Ike is fully initiated the chase begins.
6. A certain coffee commercial is amusing because it uses puppets, and is different from other advertisements.
7. The skeptical writer proposes questions hoping for answers.
8. I could readily understand for instance, that primitive man who was ignorant and easily terrified, might develop a caste of medicine men.
9. The band, bunting and fireworks were planned but these were not enough to assure the parade's success.
10. It is soon evident, in the story, *Lucky Jim,* by Kingsley Amis, that Margaret is unstable, and that Dixon feels insecure and inferior.
11. He is apparently disgusted with his job, and the rest of his environment.
12. Their faces, like the faces of the rest of the villagers are grotesque and primitive.

7c The Semicolon

The semicolon indicates a greater break in the sentence than the comma does, but it does not have the finality of a period. Its most important use is to separate two independent clauses not joined by a conjunction. As a device for creating compound sentences from shorter sentences, the semicolon may easily be overworked. If a conjunction expresses the relationship between the two parts of your sentence, use the conjunction. The semicolon should be reserved for use when the relationship between two statements is so clear that it is unnecessary to state it explicitly.

(1) To Separate Principal Clauses

When the independent clauses of a compound sentence are not joined by a conjunction, a semicolon is required.

CORRECT I do not say that these stories are untrue; I only say that I do not believe them.

CORRECT In India fourteen main languages are written; several hundred dialectical variations are spoken.

The conjunctive adverbs (*so, therefore, however, hence, nevertheless, moreover, accordingly, besides, also, thus, still, otherwise,* etc.) are inadequate to join two independent clauses. A semicolon is required to separate two independent clauses not connected by a pure conjunction. Using a comma instead produces a comma splice (see section 2c).

COMMA SPLICE Our plan was to sail from Naples to New York, however, an emergency at home forced us to fly instead.

CORRECT Our plan was to sail from Naples to New York; however, an emergency at home forced us to fly instead.

CORRECT From the high board, the water looked amazingly far away; besides, I was getting cold and tired of swimming.

CORRECT The loan account book must be sent with each monthly payment; otherwise, there may be disputes as to the amount still owing.

If the clauses are short and closely parallel in form, commas are frequently used between them even if conjunctions are omitted.

CORRECT The picture dimmed, the sound faded, the TV failed.

CORRECT The curtains fluttered, the windows rattled, the doors slammed.

(2) To Separate Clauses When Commas Are Inadequate

Even when two independent clauses are joined by a coordinating conjunction, a semicolon may be used to separate the clauses if the clauses are long or are subdivided by commas.

CORRECT The Northwest Ordinance of 1787, drafted by Jefferson, is generally noted because it established government of territory north of Ohio and west of New York; ***yet*** one of its most important statutes was the allocation of land and support for public schools.

CORRECT In recognition of her services, the principal was given a farewell dinner, a record, and a scroll; ***and*** a new elementary school was named after her.

A semicolon is used to separate elements in a series when the elements contain internal commas. That is, when a comma is not a strong enough mark of separation to indicate the elements of a series unmistakably, a semicolon is used instead.

AMBIGUOUS One day of orientation was led by Mr. Joseph, the chaplain, Mrs. Smith, a French teacher, and the Dean.
How many led orientation?

CORRECT One day of orientation was led by Mr. Joseph, the chaplain; Mrs. Smith, a French teacher; and the Dean.

CORRECT Bibliography may include Randall Jarrell, *Poetry and the Age*; Northrup Frye, *Anatomy of Criticism*; and Edmund Wilson, *The Shock of Recognition.*

Be sure that semicolons separate coordinate elements. Using a semicolon to separate an independent clause and a subordinate clause is an error similar to writing a sentence fragment, and just as serious.

INCORRECT Young people tend to reject parental authority; although they are searching for other adults as models.

CORRECT Young people tend to reject parental authority, although they are searching for other adults as models.

Exercise 5

Some of the following sentences contain semicolons which are unnecessary or incorrect, while other sentences lack needed semicolons. Correct the punctuation and be able to justify each semicolon you use or omit.

1. Joseph is reluctantly picked up by a passing stagecoach; and then only after one of the passengers notes that they could be held legally responsible if a naked stranger should die for lack of aid.

2. More understandable than any of her other criticisms are her remarks about the educational system, however, even these are not very specific.
3. Our technology has developed the telephone for the talebearer; the car for the speedster; and the elevator for children.
4. A novel dealing with the affectations of a past society may become dated, and one must consider this possibility when judging it, otherwise, the book will suffer undue criticism.
5. He was not admitted to the honor society; although he was a good athlete and a top student.
6. The second edition of the book, published in 1922, is relatively scarce and hard to find; but the third edition, published four years later, can be seen in almost any store selling old books.
7. Sometimes I get so interested in a book that I stay up until I finish it; regardless of whether I have classes the next morning or not.
8. Since air is dissolved by water at the surface only, the shape of an aquarium is important, too small an opening may cause an oxygen deficiency.
9. I might ask here; "What is the most important thing in life?"
10. The sculptor can work for more than a week on the same clay model; because clay can be kept soft and pliable for a long time.

Exercise 6

Explain the punctuation in the following sentences. In order to do so, you will need to distinguish between principal clauses, subordinate clauses, and phrases.

1. There are no set rules which actors must follow to become proficient in their art; however, there are certain principles regarding the use of mind, voice, and body which may help them.
2. The book covered the life of Lotta Crabtree from birth to death; it painted her as one of the most colorful figures of early California.
3. Her forehead was wrinkled, her mouth was firm and tense, but her eyes had a dreamy, reminiscent look.
4. The unconscious sailor would then be taken to an outbound ship to be sold to the captain at a price ranging from $100 to $300, depending on how pressed the captain was for men; and he would regain consciousness somewhere in the Pacific Ocean, without the slightest idea of where he was or where he was going.

5. Among the colorful figures in the book are Johnny Highpockets, a simple-minded settler; Charley Tufts, formerly a professor at Yale; and the author of the book himself.
6. A grove of cypress trees, wind-blown and shaggy with Spanish moss, still grows on the headland, as it did when Stevenson first explored the area.
7. Somervell, the only son of a hard-working country doctor and a mother who had been trained as a school teacher, was born in a quiet, secluded farming town in Arkansas on August 21, 1892.
8. In most respects the hotel is admirably located; it is near the corner of Fifth Avenue and 52nd Street, within walking distance of convention headquarters.
9. On the postcard was a reproduction of a watercolor by John Piper; it showed the interior of Ingelsham Church.
10. Since air is dissolved by water at the surface only, the shape of an aquarium is important; too small an opening may cause an oxygen deficiency.

7d Quotation Marks

(1) To Enclose Direct Quotation

Use quotation marks to enclose a direct quotation, but not an indirect quotation. A direct quotation gives the exact words of a speaker. An indirect quotation is the writer's paraphrase of what someone said.

INDIRECT QUOTATION He said that he would call.

DIRECT QUOTATION He said, "I will call."

The indirect quotation does not give the speaker's exact words; the direct quotation does and is enclosed with quotation marks.

The expression *he said* is never included within the quotation marks. If the actual quotation is interrupted by such an expression, both halves must be enclosed by quotation marks.

CORRECT "I am interested," he said, "so let's talk it over."

CORRECT "It all began accidentally," Jackson said. "My remark was misunderstood."

(2) To Quote Several Sentences

If a quotation consists of several sentences, uninterrupted by a *he* or *she said* expression, use one set of marks to enclose the entire quotation. Do not enclose each separate sentence. If a quotation consists of several paragraphs, put quotation marks at the beginning of each paragraph and at the end of the last paragraph.

CORRECT Barbara replied, "Right now? But I haven't finished my paper for Economics. Call me in a couple of hours."

CORRECT Poor Richard has a number of things to say about diet:

"They that study much, ought not to eat so much as those that work hard, their digestion being not so good.

"If thou art dull and heavy after meat, it's a sign thou hast exceeded the due measure; for meat and drink ought to refresh the body and make it chearful, and not to dull and oppress it.

"A sober diet makes a man die without pain; it maintains the senses in vigour; it mitigates the violence of the passions and affections."

A quotation within a quotation is enclosed with single quotation marks. Be sure to conclude the original quotation with double marks.

CORRECT The lecture began, "As Proust said, 'Any mental activity is easy if it need not take reality into account.'"

(3) To Indicate Implied Speech

Quotation marks are frequently used for implied speech, but are not customarily used for unspoken thoughts.

CORRECT He tried to cry, "She is there, she is there," but he couldn't utter the words, only the sounds.

—Jan de Hartog

CORRECT It was a momentary liberation from the pent-up anxious state I usually endured to be able to think: At least I'm not them! At least I'm not those heavy, serious, righteous people upstairs.

—Robert Lowry

(4) Misuse in Paraphrase

Use quotation marks around material directly quoted from another writer, but not around a paraphrase of an author's ideas.

CORRECT John Selden pinpoints our attitude toward virtues when he defines humility: "Humility is a virtue all preach, none practise, and yet everybody is content to hear. The master thinks it good doctrine for his servant, the laity for the clergy, and the clergy for the laity."

CORRECT John Selden describes humility as a virtue we all praise, but few practice. We expect to observe it in those who deal with us, while overlooking our own chances to be humble.

If you quote only a few words from a well-known writer and work them into your own sentence, quotation marks may be omitted.

CORRECT During childhood it was easy to see that others should share toys, but during adulthood it is not easy to do unto others as you would have them do unto you.

(5) Longer Quotations

When a borrowed quotation runs to several lines of print, it should be set off by indenting and single-spacing. Quotation marks should not be used to set off such material, though they may be required within the quotation.

CORRECT T. S. Eliot begins the essay "Tradition and the Individual Talent":

> In English writing we seldom speak of tradition, though we occasionally apply its name in deploring its absence. We cannot refer to "the tradition" or to "a tradition"; at most, we employ the adjective in saying that the poetry of So-and-so is "traditional" or even "too traditional." Seldom, perhaps, does the world appear except in a phrase of censure. If otherwise, it is vaguely approbative, with the implication, as to the work approved, of some pleasing archaeological reconstruction.

(6) Verse Quotations

A quotation of more than one line of poetry should be set off by indenting and single-spacing, without quotation marks. Be sure to keep the line lengths exactly as they are in the original.

CORRECT Boileau has captured a quality inseparable from fine satire:

> But satire, ever moral, ever new.
> Delights the reader and instructs him too.
> She, if good sense refine her sterling page,
> Oft shakes some rooted folly of the age.

A quotation of one line of verse, or part of a line, should be enclosed in quotation marks and run in as part of your text.

CORRECT Lytton disliked the false heroics of Henley's "My head is bloody but unbowed."

If parts of two lines of verse are run in to the text, indicate the line break by a slash (/):

CORRECT Stark Young and Rex Stout both found book titles in Fitzgerald's "never grows so red / The rose as where some buried Caesar bled."

(7) Punctuation with Quotation Marks

At the end of a quotation, a period or comma is placed inside the quotation mark; a semicolon or colon is placed outside the quotation mark.

CORRECT "Quick," said my cousin, "hand me the flashlight."

CORRECT The bride and groom said, "I do"; the ladies in the audience wept.

CORRECT I have only one comment when you say, "All people are equal": I wish it were true.

A question mark or exclamation mark goes inside the quotation mark if it applies to the quotation only, and outside the quotation mark if it applies to the whole sentence.

CORRECT My mother asked, "Did you arrive on time?"

CORRECT Did the invitation say "R.S.V.P."?

CORRECT He called irritably, "Move over!"

CORRECT Above all, don't let anyone hear you say, "I give up"!

(8) To Indicate Titles

Titles of books, poems, plays, musical compositions, etc., may be enclosed in quotation marks, but the preferred practice is to italicize titles of books, journals, plays, and major poetic or musical works, and to use quotation marks for the titles of chapters, articles, short poems, and songs. Titles of paintings and other objects of art are regularly enclosed in quotation marks.

CORRECT The fourth section of Isak Dinesen's ***Out of Africa*** is entitled "From an Immigrant's Notebook."

CORRECT Carl Orff's cantata ***Carmina Burana*** opens and closes with "Fortune, Empress of the World."

(9) Misuse for Humorous Emphasis or with Slang

If occasionally you want to indicate that a word or phrase should be heavily stressed or deserves special attention, use italics, not quotation marks. Humor or irony should be indicated by the context. Using quotation marks to call attention to an ironic or humorous passage is like poking your listener in the ribs when you have reached the point of a joke. If you use slang at all, take full responsibility for it. Do not apologize for a phrase by putting it in quotation marks.

Exercise 7

Insert quotation marks where they are necessary in the following sentences.

1. The Dean replied that he knew very well freshmen had trouble getting adjusted. But, he added, it doesn't usually take them eight months to find themselves.
2. I hope said Professor Painter that someone can identify a quotation for me. It's from the end of a sonnet, and all I can remember is Like a lean knife between the ribs of Time.
3. President Turini, according to the *Alumni Magazine,* believed that the chief values of a liberal education were nonmaterial; but on another page she was quoted, in the course of a speech delivered in Seattle, as saying that a college education is essential for any person who does not plan to marry money.
4. I asked whether Professor Lawrence still began his first lecture by saying My name is Lawrence and I wish I were not here, as he always did when I was in college.
5. The program said that the musical Hello, Dolly is based on Thornton Wilder's play The Matchmaker.
6. Take a chair, said my tutor, and smoke if you like. He picked up my paper. Tell me honestly, he said; is this the best you can do?
7. Madame Lenoir said, As my first number I will sing the song Der Leiermann, from Schubert's *Winterreise*.
8. When asked To what do you attribute your success? Henderson always answered Sleeping late in the morning.

7e Other Punctuation Marks: Apostrophe, Colon, Dash, Parentheses, Brackets

(1) The Apostrophe

The chief uses of the apostrophe are to indicate the possessive case of nouns and indefinite pronouns, to mark the omission of letters in a contracted word or date, and to indicate the plural of letters or numerals.

Possessive Case

Nouns and indefinite pronouns which do not already end in *s* form the possessive by adding an apostrophe and an *s*.

CORRECT a child'**s** toy children'**s** toys
one'**s** dignity Cole Porter'**s** songs

Plural nouns which end in *s* (*boys, girls*) form the possessive by adding an apostrophe only.

CORRECT girls' hockey the Ellises' orchard
boys' jackets the Neilsons' garage

Singular nouns which end in *s* (*Thomas, kiss*) form the possessive by adding an apostrophe and an *s* if the *s* is to be pronounced as an extra syllable.

CORRECT Thomas's poems King James's reign the kiss's effect

But if an extra syllable would be awkward to pronounce, the possessive is formed by adding the apostrophe only, omitting the second *s*.

CORRECT Socrates' questions Moses' life Euripides' plays

The personal pronouns *never require an apostrophe,* even though the possessive case ends in *s: his, hers, its, ours, yours, theirs.*

In joint possession the last noun takes the possessive form. In individual possession each name should take the possessive form.

JOINT POSSESSION Marshall and Ward's St. Paul branch

INDIVIDUAL POSSESSION John's, George's, and Harold's separate claims.

Note also these preferred forms: *someone else's book; my sister-in-law's visit; nobody else's opinion.*

Contractions

Use an apostrophe to indicate omissions in contracted words and dates.

CORRECT	haven't	doesn't	isn't	it's	o'clock
	have not	does not	is not	it is	of the clock

CORRECT the class of '38

Plural of Letters and Numerals

The plural of letters and of numerals is formed by adding an apostrophe and an *s*. The plural of a word considered as a word may be formed in the same way.

CORRECT Her ***w***'s were like ***m***'s, and her ***6***'s like ***G***'s.

CORRECT His conversation is too full of ***you know***'s punctuated by ***well***'s.

(2) The Colon

The colon is a formal mark of punctuation, used primarily to introduce a formal enumeration or list, a long quotation, or an explanatory statement.

CORRECT Consider these three viewpoints: political, economic, and social.

CORRECT Tocqueville expresses one view: "In the United States we easily perceive how the legal profession is qualified by its attributes . . . to neutralize the vices inherent in popular government. . . ."

CORRECT I remember which way to move the clock when changing from Daylight Saving Time to Standard Time by applying a simple rule: spring ahead, fall backwards.

Note that a list introduced by a colon should be in apposition to a preceding word; that is, the sentence preceding the colon should be grammatically complete without the list.

UNDESIRABLE We provide: fishing permit, rod, hooks, bait, lunch, boat, oars.

CORRECT We provide the following items: fishing permit, rod, boat, oars, etc.

CORRECT We provide the following: fishing permit, rod, lunch, boat, etc.

CORRECT The following items are provided: fishing permit, rod, lunch, boat, etc.

The colon may be used between two principal clauses when the second clause explains or develops the first.

CORRECT Intercollegiate athletics continues to be big business, but Robert Hutchins long ago pointed out a simple remedy: colleges should stop charging admission to football games.

A colon is used after a formal salutation in a business letter.

CORRECT Dear Sir: Dear Mr. Harris: Gentlemen:

A colon is used to separate hour and minutes in numerals indicating time.

CORRECT The train leaves at 9:27 A.M., and arrives at Joplin at 8:15 P.M.

In bibliographical references, a colon is used between the place of publication and the name of the publisher.

CORRECT New York: Oxford University Press

Between the parts of a Biblical reference a colon may be used.

CORRECT *Proverbs* 28:20

(3) The Dash

The dash, as its name suggests, is a dramatic mark. Like the comma and the parentheses, it separates elements within the sentence, but what the parentheses says quietly the dash exclaims. To signal a summary statement, the dash is more informal than the dignified colon—and more emphatic. Use the dash cautiously. Its flashy interruption can create suspense and energy in a sentence, but its frequent use often indicates a writer who has not learned how to punctuate with discrimination.

A dash is used, as a separator, to indicate that a sentence is broken off or to indicate a sharp turn of thought.

CORRECT The application requested a transcript and had space to enter extracurricular activities, interests, hobbies—need I say more?

CORRECT From noon until three o'clock, we had an excellent view of all that can be seen of a battle—i.e., nothing at all.

—STENDHAL

Dashes may be used to set off appositives or parenthetic elements when commas are insufficient.

CORRECT Three pictures—a watercolor, an oil, and a silk screen—hung on the west wall.

If the commas were used to set off "a watercolor, an oil, and a silk screen" the sentence might be misunderstood to refer to six pictures. The dashes make it clear that only three pictures are meant.

CORRECT By the time the speech was over—it lasted almost two hours—I was dozing in my chair.

Since the parenthetic element is an independent clause, commas would be insufficient to set it off clearly.

When a sentence begins with a list of substantives, a dash is commonly used to separate the list from the summarizing statement which follows.

CORRECT Relaxation, repose, growth within—these are necessities of life, not privileges.

CORRECT The chance to sit on a committee with no big issues to debate, the prospect of introducing bills which will never be reported, the opportunity to write speeches that will rarely be delivered—these are not horizons toward which an able man will strain.

—HAROLD LASKI

(4) Parentheses

Parentheses, like dashes and commas, are used to enclose or set off parenthetic, explanatory, or supplementary material. Arbitrary rules indicating which marks to use cannot be laid down. Commas are most frequently used, and are usually sufficient, when the parenthetic material is very closely related in thought or structure to the rest of the sentence. If the parenthetic material is long or if it contains commas, dashes would customarily be used to set it off. Parentheses are most often used for explanatory or supplementary material of the sort which might be put in a footnote—useful information which is not essential. Parentheses are also used to enclose numbers which mark an enumeration within a sentence.

CORRECT It was, perhaps, this very sensibility to the surrounding atmosphere of feeling and speculation which made Rousseau more directly influential on contemporary thought **(**or perhaps we should say sentiment**)** than any writer of his time.

—James Russel Lowell

CORRECT His last story **(**"Success à la Steinberg"**)** lacked imagination and any relevance to the cartoonist named in the title.

CORRECT In general, the war powers of the President cannot be precisely defined, but must remain somewhat vague and uncertain. **(**See Wilson's *Constitutional Government in the United States.***)**

CORRECT The types of noncreative thinking listed by Robinson are **(**1**)** reverie, or daydreaming, **(**2**)** making minor decisions, **(**3**)** rationalizing, or justifying our prejudices.

(5) Brackets

Brackets are used to enclose a word or words inserted in a quotation by the person quoting.

CORRECT "For the First Amendment does not speak equivocally. It prohibits any law 'abridging the freedom of speech, or of the press.' *It must be taken as a command of the broadest scope that explicit language, read in the context of a liberty-loving society, will allow.*" **[**Italics added.**]**

CORRECT "It is clear **[**the message read**]** that the Muscle Shoals development is but a small part of the potential public usefulness of the entire Tennessee River."

CORRECT "We know more about its state **[**the state of the language**]** in the later Middle Ages; and from the time of Shakespeare on, our information is quite complete."

The word *sic* (meaning *thus*) enclosed in brackets is sometimes inserted in a quotation after a misspelling or other error to indicate that the error occurs in the original.

CORRECT He sent this written confession: "She followed us into the kitchen, snatched a craving **[***sic***]** knife from the table, and came toward me with it."

If one parenthetical expression falls inside another, then brackets replace the inner parentheses. **(**Avoid this situation whenever possible; usually **[**as here**]** it is distracting.**)**

Exercise 8

Insert colons, dashes, parentheses, and brackets as they are needed in the following sentences.

1. Each of its large rooms there were no separate cells in this prison housed some twenty prisoners.
2. I took part in a number of activities in high school the rally committee, dramatics, *Ayer* staff the *Ayer* is our annual, and glee club.
3. He joined the Quakers and became an occasional speaker the Quakers have no ordained ministers at their meetings in Philadelphia.
4. According to an inscription on the flyleaf, the book had been owned by Alburt *sic* Taylor.
5. The sect permits dancing but forbids some other seemingly innocent recreations card playing, for example, is banned as being the next thing to gambling.
6. According to the *Mason Report* Stearns testified as follows "I made his John Brown's acquaintance early in January 1857, in Boston."
7. The midnight programs at the Varsity Theater feature horror films, science-fiction thrillers, movies of strange monsters from the sea you know the kind of thing.

Exercise 9

Some of the following student sentences contain incorrect or misleading punctuation, while others lack needed punctuation. Correct each sentence and be prepared to justify your changes.

1. The author mentions spontaneous and joyous effort, but what is a spontaneous and joyous effort.
2. Lincoln born in 1809 in Kentucky, was brought up in a poor family in the woods.
3. What would imply greater silence and quiet meditation than the numerous s's in the sentence.
4. You have a carwash for your car; a combination washer and dryer for your laundry; and a portable dishwasher for your dishes.
5. His goal had been to set up camp at this particular place along the river–No other place would do even though other places would have been faster to get to, and now he had done it.

6. It is the setting that is significant, without the setting there would be no story.
7. Now we reach the inevitable question, how does our liberally educated man make use of his knowledge when he enters the business world?
8. However, Bernard Shaw's main purpose is not to show the tragedy of St. Joan (that is already quite evident)—but to explain the character of St. Joan.
9. In our new house, the kitchen the bathroom and the utility rooms, will have plain wood floors
10. Under the system just established a student from a family which cannot afford to send a child away to college, will have a chance for a scholarship, especially if he or she is interested in science or engineering.

Exercise 10

Punctuate the following paragraphs and be ready to give a reason for each mark used.

1. I could tell without turning who was coming. There wasnt a big flat-footed clop-clop like horses make on hard-pack but a kind of edgy clip-clip-clip. There was only one man around here would ride a mule at least on this kind of business. That was Bill Winder who drove the stage between Reno and Bridgers Wells. A mule is tough all right a good mule can work two horses into the ground and not know it. But theres something about a mule a man cant get fond of. Maybe its just the way a mule is just as you feel its the end with a man whos that way. But you cant make a mule part of the way you live like your horse is its like he had no insides no soul. Instead of a partner youve just got something else to work on along with the steers. Winder didnt like mules either but thats why he rode them. It was against his religion to get on a horse horses were for driving

Its Winder Gil said and looked at Davies and grinned. The news gets around dont it

I looked at Davies too in the glass but he wasnt showing anything just staring at his drink and minding his own thoughts.

—WALTER VAN TILBURG CLARK

2. A few teachers and college administrators have begun to discover that student-made films say as much . . . about students, their present frustrations and aspirations, as about film-making itself. Some contend that these movies are the best guides to the

intellectual and emotional world of students and that even a cursory glance will provide penetrating insights into what is really behind the recent upheavals at Berkeley and other institutions. On a kind of hunch the American Council on Education a relatively conservative organization in higher education has screened dozens of student-made films to learn more about what undergraduates are thinking. No one has clarified the reasons why these films are so revealing but most people believe that it has a great deal to do with the fact that students are expressing themselves in a medium which they feel is their own and which therefore they can trust.

Not unexpectedly student films are characterized by a spirit of revolt they are anti-establishment anti-system anti-conformity. In some pictures this takes the form of a relatively clear statement. Take The Bulb Changer a whimsical comedy produced by a Northwestern student in which the title character completely fouls up an entire community's traffic-light system after he suffers an injustice at the hands of his superior at the local bureaucracy.

More often however the "message" in a student film is stated obliquely. A film entitled Another Yesterday made by two undergraduates at the University of Pennsylvania's Annenberg School of Communication is ostensibly a documentary account of the humdrum life of a young Negro prizefighter. We follow him from the time he awakes at 600 A.M. and starts his roadwork until he returns from the gym to his dingy one-room apartment following a 900 P.M. workout. Boxing is his profession but most of the time he devotes to it is actually moonlighting before and after his regular job as a stevedore. Part of the sound track gives us the highlights of a boxer's day a straightforward professionally composed narrative. The startling element however is an interwoven narration spoken flatly and without emotion from Camus' novel The Stranger for example Mother died today or was it yesterday it doesn't really matter.

In this second narrative thread the film-makers felt they had captured the essence of what was really going on. Predictably they waited until the last minute to add the sound assuming that their teacher wouldn't understand and would veto the whole project.

—DAVID C. STEWART

8 Spelling

Misspelling of common words is regarded by the general public as a sure sign of lack of education. College graduates cannot afford to be poor spellers. They need not be, since most misspelling is a habit and habits can be changed with a little effort.

The first step is to make a list of words which you misspell. Have someone give you a series of spelling tests on the words listed in section 8e. These are all common words frequently misspelled. Difficult words like *asphyxiate* or *symbiosis,* which occur infrequently in ordinary writing, need not be learned, since you can consult a dictionary for the spelling of any word which is obviously difficult.

Add to the list all words which are misspelled on your themes, and study the list. Look carefully at the letters of each word, pronounce the word a syllable at a time, write the word repeatedly to fix the pattern in your mind. Invent mnemonic devices—pictures, jingles, associations—to help you remember particular spellings. For example, a student might remember the distinction between *capital* and *capitol* by associating capitAl with WAshington and capitOl with dOme. Learn the common prefixes and suffixes, and analyze words to see how they are formed. For example:

disappoint = dis + appoint
dissatisfied = dis + satisfied
misspelling = mis + spell + ing
really = real + ly

unnecessary = un + necessary
undoubtedly = un + doubt + ed + ly
government = govern + ment
carefully = care + ful + ly
incidentally = incident + al + ly

See how many words in the list of *Words Commonly Misspelled* can be analyzed into a root word with prefixes or suffixes. If you find exceptions, look for an explanation in the Spelling Rules.

When you have finished the final draft of a paper, proofread it carefully before you hand it in. (Proofread for spelling errors separately if you have trouble with spelling.) It is no excuse to say that you knew the correct spelling of a word but that your pen slipped. Misspellings due to typographical errors or general carelessness are still misspellings.

8a Trouble Spots in Words

Learn to look for the trouble spots in words and concentrate on them. Common words are almost always misspelled in the same way. That is, a particular letter or combination of letters is the trouble spot, and if you can remember the correct spelling of the trouble spot, the rest of the word will take care of itself. *Receive,* like *deceive, perceive,* and *conceive,* is troublesome only because of the *ei* combination; if you can remember that it is *ei* after *c,* you will have mastered these words. To spell *beginning* correctly, all you need to remember is the double *n.*

Careful pronunciation may help you to avoid errors at trouble spots. In the following words, the letters in italics are often omitted. Pronounce the words aloud, exaggerating the sound of the italicized letters:

accident***al***ly	Feb***r***uary	li***a***ble
can***d***idate	gener***al***ly	lib***r***ary
ever***y***body	lab***o***ratory	liter***a***ture
occasion***al***ly	reco***g***nize	su***r***prise
proba***b***ly	soph***o***more	temper***a***ment
quan***t***ity	stric***t***ly	us***u***ally

Many people add letters incorrectly to the following words. Pronounce the words, making sure no extra syllable creeps in at spots indicated by italics.

a**th**letics	en**tr**ance	mischie**v**ous
disas**tr**ous	heigh**t**	remem**br**ance
drown**ed**	hin**dr**ance	simil**ar**
e**lm**	ligh**tn**ing	um**br**ella

Trouble spots in the following words are caused by a tendency to transpose the letters italicized. Careful pronunciation may help you to remember the proper order.

child**re**n	p**er**form	pre**jud**ice
hund**re**d	p**er**spiration	p**re**scription
irre**l**e**v**ant	p**re**fer	trage**d**y

8b Similar Words Frequently Confused

Learn the meaning and spelling of similar words. Many errors are caused by confusion of such words as *effect* and *affect*. It is useless to spell *principal* correctly if the word that belongs in your sentence is *principle*. The following list distinguishes briefly between words which are frequently confused.

accept	***receive***
except	***aside from***
access	***admittance***
excess	***greater amount***
advice	noun
advise	verb
affect	***to influence*** (verb)
effect	***result*** (noun)
effect	***to bring about*** (verb)
aisle	in church
isle	***island***
all ready	***prepared***
already	***previously***
allusion	***reference***
illusion	***misconception***
altar	***shrine***
alter	***change***
alumna	a woman
alumnae	women
alumnus	a man
alumni	men
angel	***celestial being***
angle	***corner***
ascent	***climbing***
assent	***agreement***
berth	***bed***
birth	***being born***
boarder	***one who boards***
border	***edge***
breath	noun
breathe	verb

capital	*city*
capitol	*building*
choose	present
chose	past
clothes	*garments*
cloths	*kinds of cloth*
coarse	*not fine*
course	*path, series*
complement	*to complete*
compliment	*to praise*
conscience	*sense of right and wrong*
conscious	*aware*
corps	*group*
corpse	*dead body*
costume	*dress*
custom	*manner*
council	*governmental group*
counsel	*advice*
decent	*proper*
descent	*slope*
desert	*wasteland*
dessert	*food*
device	noun
devise	verb
dairy	*milk supply*
diary	*daily record*
dual	*twofold*
duel	*fight*
formally	*in a formal manner*
formerly	*previously*

forth	*forward*
fourth	*4th*
ingenious	*clever*
ingenuous	*frank*
its	*of it*
it's	*it is*
later	*subsequently*
latter	*second of two*
lead	*metal*
led	past tense of verb ***lead***
loose	adjective
lose	verb
peace	*not war*
piece	*a portion*
personal	adjective
personnel	noun
principal	*most important*
principle	*basic doctrine*
quiet	*still*
quite	*entirely*
respectfully	*with respect*
respectively	*in the order named*
shone	from ***shine***
shown	from ***show***
stationary	adjective
stationery	noun
their	possessive
there	*in that place*
they're	*they are*
than	comparison
then	*at that time*

to	go *to* bed	who's	***who is***
too	***too*** bad, me ***too***	whose	possessive
two	2	you're	***you are***
		your	possessive
weather	***rain*** or ***shine***		
whether	***which of two***		

8c Spelling Rules

Learn the available spelling rules. Spelling rules apply to a relatively small number of words, and unfortunately almost all rules have exceptions. Nevertheless, some of the rules may help you to spell common words which cause you trouble, especially those words formed with suffixes.

It is as important to learn when a rule may be used as it is to understand the rule itself. Applied in the wrong places, rules will make your spelling worse, instead of better.

(1) Final Silent e

Drop a final silent *e* before suffixes beginning with a vowel (*-ing, -age, -able,*). Keep a final silent *e* before suffixes beginning with a consonant (*-ful, -ly, -ness*).

hope + ing = hoping	hope + ful = hopeful
love + able = lovable	nine + teen = nineteen
stone + y = stony	arrange + ment = arrangement
guide + ance = guidance	late + ly = lately
plume + age = plumage	pale + ness = paleness
white + ish = whitish	white + wash = whitewash
write + ing = writing	sincere + ly = sincerely
dote + age = dotage	bale + ful = baleful

Learn the following exceptions:

dyeing	hoeing	judgment	awful
ninth	truly	duly	wholly

The *e* is retained in such words as the following in order to keep the soft sound of *c* and *g*:

noticeable	courageous
peaceable	outrageous

Exercise 1

Following the rule just given, write the correct spelling of each word indicated below.

use + ing
use + ful
argue + ment
guide + ance
nine + ty
pale + ness
immediate + ly
please + ure
manage + able
pale + ing
manage + ment
write + ing
advantage + ous
refuse + al
waste + ful
hope + less
absolute + ly
sure + ly

(2) Doubling Final Consonant

When adding a suffix beginning with a vowel to words ending in one consonant preceded by one vowel (*red, redder*), notice where the word is accented. If it is accented on the last syllable or if it is a monosyllable, *double* the final consonant.

pre**fér** + ed = preferred
o**mít** + ing = omitting
oc**cúr** + ence = occurrence
réd + er = redder
bénefit + ed = benefited
prófit + ing = profiting
díffer + ence = difference
trável + er = traveler

Note that in some words the accent shifts when the suffix is added.

re**fér**red
pre**fér**ring
réference
préference

There are a few exceptions to this rule, like *transferable* and *excellent;* and a good many words that should follow the rule have alternative spellings: either *worshiped* or *worshipped; traveling, traveler,* or *travelling, traveller.*

Exercise 2

Make as many combinations as you can of the following words and suffixes. Give your reason for doubling or not doubling the final consonant. Suffixes: *-able, -ible, -ary, -ery, -er, -est, -ance, -ence, -ess, -ed, -ish, -ing, -ly, -ful, -ment, -ness, -hood.*

occur	scrap	ravel	man	libel	glad
happen	red	kidnap	defer	will	profit
begin	equip	hazard	sum	skill	avoid
god	commit	read	stop	expel	level
shrub	equal	rid	clan	rival	jewel

(3) Words Ending in *y*

If the *y* is preceded by a consonant, change the *y* to *i* before any suffix except *-ing*.

lady + es = ladies
try + ed = tried
study + ing = studying
lonely + ness = loneliness
accompany + es = accompanies

The *y* is usually retained if it is preceded by a vowel:

valleys monkeys displayed

SOME EXCEPTIONS laid, paid, said, ladylike

Exercise 3

Add suffixes to the following words. State your reason for spelling the word as you do.

mercy	relay	hardy	bounty	medley
duty	study	wordy	jockey	galley
pulley	essay	fancy	modify	body

(4) *ie* or *ei*

When *ie* or *ei* is used to spell the sound *ee*,
Put *i* before *e*
Except after *c*.

ach***ie***ve	gr***ie***ve	retr***ie***ve	c***ei***ling
bel***ie***f	n***ie***ce	sh***ie***ld	conc***ei***t
bel***ie***ve	p***ie***ce	shr***ie***k	conc***ei***ve
br***ie***f	p***ie***rce	s***ie***ge	dec***ei***t
ch***ie***f	rel***ie***f	th***ie***f	dec***ei***ve
f***ie***ld	rel***ie***ve	w***ie***ld	perc***ei***ve
gr***ie***f	repr***ie***ve	y***ie***ld	rec***ei***ve

SOME EXCEPTIONS ***ei***ther, l***ei***sure, n***ei***ther, s***ei***ze, w***ei***rd.

8d Hyphenation

A hyphen is used, under certain circumstances, to join the parts of compound words. Compounds are written as two separate words (*city hall*), as two words joined by a hyphen (*city-state*), or solid as one word (*townspeople*). In general, the hyphen is used in recently made compounds and compounds still in the process of becoming one word. Because usage varies considerably, no arbitrary rules can be laid down. When in doubt consult the latest edition of an unabridged dictionary. The following "rules" represent the usual current practice.

(1) Compound Adjectives

Words used as a single adjective *before* a noun are usually hyphenated.

fine-grained wood	three-quarter binding
strong-minded woman	matter-of-fact statement
far-sighted proposal	so-called savings
well-informed leader	old-fashioned attitude

When these compound adjectives *follow* the noun, they usually do not require the hyphen.

CORRECT The snow-covered mountains lay ahead.

CORRECT The mountains are snow covered.

When the adverb ending in *-ly* is used with an adjective or a participle, the compound is not usually hyphenated.

CORRECT highly praised organization, widely advertised campaign.

(2) Prefixes

When a prefix still retains its original strength in the compound, use a hyphen. In most instances, however, the prefix has been absorbed into the word and should not be separated by a hyphen. Contrast the following pairs of words:

ex-president, excommunicate	pre-Christian, preconception
vice-president, viceroy	pro-British, procreation

Note that in some words a difference of meaning is indicated by the hyphen:

She recovered her strength.

She re-covered her quilt.

(3) Compound Numbers

A hyphen is used in compound numbers from twenty-one to ninety-nine.

CORRECT twenty-six, sixty-three, *but* one hundred thirty.

(4) Hyphen to Prevent Misreading

Use a hyphen if necessary to avoid ambiguity.

AMBIGUOUS A detail of six foot soldiers was on duty.

CLEAR A detail of six foot-soldiers was on duty.

OR

CLEAR A detail of six-foot soldiers was on duty.

Exercise 4

Should the compounds in the following sentences be written solid, with a hyphen, or as two words? Consult a recent edition of a good dictionary, if necessary.

1. We need an eight foot rod.
2. All the creeks are bone dry.
3. She gave away one fourth of her income.
4. The United States is a world power.
5. Who was your go between?
6. He is very good looking.
7. The younger son was a ne'er do well.
8. Let us sing the chorus all together.
9. They are building on a T shaped wing.
10. She is getting a badly needed rest.
11. Are you all ready?
12. The leak was in the sub basement.
13. He was anti British.
14. She does her work in a half hearted manner.
15. I don't like your chip on the shoulder manner.

16. They always were old fashioned.
17. A high school course is required for admission.
18. I do not trust second hand information.
19. He is as pig headed a man as I ever knew.
20. She will not accept any thing second rate.

8e Words Commonly Misspelled

The following list is composed of some ordinary words that are often misspelled. If you learn to spell correctly those which you usually misspell, and if you will look up in a dictionary words which are obviously difficult or unfamiliar, your spelling will improve remarkably.

Have a friend test you on these words—fifty at a time. Then concentrate on the ones you miss. To help you remember correct spellings, trouble spots are indicated by boldface italic type in most of the words.

ab***s***en***c***e
absor***p***tion
ab***su***rd
abund***a***nt
ac***a***demic

accident***al***ly
a***cc***o***mm***odate
a***cc***umulate
a***cc***urate
ach***ie***vement

a***c***quainted
a***c***quire
a***c***ross
a***dd***ition***al***ly
a***dd***ress

ad***e***quat***e***ly
a***gg***ravate
airplane
a***ll***o***t***ment
allo***tt***ed

a***ll*** right
a***l***ready
a***l***tog***e***ther
a***l***ways
am***a***t***eu***r

am***on***g
anal***y***sis
a***nn***ua***ll***y
a***p***ol***o***gy
a***pp***ar***a***t***u***s

a***pp***ar***e***nt
appear***a***nce
app***e***tite
appr***ec***iate
a***pp***ro***pr***iate

ar***c***tic
arg***u***ment
arithm***e***tic
a***rr***ang***e***ment
arti***cle***

as***c***end
a***ss***o***c***iation
a***thl***etic
attack***ed***
attend***a***nce

audi***e***nce
av***ai***l***a***ble
awkward
barg***ai***n
basic***all***y

beco***m***ing
begi***nn***ing
bel***ie***ve
ben***e***fi***t***ed
bound***a***ry

brill***ia***nt
Brit***ai***n
bus***i***ness
cal***e***nd***a***r
can***d***idate

ca***r***eer
cat***e***gory
cemet***e***ry
cert***ai***n
chall***e***nge

chang***ea***ble
chang***i***ng
Christ***ia***n
colu***mn***
co***m***ing

co***mm***i***ss***ion
co***mm***i***tt***ee
compar***a***tively
compet***e***nt
comp***eti***tion

conc***ei***t
con***c***entrate
conde***mn***
confid***e***nce
conqu***ero***r

conscientious
con***scious***
con***s***ider
consist***e***nt
contempor***a***ry

contin***uous***
contro***ll***ed
conv***e***n***ie***nce
coo***ll***y
cop***ie***s

court***eous***
crit***icis***m
d***ea***lt
dec***ei***ve
dec***is***ion

def***i***nit***e***ly
de***sc***end***a***nt
d***e***scribe

d***e***scri***p***tion
desir***a***ble

desp***ai***r
desp***e***rate
diction***a***ry
di***ff***er***e***nt
di***ffi***cult

di***n***ing room
di***s***a***pp***ear
di***s***a***pp***oint
disas***tr***ous
dis***ci***pline

di***s***ease
di***ss***atisfied
di***ssi***pate
d***i***vide
doct***o***r

dying
effect
eig***hth***
el***i***m***i***nate
emba***rr***a***ss***

em***ph***asize
entir***e***ly
en***tr***ance
envi***ron***ment
equi***pp***ed

especially
e***tc.*** (***et cetera***)
exa***gg***erate
exc***ee***d
exce***ll***ent

exceptio***nal***ly
e***x***ercise
e***x***ist***e***nce
e***x***orbitant
expen***s***e

exp***e***r***ie***nce
expl***an***ation
famili***ar***
fa***sc***inate
feas***i***ble

Feb***r***uary
fict***it***ious
fina***ll***y
for***ei***gn
f***o***rty

fr***ie***nd
g***au***ge
gover***nm***ent
gramm***a***r
g***ua***rd

ha***r***a***ss***
hard***e***ning
hei***ght***
hin***dr***ance
hum***o***rous

hurr***ie***dly
h***y***pocr***i***sy
i***ll***iterate
i***m***agination
i***m***itation

i***mm***ediat***e***ly
incident***al***ly
incred***ibl***y
independ***e***nt
indispens***a***ble

inf***i***nite
init***ia***tive
intell***i***gence
inter***e***st
involve

irre***lev***ant
i***rr***esist***i***ble
itself

j***ea***l***ou***sy
knowle***d***ge

lab***o***ratory
laid
l***e***d
l***ei***sure
library

li***c***en***s***e
literature
lon***e***liness
l***o***se
lux***u***ry

mag***az***ine
maint***e***nance
manufact***urer***
marr***ia***ge
math***e***matics

ma***tt***ress
m***ea***nt
med***ieva***l
m***e***r***e***ly
min***ia***ture

munici***pal***
murm***u***r
m***y***steri***ou***s
ne***c***e***ss***ary
n***ei***ther

nin***e***teen
notic***ea***ble
now***a***days
nucleus
obst***a***cle

o***cc***a***s***ion***al***ly
o***cc***u***rr***ed
occurr***e***nce
o***m***i***ss***ion
o***m***i***tt***ed

o***p***inion
o***ppor***tunity
opt***i***mism
or***i***gin
pa***i***d

pam***ph***let
para***ll***el
paral***y***zed
parl***i***ament
p***a***rticularly

par***t***ner
pa***s***time
p***er***form
p***er***haps
perm***a***n***e***nt

permiss***i***ble
persist***e***nt
perso***nnel***
p***e***rsuade
ph***y***sical

pleas***a***nt
politic***ia***n
po***ss***e***ss***
po***ssi***ble
practic***al***ly

prec***e***ding
predomin***ant***
pre***j***udice
prep***a***ration
prev***a***l***e***nt

prim***i***tive
priv***i***l***e***ge
prob***ab***ly
pro***ce***dure
proc***ee***d

pro***f***e***ss***ion
pro***f***ess***o***r
promin***e***nt

pron***u***nciation
pr***o***ve

psychology
p***u***rsue
qui***zz***es
rea***ll***y
rec***ei***ve

reco***g***nize
re***c***o***mm***end
refe***r***ence
refe***rr***ed
rel***i***g***i***ous

reminis***c***e
rep***e***tition
represen***t***ative
r***h***ythm
r***i***diculous

sacr***i***fice
saf***e***ty
scene
sched***ule***
secretary

s***ei***ze
sen***s***e
sep***a***rate
s***e***rg***ea***nt
sever***e***ly

shi***n***ing
s***ie***ge
simil***a***r
sincer***e***ly
soliloquy

soph***o***more
specim***e***n
sp***ee***ch
sto***pp***ing
stren***uou***s

st***re***tch
stud***y***ing
su***cc***eed
su***pp***ress
su***r***prise

suscept***i***ble
syllable
sympathize
temper***a***ment
tend***e***ncy

th***o***rough
tog***e***ther
tra***g***edy
transfe***rr***ed
tr***u***ly

typical
tyra***nn***y
undoubt***ed***ly
un***n***e***c***e***ss***ary
unti***l***

u***s***ing
usua***ll***y
veng***ea***nce
vi***ll***age
vill***ai***n

w***ei***rd
wri***t***ing

Exercise 5

Write the infinitive, the present participle, and the past participle of each of the following verbs (e.g., ***stop, stopping, stopped***):

prefer slam hop acquit
profit begin differ commit
drag equip recur confer

Exercise 6

Write the following words together with the adjectives ending in ***-able*** derived from them (e.g., ***love, lovable***):

dispose compare imagine
move console cure
prove blame measure

Exercise 7

Write the following words together with their derivatives ending in ***-able*** (e.g., ***notice, noticeable***):

trace marriage damage
service charge peace
change place manage

Exercise 8

Write the singular and the plural of the following nouns (e.g., ***lady, ladies***):

baby	remedy	treaty	turkey
hobby	enemy	delay	decoy
democracy	poppy	alley	alloy
policy	diary	attorney	corduroy
tragedy	laundry	journey	convoy

Exercise 9

Write the first and third persons present indicative, and the first person past, of the following verbs (e.g., ***I cry, he cries, I cried***):

fancy	spy	vary	worry
qualify	reply	dry	pity
accompany	occupy	ferry	envy

Exercise 10

Study the following words, observing that in all of them the prefix is not ***diss-*** but ***dis-:***

dis + advantage	dis + obedient
dis + agree	dis + orderly
dis + approve	dis + organize
dis + interested	dis + own

Exercise 11

Study the following words, observing that in all of them the prefix is not ***u-*** but ***un-:***

un + natural	un + numbered
un + necessary	un + named
un + noticed	un + neighborly

Exercise 12

Study the following words, distinguishing between the prefixes ***per-*** and ***pre-***. Keep in mind that ***per*** means ***through, throughout, by, for;*** and that ***pre-*** means ***before.***

perform	perhaps	precept
perception	perspective	precipitate
peremptory	perspiration	precise
perforce	precarious	precocious
perfunctory	precaution	prescription

Exercise 13

Study the following adjectives, observing that in all of them the suffix is not ***-full,*** but ***-ful:***

peaceful	forceful	healthful
dreadful	shameful	pitiful
handful	grateful	thankful
graceful	faithful	plentiful

Exercise 14

Study the following words, observing that in all of them the ending is not ***-us,*** but ***-ous:***

advantageous	specious	fastidious
gorgeous	precious	studious
courteous	vicious	religious
dubious	conscious	perilous

Exercise 15

Study the following words, observing that in all of them the suffix ***-al*** precedes ***-ly:***

accidentally	terrifically	exceptionally
apologetically	specifically	elementally
pathetically	emphatically	professionally
typically	finally	critically

Exercise 16

Study the following words, observing that the suffix is not ***-ess,*** but ***-ness:***

clean + ness	plain + ness	stern + ness
drunken + ness	stubborn + ness	keen + ness
mean + ness	sudden + ness	green + ness

Exercise 17

Study the following words, observing that the suffix is not ***-able,*** but ***-ible:***

accessible	discernible	imperceptible
admissible	eligible	impossible
audible	feasible	incompatible
compatible	flexible	incredible
contemptible	forcible	indefensible
convertible	horrible	indelible
intelligible	perceptible	responsible
invincible	permissible	sensible
invisible	plausible	susceptible
irresistible	possible	tangible
legible	reprehensible	terrible

Exercise 18

Study the following groups of words:

-ain	***-ain***	***-ian***	***-ian***
Britain	curtain	barbarian	guardian
captain	fountain	Christian	musician
certain	mountain	civilian	physician
chieftain	villain	collegian	politician

Exercise 19

Study the following groups of words:

-ede	***-ede***	***-eed***
accede	precede	exceed
antecede	recede	proceed
concede	secede	succeed

Exercise 20

Fill the blanks with ***principal*** or ***principle. Principle*** is always a noun; ***principal*** is usually an adjective. ***Principal*** is also occasionally a noun: the ***principal*** of the school, both ***principal*** and ***interest.***

1. The __________ will be due on the tenth of the month.
2. Her refusal was based on __________.
3. This is my __________ reason for going.
4. The __________ has asked that we hold our meeting tomorrow.

5. He did not even know the first __________ of the game.
6. Can you give the __________ parts of the verb?

Exercise 21

Fill the blanks with ***affect*** or ***effect:***

1. I do not like his __________ed manner.
2. An entrance was __________ed by force.
3. The __________ upon her is noticeable.
4. The law will take __________ in July.
5. It will be an __________ive remedy.
6. The hot weather will __________ the crops.
7. There was no serious after__________.
8. She __________ed ignorance of the whole matter.

Exercise 22

Fill the blanks with ***passed*** or ***past. Passed*** is the past tense or past participle of the verb ***pass; past*** can be an adjective, noun, adverb, or preposition.

1. We __________ your house.
2. She went __________ me.
3. They whistled as they __________ by.
4. He is a man with a __________.
5. My cousin is a __________ master at the art of lying.
6. That vocalist is __________ her prime.
7. Many years __________ before he returned.
8. It is long __________ bedtime.

Exercise 23

Fill the blanks with:
(a) ***Its*** (pronoun in the possessive case) or ***it's*** (contraction of ***it is***).

1. __________ raining.
2. The cat has had __________ supper.
3. The clock is in __________ old place again.
4. __________ now six years since the accident.
5. I think that __________ too late to go.

(b) ***Your*** (pronoun in the possessive case) or ***you're*** (contraction of ***you are***).

1. __________ mistaken; it is __________ fault.
2. __________ position is assured.
3. __________ to go tomorrow.
4. I hope that __________ taking __________ vacation in July.

(c) ***There*** (adverb or interjection), or ***their*** (pronoun in the possessive case), or ***they're*** (contraction of ***they are***).

1. It is __________ turn.
2. __________ ready to go.
3. __________, that is over with.
4. __________ car was stolen.
5. __________ back from __________ trip.

(d) ***Whose*** (pronoun in the possessive case) or ***who's*** (contraction of ***who is***).

1. __________ turn is it?
2. There is the woman __________ running for mayor.
3. __________ responsible for this?
4. __________ book is this?
5. He is one __________ word can be trusted.
6. Bring me a copy of __________ *Who.*
7. __________ ready to go?

Exercise 24

Circle the italicized word which is spelled correctly in each of the following sentences. Consult section 16b if necessary.

1. Everyone is going ***accept, except*** me.
2. People came to her every day for ***advice, advise,*** and she was always ready to ***advice, advise*** them.
3. At so high an altitude it was hard to ***breath, breathe.***
4. His ***breath, breathe*** came in short gasps.
5. One of the sights of Washington, D.C. is the ***Capital, Capitol.***
6. Albany is the ***capital, capitol*** of New York.
7. Before dinner I had time to change my ***clothes, cloths.***
8. The tickets were sent with the ***complements, compliments*** of the manager.

9. The country was as dry and dreary as a ***desert, dessert.***
10. The shack in which we ***formally, formerly*** lived is still standing.
11. It's ***later, latter*** than you think.
12. The winners were ***lead, led*** up onto the stage.
13. Button the money in your pocket so you won't ***lose, loose*** it.

Mechanics 9

Before a paper is handed in, it should be carefully edited and corrected. An instructor has no way of knowing whether an error—in spelling, for example—is a result of ignorance or of hasty typing and careless editing. Do not expect to receive the benefit of the doubt. The following rules are designed to make your paper easier to read.

9a Manuscript

Paper should be 8½ × 11 inches in size, unless your instructor specifies some other kind. It should be unruled if you type your themes. If you use ruled paper for handwritten themes, the lines should be widely spaced to prevent crowding. Themes should be either typed or written in ink—black or blue-black; pencil is difficult to read. Write legibly. An instructor or an editor cannot do full justice to a manuscript which has to be puzzled out, one word at a time. Do not crowd your writing. Leave enough space between consecutive lines to permit editing. Write each word as an entity without gaps between the letters. Do not decorate letters with unnecessary flourishes; use plain forms. Simple, clear handwriting which can be easily read predisposes the reader in your favor. Conversely, handwriting which must be deciphered word by word makes it almost impossible for a reader to appreciate what you have written.

Observe the following conventions for arrangement of material on the page:

1. Write on one side of the sheet only.
2. Leave a generous margin—at least an inch and a half—at the left side of each page and at the top. Leave about an inch of margin at the right side and at the bottom.
3. In typewritten manuscript, double-space the lines throughout, including footnotes or endnotes. In handwritten manuscript, leave an equivalent space between lines. Use alternate lines on narrow lined paper.
4. Number all pages except the first in the upper right-hand corner. Use arabic numerals, not roman.
5. Indent uniformly for paragraphs. The usual indentation for typewritten manuscript is five spaces. Indent about an inch in handwritten manuscript.
6. Center the title at least two inches from the top of the page, or on the first line if you use ruled paper. Leave extra space between the title and the first line of the composition.

Do not underline your title or put quotation marks around it (unless it is a quotation or the title of a book). Capitalize all words in the title except articles, short conjunctions, and short prepositions.

(1) Arrangement of Quotations

Observe the following conventions in reproducing quotations:

1. A quotation of only a few words may be incorporated into the text.

CORRECT

> Irma Rombauer describes the Dobos Torte as a cake that "looks rich, is rich, and enriches all who eat it."

CORRECT

> In Childhood and Society, Erik Erikson says that the young adult, "emerging from

the search for and insistence on identity," is now "ready for intimacy."

2. A quotation of more than two lines of verse or more than 100 words of prose should be set off from the main text, without quotation marks. It should be introduced by a colon if the preceding sentence has referred to the quotation, and it should begin on a new line. It should be indented from the left-hand margin. (Poetry should be centered on the page.) It should be single-spaced.

CORRECT

Ruth Benedict's strong belief that individual rituals reflect a larger cultural whole is apparent in her description of the dance of the Zuni Indians in New Mexico:

> The dance, like their ritual poetry, is a monotonous compulsion of natural forces by reiteration. The tireless pounding of their feet draws together the mist in the sky and heaps it into the piled rain clouds. It forces out the rain upon the earth. They are bent not at all upon an ecstatic experience, but upon so thorough-going an identification with nature that the forces of nature will swing to their purposes. This intent dictates the form and spirit of Pueblo dances. There is nothing wild about them. It is the cumulative force of the rhythm, the perfection of forty men moving as one, that makes them effective.

As an anthropologist, Benedict is particularly drawn to rituals because. . . .

3. A quotation of poetry should be divided into lines exactly as the original is divided. If an entire line of verse cannot be written on one line of the page, the part left over should be indented.

CORRECT

```
Allons! the inducements shall be greater,
We will sail pathless and wild seas,
We will go where winds blow, waves dash, and
     Yankee clipper speeds by under full sail

                                  --Walt Whit
```

4. When quoting a conversation from a story, novel, or play, be sure the quotation is exactly as it appears in the original, including the paragraphing and punctuation. (British writers commonly use a single quotation mark where we would use two.)

CORRECT

```
  "Would you like some whisky?" Honora
asked.
  "Yes, please," Leander said.
  "There isn't any," Honora said. "Have a
cookie."
  Leander glanced down at the plate of
cookies and saw they were covered with
ants. "I'm afraid ants have gotten into
your cookies, Honora," he said.
  "That's ridiculous," Honora said. "I
know you have ants at the farm, but I've
never had ants in this house." She picked
up a cookie and ate it, ants and all.
                          --John Cheever
```

(2) Correcting the Manuscript

If a reading of your final draft shows the need of further alterations or revisions, make them unmistakably clear. It is not necessary to recopy an entire page for the sake of one or two insertions or corrections. Copying is necessary only when there are so many corrections as to make the page difficult to read or messy in appearance.

Words to be inserted should be written above the line, and their proper position should be indicated by a caret (∧) placed below the line. Words so inserted should not be enclosed in parentheses or brackets unless these marks would be required if the words were written on the line. Cancel words by drawing a neat line through them. Parentheses or brackets should never be used for this purpose.

9b Capital Letters

The general principle is that proper nouns are capitalized; common nouns are not capitalized. A proper noun is the name of a particular person, place, or thing: *Richard Wright, Virginia Woolf, Alaska, New Orleans, the Capitol, the United States Senate, Colorado River.* A common noun is a more general term which can be used as a name for a number of persons, places, or things: *engineer, doctor, county, town, court house, legislative body, harbor.*

Note that the same word may be used as both a proper and a common noun.

CORRECT Of all the peaks in the Rocky Mountains, Pike's Peak is the mountain I would most like to climb.

CORRECT Our beginning history class studied legislative procedure and the part our representatives play in it. When I took History 27 our class visited the Legislative Committee hearing in which the Representative from Ohio expressed his views on the Alliance for Progress.

Abbreviations are capitalized when the words they stand for would be capitalized: USN, ROTC, NBC.

(1) Proper Nouns

Capitalize proper nouns and adjectives derived from them. Proper nouns include the following:

1. Days of the week, and months
2. Organizations such as political parties, governmental bodies and departments, societies, institutions, clubs, churches, and corporations

   CORRECT the Socialist Party, the Senate, the Department of the Interior, the American Cancer Society, the Boy's Republic, the Optimists' Club, the J. E. Caldwell Company

3. Members of such organizations: Republicans, Lions, Presbyterians, Catholics
4. Historical events and periods: the Battle of Hastings, the Medieval Age, the Baroque Era
5. Geographic areas: the East, the Midwest, the Northwest
6. Race and language names: Japanese, English, Indian, Caucasian
7. Many words of religious significance: the Lord, the Son of God, the Trinity
8. Names of members of the family when used in place of proper names: a call from Mother telling about my father's trip.
9. In biological nomenclature, the names of genera but not of species: *Homo sapiens, Salmo irideus, Equus caballus*
10. Stars, constellations, and planets, but not the earth, sun, or moon unless used as astronomical names

(2) Titles

1. Capitalize titles of persons when they precede proper names. When used without proper names, titles of officers of high rank should be capitalized; other titles should not.

CORRECT Senator Marsh, Professor Stein, Admiral Byrd, Aunt Elsa. Both the Governor and the Attorney General endorsed the candidacy of our representative. The postmaster of our town appealed to the Postmaster General.

2. Capitalize the first word and the important words of the titles of books, plays, articles, musical compositions, pictures, and other literary or artistic works. The unimportant words are the articles *a, an* and *the;* short conjunctions and short prepositions.

CORRECT *I, Claudius; Summer in Williamsburg; Friar Felix at Large; Childhood and Society; Measure for Measure;* Beethoven's *Third Symphony;* Brancusi's "Bird in Flight"; Joni Mitchell's *For the Roses.*

3. Capitalize the first word and any titles of the person addressed in the salutation of a letter.

CORRECT Dear Sir, Dear President Stark, My dear Sir.

In the complimentary close, capitalize the first word only.

CORRECT Very truly yours, Yours sincerely, Yours very truly,

(3) Sentences and Quotations

1. Capitalize the first word of every sentence and of every direct quotation. Note that a capital is not used for the part of a quotation that follows an interpolated expression like "he said" unless that part is a new sentence.

CORRECT "Mow the lawn diagonally," said Mrs. Grant, "and go over it twice."

CORRECT "Mow the lawn twice diagonally," said Mrs. Grant. "It will be even smoother if the second mowing crosses over the first one."

CORRECT Mrs. Grant said, "Mow the lawn twice."

Following a colon, the first word of a series of short questions or sentences may be capitalized.

CORRECT The first aid questions were dull but important: What are the first signs of shock in an accident victim? should he be kept warm? should he eat? should he drink?

2. Capitalize the first word of every line of poetry except when the poem itself does not use a capital.

CORRECT I am a part of all that I have met;
Yet all experience is an arch wherethrough
Gleams that untraveled world whose margin fades
Forever and forever when I move.
How dull it is to pause, to make an end,
To rust unburnished, not to shine in use!
—TENNYSON

CORRECT last night i heard
a pseudobird;
or possibly
the usual bird
heard pseudome.
—EBENEZER PEABODY

Exercise 1

What words in the following sentences should be capitalized? Why?

1. A canary-colored buick convertible was driving north on fountain avenue.

2. Although many of the natives can speak spanish, they prefer their own indian dialect.
3. A novel experiment in american education was announced on monday by the yale school of law and the harvard school of business administration.
4. "I'm going out to the country club," said chris; "want to come along?"
5. Although technically a veteran, he had served in the coast guard for only two weeks toward the end of the second world war.
6. the douglas fir, often sold under the name oregon pine, is neither a fir nor a pine.
7. He makes these regional divisions: the east, the old south, the middle west, and the far west.
8. When I left high school I intended to major in economics, but in college I became interested in science and graduated as a biology major.
9. Buddhists, christians, jews, and moslems attended the conference, which was held at ankara, the capital of turkey.
10. Both the rotarians and the lions meet in the private dining room of the piedmont inn.

9c Writing Numbers

Usage varies somewhat, but the following practices are widely accepted. One general principle is that all related figures in a particular context should be treated similarly: for consistency, do not use figures for some and words for others.

1. Numbers from one to ten and round numbers which can be expressed in one or two words are usually written out: ***three** people in line, **seven hundred** reserved seats, **five thousand** tickets.* All numbers that begin a sentence are spelled out, even though they would ordinarily be represented by figures: ***Four hundred sixty** dollars was too high a price.*

2. For ordinary usage, figures are appropriate for the day of the month (*June **23***), the year (***1929***), and street numbers (***400** University Circle*).

3. Figures are used for long numbers (*a capacity of **1,275** gallons*), page and chapter numbers (*chapter **14**, page **372***), time expressed

by A.M. and P.M. (*from **11** A.M. to **2** P.M.*), and exact percentages, decimals and technical numbers (***7.31** inches, **8.5** percent interest, 38th parallel*).

4. After a dollar sign ($) figures are always used: *My share of the job paid **$177.90**, but I had **$27.50** in expenses.* If a number is short and followed by dollars or cents, it may be spelled out: *I paid **twelve dollars** for the reservation.*

9d Abbreviations

Minimize the use of abbreviations in ordinary expository prose. Spell out Christian names, the words in addresses (***Street, Avenue, New Jersey***), the days and months of the year, units of measurement (***ounces, pounds, feet, hour, gallon***). Volume, chapter, and page should be spelled out in references in the text, but abbreviated in footnotes, parenthetical citations, and bibliographies.

CORRECT Eliott Brodie of 372 West 27th ***Avenue,*** Kenosha, moved on ***December*** 16, 1970.

CORRECT The quotation is on ***page*** 267 of the ***third edition.***

CORRECT For further information on proper terms for addressing dignitaries, consult the appropriate section in the latest Webster unabridged dictionary ("Forms of Address," ***pp.*** 51a–54a).

The following conventions are generally observed:

1. A few standard abbreviations are in general use in all kinds of writing: ***i.e.*** (that is), ***e.g.*** (for example), ***etc.*** (and so forth), ***vs.*** (versus), **A.D., B.C., A.M., P.M.,** (or ***a.m., p.m.***), Washington, ***D.C.*** Names of some organizations and of many government agencies are commonly represented by their initials: ***CIA, GOP, NATO, CAA, TVA,*** etc. Dictionaries vary in their preferences for using periods with these abbreviations.

Some abbreviations require periods (***Ph.D., N.Y., Col., oz.***), but others are regularly written without periods (***FBI, Na, ROTC***). The correct form of standard abbreviations can be found in your dictionary, usually in regular alphabetical order, sometimes in a separate appendix.

2. Civil, religious, and military titles are spelled out except the following ones:

a. Preceding names: ***Mr., Messrs., Ms., Mrs., Dr., St.*** (for *Saint*). (***The***) ***Rev.*** and (***The***) ***Hon.*** are used only when the surname is preceded by a Christian name: ***Rev. Henry Mitchell,*** (or ***Mr. Mitchell*** or ***Father Mitchell***), not ***Rev. Mitchell.***
b. Following names: ***Esq., M.D., Sr., Jr., Ph.D., M.A., LL.D.,*** etc. Do not duplicate a title before and after a name.

WRONG ***Dr.*** Rinard Z. Hart, ***M.D.;***

CORRECT ***Dr.*** Rinard Z. Hart, or Rinard Z. Hart, ***M.D.***

For the correct forms of titles used in addressing officials of church and state, consult an unabridged dictionary.

3. In technical writing, directions, recipes, and the like, terms of measurement are often abbreviated when used with figures.

CORRECT 32°**F.;** 1,500 **rpm;** 25 **mph;** ½ **tsp.** salt and 2 **tbs.** sugar; 12 **ft.** 9 **in.;** 5**cc.;** 2 **lb.** 4 **oz.**

Abbreviations like ***Co., Inc., Bros.,*** should be used only when business organizations use them in their official titles. The ampersand (&) is used only when the company uses the symbol in its letterhead and signature.

WRONG D. C. Heath **&** Co., D. C. Heath and **Co.,**

CORRECT D. C. Heath and Company

Exercise 2

Correct any errors in abbreviations in the following sentences.

1. Dr. Geo. C. Fryer lives on Sandy Blvd. near Walnut St.
2. I have worked for the Shell Oil Co. since Oct., '57.
3. We expected to go to N.Y. for Xmas.
4. The Acme Corp. ships mail-order goods C.O.D.
5. I was in Wash., D.C., on Aug. 10, 1975.
6. Mt. Whitney, which is 14,495 ft. high, is located in SE California.
7. The drive to Lexington, Ky., took us 3 hrs., 17 min.
8. A temperature of 32°F. is equivalent to zero on the cent. scale.
9. He bought three fl. oz. of aromatic spirits of amm.
10. Turn back to the 1st page of Ch. 3 and read pp. 18–22.

9e Use of Italics

Italics are used for certain titles, unnaturalized foreign words, scientific names, names of ships and aircraft, and words considered *as* words. To italicize a word in a manuscript, draw one straight line below it, or use the special underlining key on the typewriter, thus: `King Lear.`

1. In the titles of books, monographs, musical works, and such separate publications, italicize all words. (Do not italicize the author's name.) In the titles of newspapers, magazines, and periodicals, only the distinctive words are italicized. The article *The* in newspaper titles is usually not italicized, but printed in regular (roman) type. (Note that *The* is italicized in the preceding sentence since it refers to the word itself, used as the subject of is.)

CORRECT ***The Blithedale Romance.*** Edmund Wilson's ***The Shock of Recognition. Of Stars and Men. Dictionary of Foreign Terms.*** The ***Atlantic Monthly. Christian Science Monitor.*** The ***Southern Review.*** The ***New York Times.***

Titles of parts of published works and articles in magazines are enclosed in quotation marks.

CORRECT The assignment is "Despondency" from William Wordsworth's long narrative poem, ***The Excursion.***

CORRECT I always read filler material in the ***New Yorker*** entitled "Letters We Never Finished Reading."

CORRECT She hoped to publish her story entitled "Nobody Lives Here" in a magazine like ***Harper's.***

2. Italicize foreign words which have not yet become accepted in the English language. If you are not certain whether a foreign word has become naturalized, consult a dictionary. Be sure to consult the Explanatory Notes to see how foreign words are indicated. Scientific names for plants and animals are italicized.

CORRECT The dancer unties a knot with her feet in the Mexican ***reboza.***

CORRECT The technical name of Steller's jay is ***Cyanocitta stelleri.***

3. Italicize the names of ships and aircraft, but *not* the names of the companies that own them.

CORRECT The liner ***S. S. Constitution*** sails for Africa tomorrow.

CORRECT He went to Hawaii on a Matson liner and returned on one of United's ***Royal Hawaiian*** flights.

4. When words, letters, or figures are spoken of as such, they are usually italicized.

CORRECT The misuse of ***cool*** and ***real*** is a common fault.

CORRECT The letter ***e*** and the figure **2** on my typewriter are worn.

9f Syllabication

Dividing a word at the end of a line is mainly a printer's problem. In manuscripts it is not necessary to keep the right-hand margin absolutely even, and so it is seldom necessary to divide a word at the end of a line. If such a division is essential, observe the following principles, and mark the division with a hyphen (-) at the end of the line.

1. Divide words only *between* syllables—that is, *between* the normal sound-divisions of a word. When in doubt as to where the division between syllables comes, consult a dictionary. One-syllable words, like *through* or *strength,* cannot be divided. Syllables of one letter should not be divided from the rest of the word. A division should never be made between two letters that indicate a single sound. For example, never divide *th* as in *brother, sh* as in *fashion, ck* as in *Kentucky, oa* as in *reproaching, ai* as in *maintain*. Such combinations of letters may be divided if they indicate two distinct sounds: *post-haste, dis-hon-or, co-au-thor,* etc.

WRONG li-mit, sinec-ure, burg-lar-ize, ver-y, a-dult

CORRECT lim-it, sine-cure, bur-glar-ize, very, adult, co-or-di-na-tion

2. The division comes at the point where a prefix or suffix joins the root word, if pronunciation permits.

CORRECT be-half, sub-way, anti-dote, con-vene, de-tract

CORRECT lik-able (or like-able), like-ly, place-ment, Flem-ish, en-force-ment, tall-er, tall-est, fall-en

EXCEPTIONS BECAUSE OF PRONUNCIATION prel-ate, pred-e-cessor, res-ti-tu-tion, bus-tling, prej-u-dice, twink-ling, jog-gled

3. When two consonants come between vowels (me*mb*er), the division is between the consonants if pronunciation permits (*mem-ber*). If the consonant is doubled before a suffix, the second consonant goes with the suffix (*plan-ning*).

CORRECT remem-ber, pas-sage, fas-ten, disman-tle, symmet-rical (***but*** symme-try), prompt-er (***but*** promp-ti-tude), impor-tant, clas-sic, rum-mage, as-surance, oc-cident, at-tend, nar-ration, of-fi-cial-ly, com-pen-di-um, fit-ting, tel-ling.

BUT NOTE knowl-edge

4. The division comes after a vowel if pronunciation permits.

CORRECT modi-fier, oscilla-tor, ora-torical, devi-ate.

Exercise 3

Correct in the following sentences any errors in abbreviations, numbers, capitals, and italics.

1. He made a survey of Athletics in the Universities and Colleges in the U.S.
2. When grandmother was a girl, she lived in Lincoln, Nebr.
3. She always adds a P.S. to her letters.
4. He was traveling in the East last Winter.
5. I spent fifty cents for a pattern, $6.80 for my material, and a dollar and ten cents for trimming; so you see that my dress will cost only $8.40.
6. 1975 brought us good fortune.
7. "You will surely decide to go," he said, "For you will never have such a chance as this again."
8. After each war we resolve "That these dead shall not have died in vain."
9. Our country entered the second world war in nineteen hundred and forty-one.
10. The use of the word like as a conjunction is a very common error.
11. My Chemistry and Math. grades were high, and my grade point average was 3.2.
12. Roosevelt was elected president for a 2nd term by an Overwhelming Majority.

13. They discussed the eighteenth amendment and the methods of repealing an amendment to the constitution.
14. The president of the United States rose to greet the president of our university.
15. Queen Elizabeth 1 tried to preserve the status quo.

10 The Long Paper

A theme in a freshman composition course is usually short, from 500 to 700 words. It fills two or three typed double-spaced pages, and a first draft of it can be written at one sitting. Most often you write a short theme out of your own head, the material coming from your own experience, knowledge, or reading. In any case, if you are writing on something you know about at first hand, collecting information on the subject is no problem.

In upper-division courses, and later in "real" life, you will probably need to write at greater length. A long paper may be required in a seminar or as a report on independent study; business and professional men and women have to write reports, digests and summaries, legal briefs, or feature articles. Such an assignment, often running to more than a thousand words, presents special problems. You will be writing, not fiction or reminiscence or personal experience, but some form of exposition—descriptive or analytic or argumentative.

An essential first step, before you begin to write, is to get together the information you need. Even if you already know something about the subject, you will want to check on recent developments, and in most cases you will have to do some digging around in the library if you are to know what you are talking about. You can't even decide on your particular topic, nor adapt it to fit the space available, until you know something about the subject. Part of this chapter, accordingly, will be about locating material in books and magazines.

You will also need to know the conventional methods of documentation—that is, indicating to the reader by footnotes or other references the sources of your material. Failure to indicate the source of a quotation or paraphrase will lead the reader to assume that it is your own writing, and if it is not, you will be guilty of plagiarism. Passing off other people's words, sentences, or ideas as your own, whether it is deliberately or ignorantly done, is a serious offense. In college it can lead to dismissal; in the business world it can lead to a damage suit. Various safeguards against this misfortune will be discussed later in this chapter.

A long paper cannot ordinarily be written at a single sitting, and you will need to plan your time accordingly. The venerable but foolish custom of neglecting an assignment till the day before and then sitting up all night to finish it simply will not work here. After three or four hours, even experienced professional writers feel fatigue and know that whatever they write thereafter will be poorer and poorer. So the first rule is to plan ahead and begin writing early enough so that you can finish in several sessions, a day apart, instead of in one desperate coffee-soaked night.

Ernest Hemingway long ago laid down two basic rules for writers. First, always stop when you are going good. Don't write yourself out at any session, for if you say everything you have in mind, you may have trouble getting started next day when you return to the job. Make yourself stop when you still know exactly what is to come next, and you will find it easy to pick up the thread of your discourse next day. Second, to insure continuity, begin each writing session by reading everything that has gone before, or at least the preceding five or ten pages. By the time you come to the place where you stopped writing, you should be back into the mood and spirit of the piece, and you may even have recovered your momentum. This is as important to a writer as to a football team.

But the first problem when you begin a long paper is to get some information together, and the first place to go is the library.

10a The Library

The library is the heart of a college or university, and students should learn to use it effectively. Since the amount of information one can carry in his head is small compared with the vast amount stored in print, an important part of one's college education is learning how to find needed information. Every student should be able to use the card catalog, be familiar with important reference books, and know how to use bibliographies and periodical indexes.

(1) The Card Catalog

The card catalog is the index of the library. All books and bound periodicals are listed on 3 × 5 cards, which are filed in alphabetical order in labeled drawers. A book is often listed three times: by author's name, by title, and by general subject. In large university libraries, the subject cards may be filed in a separate alphabetical order and kept in a separate Subject Catalog. Author and title cards usually make up the main catalog, in one single alphabetical listing.

Subject cards are intended to help you find books on a particular subject when you don't know the authors or the titles. The chief value of subject cards is to direct you to the section of the stacks where books on your topic are kept. A little browsing around the area indicated by one call number will usually lead you to a number of relevant books. If these are serious studies of the subject, they will contain bibliographies (that is, lists of other books in the field), and soon you will have so many references that you can begin to pick and choose. The main thing is to get a start, and the subject cards can often help.

Exercise 1

a. By consulting the author cards, see if your library has the following books. If so, list the place of publication, the publisher, and the date of publication.

1. *The Culture of Cities,* by Lewis Mumford
2. *Animals as Social Beings,* by Adolf Portmann
3. *The Subversive Science: Essays toward an Ecology of Man,* by Paul Shepard.
4. *Literature and Film,* by Robert Richardson
5. *Structuralism,* by Jean Piaget
6. *Blues People,* by LeRoi Jones
7. *The Armies of the Night,* by Norman Mailer
8. *Language,* by Edward Sapir
9. *On the Contrary,* by Mary McCarthy
10. *Briefing for a Descent into Hell,* by Doris Lessing

SAMPLE CATALOG CARDS

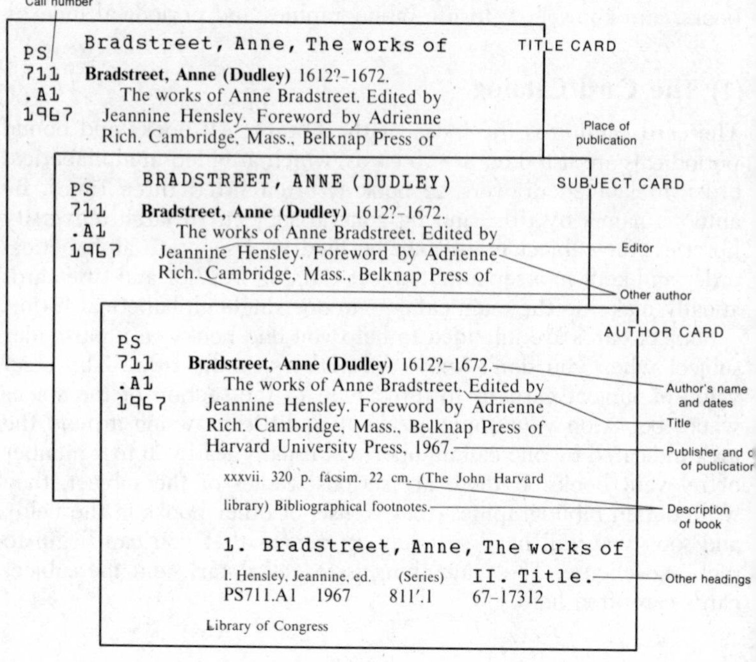

Call number
PS 711 .A1 1967
Bradstreet, Anne, The works of
TITLE CARD
Bradstreet, Anne (Dudley) 1612?–1672.
The works of Anne Bradstreet. Edited by Jeannine Hensley. Foreword by Adrienne Rich. Cambridge, Mass., Belknap Press of
Place of publication
BRADSTREET, ANNE (DUDLEY)
SUBJECT CARD
Editor
Other author
AUTHOR CARD
Harvard University Press, 1967.
xxxvii. 320 p. facsim. 22 cm. (The John Harvard library) Bibliographical footnotes.
1. Bradstreet, Anne, The works of
I. Hensley, Jeannine, ed. (Series) II. Title.
PS711.A1 1967 811'.1 67-17312
Library of Congress
Author's name and dates
Title
Publisher and d
of publicatior
Description of book
Other headings

b. Find a title card for a work of nonfiction and note any differences from the author card.

c. Select five of the books which are nonfiction and obtain the following information on each:

1. What subject headings is each book catalogued under?
2. What are at least two other books—call number, author, and title—under one of the same general subject headings?

(2) Standard Reference Books

Another way of getting a start is to use the guidebooks in the Reference Room—encyclopedias, dictionaries, indexes, bibliographies. It pays to get acquainted with such standard reference books, and their location on the shelves, early in your college career. Some of the important ones are listed below.

GUIDES TO REFERENCE BOOKS

Gates, Jean Key. *Guide to the Use of Books and Libraries.* 3rd ed. 1973.
The Reader's Adviser. 2 vols. 11th ed. 1968–69. 12th ed., Vol. I (American and British Literature), 1974.
Winchell, Constance M. *Guide to Reference Books.* 8th ed. 1967.

GENERAL ENCYCLOPEDIAS

Chambers' Encyclopedia. 15 vols. 1964.
Collier's Encyclopedia. 24 vols. 1965.
Encyclopedia Americana. 30 vols. 1971.
Encyclopaedia Britannica. 24 vols. 1968.
Encyclopedia International. 20 vols. 1964.
New Columbia Encyclopedia. 1 vol. 1975.

GAZETTEERS AND ATLASES

National Geographic Society, *Atlas of the World.* 1963.
Palmer, R. R., ed. *Rand McNally Atlas of World History.* 1970.
Pergamon World Atlas. 1968.
Seltzer, L. E., ed. *Columbia-Lippincott Gazetteer of the World.* 1962.
Shepherd, William R. *Historical Atlas,* 9th ed. 1973.
Times (London) *Atlas of the World.* 5 vols. 1958–1960.

REFERENCE BOOKS FOR SPECIAL SUBJECTS

Art and Architecture

Bryan, Michael. *Bryan's Dictionary of Painters and Engravers.* 5 vols. Rev. ed. by George C. Williamson, 1964.
Encyclopedia of World Art, 15 vols. 1959–68.
Haggar, Reginald C. *Dictionary of Art Terms.* 1962.
Hamlin, T. F. *Architecture through the Ages.* Rev. ed. 1953.
Myers, Bernard S., ed. *Encyclopedia of Painting.* 3rd ed. 1970.
Zboinski, A., and L. Tyszynski. *Dictionary of Architecture and Building Trades.* 1963.

Biography

American Men and Women of Science. 12th ed. 1971-1974. This set includes scholars in the physical, biological, and social sciences.
Current Biography. Monthly since 1940, with an annual cumulative index.
Dictionary of American Biography. 22 vols. and index. 1928-58.
Dictionary of National Biography. (British). 22 vols. and supplements.
Directory of American Scholars. 4 vols. 6th ed. 1974. This set includes scholars in the humanities.
National Cyclopaedia of American Biography. 1898-1906.
Webster's Biographical Dictionary. 1972.
Who's Who (British), *Who's Who in America, International Who's Who.* Brief accounts of living men and women, frequently revised.
Who's Who of American Women. 1958–.

Classics

Avery, C. B., ed. *New Century Classical Handbook.* 1962.
Hammond, N. G. L. & H. H. Scullard, eds. *Oxford Classical Dictionary.* 2nd ed. 1970.
Harvey, Paul, ed. *Oxford Companion to Classical Literature.* 1937.

Current Events

Americana Annual. 1923–. An annual supplement to the *Encyclopedia Americana.*
Britannica Book of the Year. 1938–. An annual supplement to the *Encyclopaedia Britannica.*
New York Times Index. 1913–.
Statesman's Year Book. 1864–. A statistical and historical annual giving current information about countries of the world.
World Almanac. 1868–.

Economics and Commerce

Coman, E. T. *Sources of Business Information.* 2nd ed. 1964.
Greenwald, Douglas, and others. *McGraw-Hill Dictionary of Modern Economics.* 2nd ed. 1973.

Historical Statistics of the United States: Colonial Times to 1957. 1960. Continuation to 1962 and revisions, 1965.
International Bibliography of Economics. 1952–.
Munn, Glenn G. *Encyclopedia of Banking and Finance.* 7th ed. 1973.
Statistical Abstract of the United States. 1879–.

Education

Burke, Arvid J. and Mary A. Burke. *Documentation in Education.* (The 5th ed., renamed, of Alexander's *How to Locate Educational Information and Data.*) 1967.
Deighton, Lee C., ed. *The Encyclopedia of Education.* 10 vols. 1971.
Ebel, Robert L., and others. *Encyclopedia of Educational* Research. 4th ed. 1969.
World Survey of Education. 5 vols. 1955–72.

History

Adams, James T., ed. *Dictionary of American History.* 2nd ed. 6 vols. 1942–61.
Cambridge Ancient History. 12 vols. 1923–39. 3rd ed. 2 vols. 1970–75.
Cambridge Mediaeval History. 8 vols. 1911–36.
Langer, William L., ed. *Encyclopedia of World History.* 5th ed. 1972.
Morris, Richard B., and Graham W. Irwin, eds. *Harper Encyclopedia of the Modern World.* 1970.
New Cambridge Modern History. 14 vols. 1975.
Sarton, George. *Horus: a Guide to the History of Science.* 1952.

Literature and Drama
A. American

Cunliffe, Marcus. *The Literature of the United States.* Rev. ed. 1967.
Hart, J. D. *Oxford Companion to American Literature.* 4th ed. 1965.
Kunitz, S. J., and H. Haycraft. *Twentieth Century Authors.* 1942. First supplement, 1955.
Leary, Lewis. *Articles on American Literature 1900–1950.* 1954; *1950–1967.* 1970.
Parrington, V. L. *Main Currents in American Thought.* 3 vols. 1927–30.
Spiller, Robert E., and others. *Literary History of the United States.* 4th ed. 2 vols. 1974.

B. British

Baugh, A. C., and others. *A Literary History of England.* 2nd ed. 1967.
Craig, Hardin, and others. *A History of English Literature.* 4 vols. 1950.
Harvey, Paul, ed. *Oxford Companion to English Literature.* 4th ed. 1967.
Sampson, George. *Concise Cambridge History of English Literature.* 3rd rev. ed. by R. C. Churchill, 1970.
Watson, George, ed. *The New Cambridge Bibliography of English Literature.* 4 vols. 1972.
Wilson, F. P., and Bonamy Dobrée, eds. *Oxford History of English Literature.* Begun in 1945, this major series of reference works will soon include all fourteen projected volumes.

C. Continental and General

Fleischmann, Wolfgang Bernard, ed. *Encyclopedia of World Literature in the 20th Century.* 3 vols. 1971.
Grigson, Geoffrey, ed. *The Concise Encyclopedia of Modern World Literature.* 1971.
Leach, Maria, and Jerome Fried, eds. *Funk & Wagnalls Standard Dictionary of Folklore, Mythology, and Legend.* 1949–50.
MacCulloch, John A., and others. *Mythology of All Races.* 13 vols. 1964.
Preminger, Alex, F. J. Warnke, and O. B. Hardison, eds. *Encyclopedia of Poetry and Poetics.* 1965.
Steinberg, Sigfrid Henry. *Cassell's Encyclopedia of World Literature.* 2 vols. 1954.

D. Drama

Gassner, John, and Edward Quin, eds. *Reader's Encyclopedia of World Drama.* 1969.
Hartnell, Phyllis, ed. *Oxford Companion to the Theatre.* 3rd ed. 1967.

Music and Dance

Apel, Willi. *Harvard Dictionary of Music.* 2nd ed. 1969.
Beaumont, Cyril W. *A Bibliography of Dancing.* 1963.
De Mille, Agnes. *The Book of the Dance.* 1963.
Ewen, David. *The World of Twentieth Century Music.* 1968.

Grove, George. *Dictionary of Music and Musicians.* 9 vols. 5th ed. 1954. Supplement. 1961.
Sachs, Curt. *World History of the Dance.* 1937.
Scholes, P. A. *Oxford Companion to Music.* 10th ed. 1970.
Thompson, Oscar. *International Cyclopedia of Music and Musicians.* 10th ed. 1974.
Westrup, J. A., ed. *The New Oxford History of Music.* 10 vols. 1957–74.

Philosophy

Copleston, Frederick. *A History of Philosophy.* 8 vols. Rev. ed. 1950.
Edwards, Paul, ed. *Encyclopedia of Philosophy.* 8 vols. 1967.
Urmson, J. O., ed. *The Concise Encyclopedia of Western Philosophy and Philosophers.* 1960.

Political Science

Burchfield, Laverne. *Student's Guide to Materials in Political Science.* 1935. Useful for earlier periods.
Frankel, Joseph. *The Making of Foreign Policy: An Analysis of Decision-Making.* Rev. ed. 1967.
Huntington, Samuel P. *Political Order in Changing Societies.* 1968.
Morgenthau, Hans. *Politics among Nations.* 4th ed. 1967.
Political Handbook of the World. 1927–.
Smith, Edward C., and A. J. Zurcher, eds. *Dictionary of American Politics.* 2nd ed. 1968.
White, Carl M. and others. *Sources of Information in the Social Sciences.* 1964.

Psychology

Drever, James. *Dictionary of Psychology.* Rev. ed. by H. Wallerstein, 1964.
The Harvard List of Books in Psychology. 4th ed. 1971. Annotated.
Psychological Abstracts. 1927–.

Religion

Buttrick, G. A., and others. *Interpreter's Dictionary of the Bible: An Illustrated Encyclopedia.* 4 vols. 1962.

Cross, F. L., ed. *Oxford Dictionary of the Christian Church*. 1961.
Ferm, Vergilius. *Encyclopedia of Religion*. 1945.
Hastings, James, ed. *Encyclopaedia of Religion and Ethics*. 12 vols. and index. 1908–27.
Jackson, S. M., and others. *New Schaff-Herzog Encyclopedia of Religious Knowledge*. 12 vols. and index. 1949–51.
McDonald, William J., and others, eds. *New Catholic Encyclopedia*. 15 vols. 1967.
Werblowsky, R. J. Z. and Geoffrey Wigoder, eds. *The Encyclopedia of the Jewish Religion*. 1965.

Science—General

Deason, Hilary. *A Guide to Science Reading*. 1963.
McGraw-Hill Encyclopedia of Science and Technology. 15 vols. 3rd ed. 1970.
Newman, James R., and others. *Harper Encyclopedia of Science*. 4 vols. Rev. ed. 1967.

Life Sciences

Benthall, Jonathan. *Ecology in Theory and Practice*. 1973.
De Bell, Garrett, ed. *The Environmental Handbook*. 1970.
Gray, Peter, ed. *Encyclopedia of the Biological Sciences*. 2nd ed. 1970.
Kerker, Ann E., and Esther M. Schlundt. *Literature Sources in the Biological Sciences*. 1961.
Smith, Roger C., and W. Malcolm Reid, eds. *Guide to the Literature of the Life Sciences*. 8th ed. 1972.

Physical Sciences

Larousse Encyclopedia of the Earth: Geology, Paleontology, and Prehistory. 1961.
Le Galley, Donald P., and A. Rosen, eds. *Space Physics*. 1964.
Parke, Nathan G. *Guide to the Literature of Mathematics and Physics*. 2nd ed. 1958.
Universal Encyclopedia of Mathematics. 1964.
Van Nostrand's International Encyclopedia of Chemical Science. 1964.

Sociology and Anthropology

Hauser, Philip M., ed. *Handbook for Social Research in Urban Areas.* 1965.

International Bibliography of Sociology. 1951–. Annual.

International Encyclopedia of the Social Sciences. 17 vols. 1968.

Kroeber, A. L., ed. *Anthropology Today: An Encyclopedic Inventory.* 1953.

Siegel, Bernard J. *Biennial Review of Anthropology.* 1959–. Contains a subject index.

Social Work Year Book.

Exercise 2

To familiarize yourself with Constance M. Winchell's *Guide to Reference Books,* pick one of the following questions and run down the answer. Consult the *Guide* for likely sources; then check the sources themselves; finally, record on a 3 × 5 card the question, the answer(s), and the sources which were most helpful. Use complete bibliographic form for sources.

1. If, in the eighteenth century, you had been convicted of "pradprigging," what would have been your crime and, in all probability, your punishment?
2. What Mexican hero-god carried a cross and what did it symbolize?
3. In what decade did the population of the United States shift from a predominantly rural to a predominantly urban one?
4. Why might a librarian view with alarm a type of book introduced in 1769 by James Granger?
5. Why are brushes made of camel hair and when did the practice begin?
6. What biographer of Johann Sebastian Bach has also written books on Jesus and Paul?

Exercise 3

Each of the following topics is too broad for a research paper of 1,500 to 2,000 words, but each has several possible, more restricted subjects within it. By using the card catalog and appropriate reference works, locate at least three books and three articles on a specialized aspect of one general topic. Then compose a thesis, a short outline, and a working bibliography for a research paper of 1,500 to 2,000 words.

1. African influences on jazz
2. American cartoon strips

3. Atomic power plants
4. Book censorship
5. Chemical basis of heredity
6. Ecology of oceans
7. Electronic computers
8. European films of the 1970's
9. Existentialism in literature
10. Ghetto schools
11. Gun control laws
12. Organic foods
13. Pesticides
14. Pop art
15. Prison riots
16. Public television
17. Sensitivity groups
18. Urban planning
19. Utopian novels
20. Women's Liberation

(3) Finding Information in Periodicals and Newspapers

Magazines and newspapers like the *New York Times* are the principal sources of information for topics of current interest and recent events. To find this information, you will need to consult periodical indexes like the following:

Readers' Guide to Periodical Literature. 1900–. Alphabetical list under author, title, and subject.
International Index to Periodicals. 1907–. Devoted chiefly to the humanities and the social sciences.
Poole's Index to Periodical Literature. 1802–1881; 1882–1906. Useful for earlier periodicals.
Book Review Digest. 1905–.
New York Times Index. 1913–.

These indexes list alphabetically, by author and by subject, important articles in magazines of general circulation. If you are investigating a more specialized subject, you may need to get information from the various scientific and learned journals. To find relevant articles in these, use specialized indexes like the following.

Applied Science and Technology Index. 1957–.
Art Index. 1929–.
Biography Index. 1946–.
Biological Abstracts. 1926–. Includes ecological materials.
Business Periodicals Index. 1958–.
Current Anthropology. 1960–.
Economic Abstracts. 1953–.
Education Index. 1929–.
Engineering Index. 1884–.
Historical Abstracts. 1955–.
Music Index. 1949–.

PMLA, "Annual Bibliography." 1921-68. Since 1969 this is entitled *MLA International Bibliography*. It is published separately from *PMLA* in four volumes: I, English and American literature; II, foreign literature; III, linguistics; IV, the teaching of foreign languages.
Psychological Abstracts. 1927–.
Public Affairs Information Service. 1915–. Political affairs, economics, and government.
Sociological Abstracts. 1953–.
Zoological Record. 1864–.

Here are two sample entries from the *Readers' Guide*. They refer to the same article, but the first is a subject entry, the second an author entry.

MASSACHUSETTS BAY colony
Anne Hutchinson versus Massachusetts. W. Newcomb. il pors Am Heritage 25:12-15+ Je '74

NEWCOMB, Wellington
Anne Hutchinson versus Massachusetts. il pors Am Heritage 25:12-15+ Je '74

Notice that these entries are not in the form you will use in your own bibliography. The abbreviations are explained on the first pages of each volume of the *Guide*. The article referred to, "Anne Hutchinson versus Massachusetts," was written by Wellington Newcomb. It appeared in June, 1974, in Volume 25 of *American Heritage* on pp. 12–15 and later pages. The article is illustrated with portraits.

10b The Long Paper

(1) Preliminary Bibliography

A list of books and articles related to a particular topic is called a bibliography, and you will need to make one of your own for a long paper. The bibliography you compile when you begin a paper is "preliminary" because you will alter it as you discover new references and discard references that turn out, as some will, to be useless. To make such changes easy, and to facilitate alphabetizing, you should put each reference on a separate card or slip of paper. A good size is 3 × 5 inches, easily distinguished from the larger slips on which you will put your actual notes.

Include on each bibliography slip all the information that will be needed for the final bibliography at the end of your paper. For a book you will need the name of the author or editor, the exact title of the book including any subtitle, the place and date of publication, and the name of the publisher. For an article in a periodical, you will need the author's name if the article is signed, the title of the article (in quotation marks), the name of the periodical (italicized), and an indication of the exact volume and pages. Ordinarily, volume number, date, and page numbers will serve, but in newspapers and in magazines like *Newsweek* which begin each issue with page 1, you will need to give the date of the particular issue in which the article appears. The standard form for bibliographic entries, which differs slightly from that of a footnote reference, is illustrated on page 215.

Use common sense in choosing the items for your preliminary bibliography. Don't waste time, for example, in collecting references to obscure publications not in your library. Inter-library loans are possible but time-consuming, and you will find it much more rewarding to explore the resources of your own library. If your topic is new—a relatively recent event or discovery or notable person—look for information in newspapers and periodicals, rather than in books. The writing and publishing of a serious book takes, usually, from two to five years; but magazines try to keep up with the times, and indexes to periodicals appear in monthly installments.

Remember, too, to check for original dates of publication whenever you are dealing with a paperback book or with a collection of essays. Some paperbacks will represent the original edition of a work, and some collections will be composed of material never printed before. But others will be reprints, or made up of reprints; and then you must be careful to get the original date of publication (which should be on the copyright page) or the source of the article (which should be either at the bottom of the first page of the article or in a list of sources at the beginning or end of the book). You need to do this for two reasons: first, because you will need this information for your footnotes and bibliography; and second, because you will feel like a fool if you refer to a 1975 paperback as "one of the latest works on this subject," only to discover too late that it's a reprint of something written in 1920.

(2) Evaluating Material

When you look into the actual books and articles referred to in your bibliography, you will find some of them unsatisfactory—too skimpy, too prejudiced, irrelevant, or just plain ignorant. Pick out the good ones and discard the rest, but be sure you are taking account of both sides of controversial issues. If your topic is, for example, "How Safe Is Nuclear Power?" you will run across pamphlets published by utility companies. These may not be actually biased, but they are almost certain to be extremely optimistic about the desirability of nuclear power plants. They should be checked with articles on the other side, which may in their turn be biased or exaggerated.

As authorities, scientists are generally preferable to public relations men, but scientists also disagree with each other. Read both sides—the scientists who signed Dr. Hans Bethe's statement in favor of nuclear energy and those members of the Union of Concerned Scientists who have come out against expanding nuclear power plants. If you feel incompetent to judge between them, present both sides. Whether your paper is meant to prove a point or just to lay out the facts, you will need to know both sides of controversial questions.

(3) Limiting the Topic

As you revise your own bibliography—discarding useless references and adding new and better ones—you should be looking ahead to the next two steps: collecting information and limiting the topic to a suitable size.

Suppose you are looking into alternate sources of energy—that is, substitutes for our rapidly disappearing stocks of oil, coal, and natural gas. The more you read about solar energy—its direct application to heating water or houses and its various secondary forms, based on winds and waves and temperature gradients, not to mention planned biological transformation and concentration of sunlight—the more surprised you may be by the breadth of the subject. If you try to include all alternative sources of energy, you won't have time or space to do a thorough account of any one of them. The solution is obvious: limit your topic by choosing three or four alternate sources, or even just one, that can be treated in detail.

How do you choose? On what principle do you select parts of a topic and discard the rest? There are many answers. You might choose those that interest you most. Or, being severely down-to-earth, you might work only on those sources that have already been tested in the laboratory.

Or you could take up those that seem most practicable, technically or economically or even politically. You may find that you will need to limit your paper still further—perhaps to the technical and economic aspects of one alternative source, like geothermal power.

Notice how these three processes—revising your bibliography, reading and evaluating material, and limiting your topic—go hand in hand. You have to find out something about the subject before you can know how to limit it, or how much limitation is needed. Limiting the subject will require changes in your bibliography, too. Not only will you discard references to articles no longer relevant, but you will be turning up new references in every book or article you read.

A useful guide in all three processes is a tentative plan. This can be a fairly detailed outline or a few notes to remind yourself what points you want to cover. The essential thing is to use the plan as a guide, but to keep it tentative and not be bound by it. The more you read, the more you may find it desirable to change this, or modify that, or emphasize some new points. No one can tell in advance what kind of material he will find, nor what will interest him most. The tentative plan should develop as your reading fills out and changes your original ideas on the subject.

(4) Taking Notes

The most important advice here is to put each note on a separate card or sheet. To organize your material, you must break it down into small units, and unless each unit is on a separate card, you will find it difficult to bring together from different sources all the notes on a single topic. Write your notes on cards (at least 4 × 6 inches) or on half sheets of theme paper. If more than one card is needed for one point, use the back or clip on another card with the subject and source as a heading.

1. State the topic of the note in the upper left-hand corner. (Other corners may be used for the library call number and other information.) The exact source, including the author, the title, and the page, can go along the bottom edge of the card. (See page 205.) It is not necessary to include the place of publication, the publisher, and the date on each card since your bibliography cards will contain full information.
2. Always put quotation marks around quoted material, and quote exactly, even to the punctuation marks and the spelling. Do not use quotation marks for paraphrases or summaries.

3. If parts of a quotation are omitted, ellipsis marks should be used to show where the omission occurs—three spaced periods (. . .) to indicate an omission within a sentence, four spaced periods (or three added to end-punctuation) to indicate an omission at the end of, or beyond the end of, a sentence. Brackets—[ ]— should enclose words which are not part of the quotation but which you have inserted for clarity. If, for example, there is an obvious error in the text, you may insert after it the word *sic* (Latin for "thus") in brackets, to show that the quotation is exact even though it contains an error: [*sic*].

A note is usually a direct quotation, a paraphrase in your own words, or a summary of main points. The disadvantage of quoting directly is that it may waste space, and hence time; a paraphrase is usually shorter. But the great advantage of direct quotation in your notes is that you can check the precise wording without going back to the book. When you actually write the paper you will use direct quotation sparingly: ordinarily a paraphrase or a summary, sometimes including a brief excerpted phrase from the original, will be more effective. But in your notes, copy out as many direct quotations as time permits, indicating them of course by quotation marks.

Direct Quotation

> *Control of smoke*
> "Smoke is... more easy to control than liquid effluents, because it proclaims itself to all the world. A stream of water running from a factory into a river or a sewer is not conspicuous, and the connivance of an official inspector may be arranged. But black smoke belching from a high stack stands out against the sky for every voter to see. The housewife in particular bristles up in wrath, and a politician recognizes a good vote-getting issue."
>
> George R. Stewart, Not So Rich as You Think, p. 125.

Paraphrase and Direct Quotation

Control of smoke
Smoke is easier to control than liquid effluents. Since dirty water draining from a factory is usually invisible to the public, "the connivance of an official inspector" can be arranged more easily than when "black smoke [is] belching from a high stack . . . for every voter to see."

George R. Stewart, Not So Rich as You Think, p. 125.

Summary

Control of smoke
Smoke can be more easily controlled than liquid effluents because it is more conspicuous. Liquid factory wastes are usually invisible to the public, but smoke from a high stack attracts the attention of voter and politician alike.

George R. Stewart, Not So Rich as You Think, p. 125.

(5) Proper and Improper Use of Source Material

The basic principle of scholarship is to make use of the discoveries and conclusions of previous investigators. Life is too short to permit repeating all the investigations of the past. What a professor tells you in class is in part a summary of the work of others, supplemented by what he has found out by his own research.

In writing a long paper, you will want to use ideas and material from a number of sources, and that is permissible so long as you name the sources. Unless you do, a reader is entitled to assume that what he is reading is your own idea, expressed in your own words. If he discovers later that it is actually the idea or the language of someone else, he will conclude that you are trying to pass this material off as your own. This is dishonesty, a moral fault. In the classroom it is called cheating, and among writers it is called plagiarism. In either case it can have serious consequences.

Avoiding plagiarism is not always as clear-cut and simple as it may sound. In practice, it is often impossible to give the sources for everything one writes. Where, for example, did I get (since I certainly was not born with) the definition of plagiarism just given? I really don't know. For years I've heard plagiarism talked about, and I have read about it and even studied examples of it in student papers. In short, my knowledge of what the term means is common knowledge, part of the vocabulary of the language I use. Generally known facts, like the discovery of America by Columbus, are also considered common knowledge. One is not required to indicate the sources of the fact that a mile is 5,280 feet and that a red light, in this country at least, means Stop.

If, however, I write that "a study of 125 randomly selected freshmen showed that only 29% considered snitching more reprehensible than cheating," my failure to indicate who made the study implies that I did it myself. And since I didn't, I could be accused of plagiarizing the work of someone else. If I write "a study by A. G. White[1] showed that 29% . . ." etc., and if I indicate in a footnote* that the source is an article entitled "Moral Judgments in the Classroom," which appeared in 1972 on page 223 of Volume 6 of the *Review of Education,* I am using White's material properly.

---

*For the proper form of such a footnote, see pp. 213–15.

Even if I indicate the source of my information, I may be plagiarizing if my paraphrase is too close to the language of the original. Suppose a paragraph in White's article reads

> The students used in the study were chosen from a middle-western university thought to be generally representative of middle-class views on ethical questions. Standard statistical techniques were employed to insure an adequate sample of the freshman class.

If in my paper this turns up as "The students were selected from a mid-western university in which middle-class views on ethical matters prevail. To insure a representative sampling of freshmen, standard statistical techniques were used," I am guilty of plagiarizing.

It is true that, in a paraphrase, I will need to use some of the words that occur in the original; it is both difficult and unnecessary to find accurate synonyms for "middle-western," "university," "freshman," and the like. But it is not enough to merely invert the order of the clauses in the second sentence of the original and to change "chosen" to "selected," and "adequate sample" to "representative sampling." To use material legitimately, you must say it in your own language, fit it into your own context, and connect it with what goes before and after in your paper. A patchwork of paraphrases and quotations, loosely connected, is not a paper you can call your own—nor, in all probability, would you want to. If it is to be your paper, you must use the source material to support, or test, or illustrate your own ideas, and in most instances, you will paraphrase rather than quote directly. When you do quote you must do so exactly.

(6) Writing the Paper

When you have collected as much information as you need, or have time for, convert your tentative plan into a final outline. Expand, cut, and reorganize so that the outline represents what you finally want to say. The new outline should be as detailed as possible, since you will actually write your paper from it.

Next, sort out your notes, putting together those that relate to the various subpoints in your outline. This will bring together the notes which explain or justify or give evidence for the points you want to make. If you find you have no notes at all for a subpoint in the outline, ask yourself some questions. Is the point really important?

Should you look for more material, should you try to write it up out of your own head, or should you simply omit the point altogether? You're in charge here. Use your judgment.

From this point on, beyond reminding you of the principles of order, coherence, emphatic statement, and careful choice of words—matters already discussed in this handbook—a teacher can only give you advice based on experience. I find, for example, Hemingway's advice very useful: write the first draft by hand, not on the typewriter. A soft pencil or a smooth-flowing ballpoint pen helps your writing to flow naturally, instead of jerking along in a staccato mechanical rhythm. It also helps to keep the first draft fluid and easy to revise. There is something final-looking about typewritten copy that discourages the impulse to make changes. Moreover, deleting a typed sentence is awkward and time-consuming, but with one satisfying swoop of the pen you can wipe out a whole sentence, or even a paragraph, and start over again. Allow plenty of space so that words or phrases can be inserted between the lines, in place of those you cross out. If the order of sentences in a paragraph needs to be changed, you can indicate this quickly and clearly with freehand lines as visual guides.

In writing the first draft, try any device that enables you to keep going rapidly so that you don't lose your train of thought. If you can't think of the right word, leave a generous blank and go on. The main idea at this stage is to get your ideas down on paper while they are hot. The time to agonize in cold blood over the exact word or the most concisely emphatic sentence pattern is in revision. Hemingway's other bit of advice is also worth remembering: Don't write yourself out. Stop while you're going good and know just what's coming next, so that you can get started readily at your next writing session.

Don't neglect transitional words, phrases, and sentences. Give the reader lots of signposts so he will know at all times where he is. *However* signals a concession to the opposite point of view; *in the second place* locates a stage in a progressive pattern. A sentence like "Two types of evidence support this theory" alerts the reader to the structure of the paragraphs that follow. If in doubt, use more transitional phrases rather than fewer. They can always be crossed out in revision, but if they seem appropriate to you, they will probably be helpful to a reader and should be retained.

If you have time, put the first draft of the whole paper in a drawer for a day or two (at least overnight) before beginning to revise it. Revision is the hardest part of a writer's task, and it is helpful to come at it refreshed and with a clear mind. This is the time for simple mechanical repairs: looking up the spelling of difficult or troublesome words, checking rules of punctuation and mechanics, looking for your likely faults in sentence structure. Decide how much direct quotation you will use, how much summary. If you see lots of long quotes on a page, look again to see if they can't be shortened. Check your paraphrases to make sure they're not uncomfortably close to plagiarism. Put footnotes into their full form now, while there's still time for a last mad dash to the library; check spellings of names and titles, correctness of page numbers. Most importantly, this is the time to test each sentence to see if it really says what you intend. Set a high standard here. Don't be satisfied with the mere hope that a reader will be able to understand your meaning. Try to write so that your reader cannot misunderstand.

The final version of your paper—the one you will hand in—should be typed, double spaced, or written neatly in ink. Follow the suggestions in section 9a (mechanics) for manuscript style. If your instructor requires it, prepare and submit a detailed outline, which will serve as a table of contents. Doublecheck footnotes for correct form, and prepare a final bibliography. When you submit the paper, put it in a folder or secure it by paper clips, but do not staple the pages together. Most instructors will want to separate the pages to facilitate checking and making corrections.

(7) Footnotes

The number of footnotes in a long paper cannot be prescribed in hard and fast rules. All quotations should be documented, of course, and all titles of books. Beyond this, use your judgment. Give references to the most important sources of your information, especially on controversial issues. If you have only four footnotes in a thousand-word paper, you probably aren't doing justice to your sources. If you have five footnotes on every page, you probably are documenting needlessly.

When a paper is to be submitted for publication, most editors prefer to have the footnotes on separate sheets at the end of the paper. Some instructors also prefer this method for term papers. Ask about it. If footnotes are placed at the bottom of each page, the first footnote should be separated from the last line of the text by triple spacing. Footnotes and bibliography entries are double spaced for college papers. Use arabic numerals rather than asterisks or other symbols to indicate the reference of the footnote in the text. Number the footnotes consecutively throughout the paper. In the text the reference numerals should be placed slightly above the line and immediately after the name, quotation, sentence, or paragraph to which the footnote refers. In the footnote itself, the reference number should also be placed slightly above the line. Information given in the text of the paper need not be repeated in the footnote. For example, if you say "Angus Wilson maintains that . . . ," the footnote would begin with the title of the book, instead of the author's name.

A footnote can be thought of as an abbreviated sentence. Its first line is indented five spaces from the left-hand margin, and the first word is capitalized. The footnote ends with a period. Only the first footnote reference to a book or periodical article needs to be written out in full. For later references, use the brief form illustrated on page 263.

The footnote form prescribed and used in this section follows that of *The MLA Style Sheet*, Second Edition. A footnote should contain the following items in the sequence here given:

1. The author's name, first name first. Since footnotes are not in alphabetical order, there is no need to put the last name first.
2. The title of the book, underlined to indicate italic type. If the reference is to an article in a periodical or in a book, the author's name is followed by the title of the article, in quotation marks, and this is followed by the name of the periodical (or book) underlined. Use commas to separate these elements.
3. Information regarding the place and date of publication. For books, this consists of the city in which the book was published, a colon, an abbreviated name of the publisher, and the date, all enclosed in parentheses. For articles, the title of the periodical underlined, followed by the volume number in arabic numerals, the date in parentheses, and the page number.
4. Page number. The abbreviation of *page* is *p.;* the plural is *pp.* If a book is printed in more than one volume, use Roman numerals to indicate numbers between one and ten. In such a case, the abbreviation *p.* is not used: e.g., II, 46.

The following six footnotes illustrate first and second footnote references.

[1]Perry Miller and T. H. Johnson, *The Puritans* (New York: Harper, 1963), II, 561–62.

[2]Rosemary M. Laughlin, "Anne Bradstreet: Poet in Search of Form," *American Literature,* 42 (1970), 16.
[3]Miller and Johnson, p. 65.
[4]Ann Stanford, "Anne Bradstreet," in *Major Writers of Early American Literature,* ed. Everett Emerson (Madison: Univ. of Wisconsin Press, 1972), p. 37.
[5]Ibid.
[6]Laughlin, p. 19.

The following additional words and abbreviations are sometimes used in footnotes, bibliographies, and references:

anon.	anonymous
b.	born
c. or ***ca.*** *(circa)*	about (used with dates)
cf. *(confer)*	compare or consult
d.	died
diss.	dissertation
ed.	edition, editor, or edited by
et al.	and others (used of people only)
f., plural ***ff.***	and following page(s)
ibid.	the same
id. or ***idem***	the same; usually the same author
l., plural ***ll.***	line(s)
loc. cit. *(loco citato)*	in the place already cited
ms., plural ***mss.***	manuscript(s)
n., plural ***nn.***	note(s)
N.B. *(nota bene)*	take notice, mark well
n.d.	no date (of publication) given
n.p.	no place (of publication) given
n. pag.	no pagination used in book

(The three preceding abbreviations tell your reader that the publisher of your reference work has omitted information you would normally include in your footnote.)

op. cit. *(opere citato)*	in the work cited

(This abbreviation must be used with the author's name, to identify the work being cited. If two works by the same author have been referred to, this abbreviation cannot be used. The general tendency today is to avoid such abbreviations altogether, and to use the author's name, plus a short title if one is needed.)

passim	here and there, throughout

rev.	revised, revision; review, reviewed by (Write out word if necessary to prevent ambiguity.)
rpt.	reprinted, reprint
sc.	scene
sic	so, thus
st., plural ***sts.***	stanza(s)
trans.	translator, translation, translated by
v., plural ***vv.***	verse(s)
vol., plural ***vols.***	volume(s)

The following list illustrates the chief footnote forms used in the first reference.

Book by One Author

[1]Elizabeth Wade White, *Anne Bradstreet: "The Tenth Muse"* (New York: Oxford Univ. Press, 1971), p. 52.

Book by One Author, Revised or Later Edition

[2]Roy Harvey Pearce, ed., *Colonial American Writing,* 2nd ed. (New York: Holt, 1969), p. 34.

Book by One Author, Reprint of an Older Edition

[3]Sumner Chilton Powell, *Puritan Village* (1963; rpt. New York: Anchor, 1965), p. 61.

Book by One Author, Translated

[4]Ursula Brumm, *American Thought and Religious Typology,* trans. John Hoaglund (New Brunswick, N.J.: Rutgers Univ. Press, 1970), pp. 49–50.

Book by One Author, Part of a Series

[5]George M. Waller, ed., *Puritanism in Early America,* 2nd ed., Problems in American Civilization (Lexington, Mass: Heath, 1973), p. 67.

[6]Josephine K. Piercy, *Anne Bradstreet,* Twayne's United States Authors Series, No. 72 (1965; rpt., New Haven, Conn: College and University Press, 1965), p. 14.

Book by Two Authors

[7]Perry Miller and T. H. Johnson, *The Puritans* (New York: Harper, 1963), II, 47.

A work with three authors would use this same style, with the authors being listed as A, B and C. If a work has more than three authors, the custom is to cite only the name of the first author mentioned on the title page and to complete it with et al. or with the English equivalent, "and others."

An Edited Text

[8]Robert Hutchinson, ed., *Poems of Anne Bradstreet* (New York: Dover, 1969), p. 48.

[9]William Bradford, *Of Plymouth Plantation: 1620–1647*, ed. Samuel Eliot Morison (New York: Knopf, 1952), pp. 101–02.

Signed Essay in a Book by Several Contributors

[10]Ann Stanford, "Anne Bradstreet," in *Major Writers of Early American Literature*, ed. Everett Emerson (Madison: Univ. of Wisconsin Press, 1972), p. 38.

[11]Robert D. Richardson Jr., "The Puritan Poetry of Anne Bradstreet," *Texas Studies in Lit. and Lang.*, 9 (1967), rpt. in Sacvan Bercovitch, ed., *The American Puritan Imagination: Essays in Revaluation* (London and New York: Cambridge Univ. Press, 1974), pp. 112–13.

Article in a Journal

[12]Rosemary M. Laughlin, "Anne Bradstreet: Poet in Search of Form," *American Literature*, 42 (1970), 5.

Article in a Weekly Magazine

[13]D. Davis, "American Hurrah: European Vision of America," *Newsweek*, 5 Jan. 1976, p. 36.

Anonymous Magazine Article

[14]"ALA Pictorial Scrapbook," *American Libraries* 7 (Jan. 1976), 42–43.

Anonymous Encyclopedia Article

[15]"Bradstreet, Anne Dudley," *Encyclopaedia Britannica,* 1974, Micropaedia II, 221.

Anonymous Newspaper Article

[16]"Women's Roles to be Featured," *Boston Sunday Globe,* 4 April 1976, p. 93, col. 5.

A Book Review

[17]John Harris, "A Free Press Underground," rev. of *The Books of the Pilgrims,* by Lawrence D. Geller and Peter J. Gomes, *Boston Sunday Globe,* 11 April 1976, p. A15, col. 1.

(8) The Final Bibliography

At the end of the paper (after the footnotes, if they are on separate sheets), add your final, alphabetized, bibliography. This may be a list of all those works mentioned in either your text or your footnotes (often called a "List of Works Cited"), or it may include all books and articles you have consulted at length, whether they were actually used in writing the paper or not. This would be a "List of Works Consulted." If your instructor does not specify one form of bibliography or the other, the choice is up to you.

The form of a bibliographic entry differs slightly from that of a footnote reference. Authors are listed with surname first, to make alphabetizing easy. The items within each reference are generally separated by periods instead of commas, but colons and semicolons remain as they were.

Sample Bibliography

"ALA Pictorial Scrapbook." *American Libraries,* 7 (Jan. 1976), 42–43.

"Bradstreet, Anne Dudley." *Encyclopaedia Britannica.* 1974. Micropaedia II, 221.

Brumm, Ursula. *American Thought and Religious Typology.* Trans. John Hoaglund. New Brunswick, N.J.: Rutgers Univ. Press, 1970.

Laughlin, Rosemary. "Anne Bradstreet: Poet in Search of Form." *American Literature,* 42 (1970), 1–17.

Miller, Perry, and others, eds. *Major Writers of America.* 2 vols. New York: Harcourt, 1962.

———————, and T. H. Johnson. *The Puritans.* 2 vols. New York: Harper, 1963.

The long dash indicates that Miller is the first-named author for this as well as for the preceding book. Books by the same author, or having the same senior author, are listed in alphabetical order.

Powell, Sumner Chilton. *Puritan Village.* 1963; rpt. New York: Anchor, 1965.

Richardson, Robert D., Jr. "The Puritan Poetry of Anne Bradstreet." *Texas Studies in Lit. and Lang.*, 9 (1967); rpt. in *The American Puritan Imagination: Essays in Revaluation.* Ed. Sacvan Bercovitch. London and New York: Cambridge Univ. Press, 1974, pp. 105–122.

Stanford, Ann. "Anne Bradstreet." *Major Writers of Early American Literature.* Ed. Everett Emerson. Madison: Univ. of Wisconsin Press, 1972, pp. 33–58.

Waller, George M., ed. *Puritanism in Early America,* 2nd ed. Problems in American Civilization. Lexington, Mass: Heath, 1973.

SAMPLE PAPER

Comments

Spacing between the lines of footnotes: in a manuscript which is going to be set in type by a printer, the footnotes are always double spaced, and for the convenience of editor and printer they are typed all together on pages at the end of the article.

If a typed manuscript is in its final form, as in a thesis or dissertation, or if it is to be duplicated by photographing or xeroxing, the footnotes are placed at the bottom of each page and made to stand out by single spacing, with double spacing between footnotes. (This is the form recommended for term papers by some handbooks.) *The MLA Style Sheet,* however, recommends double spacing the footnotes at the bottom of each page of a term paper for greater ease in reading and in making corrections. This is the form used here.

Footnote 1. Notice that an explanatory sentence may be included in a footnote.

Footnote 2. The passage in the text, quoted rather than paraphrased to preserve its vivid phrasing, could be located by the page number of Hensley's edition of the *Works*. But the author's name, Adrienne Rich, is essential to a reference, and the explanatory "foreword to" is useful, though not essential.

SAMPLE PAPER

Anne Bradstreet's Homespun Cloth:
The First American Poems

by Suzanne E. Conlon

In 1630 a young Englishwoman sailed for the New World with her husband and parents aboard the Arbella, the flagship of the Winthrop fleet carrying Puritan settlers from Southampton to the Massachusetts Bay Colony.[1] As usual, the voyage was rough and uncomfortable, "with its alternations of danger and boredom, three months of close quarters and raw nerves, sickness and hysteria and salt meats."[2] Nor was the

---

[1]Elizabeth Wade White, Anne Bradstreet: "The Tenth Muse" (New York: Oxford Univ. Press, 1971), p. 103. Biographical information is drawn from this book and from the Dictionary of American Biography, ed. Dumas Malone, I, 577–78.

[2]Adrienne Rich, "Anne Bradstreet and Her Poetry," foreword to The Works of Anne Bradstreet, ed. Jeannine Hensley (Cambridge: Harvard Univ. Press, 1967), ix.

Comments

Footnote 3. Since this second quotation is from the same page of the same article in the same book as #2, the standard abbreviation *ibid.*, "in the same place," is adequate. *The MLA Style Sheet* recommends that the abbreviation be written without underlining, since usage differs and it is easier for an editor to add underlining than to erase it.

Footnote 4. Though most of the bibliographical information repeats that of the preceding footnote, the form of reference used here is necessary to make clear that the quotation is from Anne Bradstreet herself, not from Adrienne Rich or Jeannine Hensley.

Footnote 5. The phrase "the Puritan dilemma" is widely used by American historians. The reference given here is to one of numerous discussions of the term.

landing quite what the eighteen-year-old bride had expected -- "the wild coast of Massachusetts Bay, the blazing heat of an American June, the half-dying, famine-ridden frontier village of Salem, clinging to the edge of an incalculable wilderness."[3]

Forty years later Anne Bradstreet was to report her feelings in a letter "To My Dear Children": "I found a new world and new manners, at which my heart rose [in revolt]. But after I was convinced it was the way of God, I submitted to it. . . ."[4]

This combination of revulsion and submission pervades Anne Bradstreet's poetry. It represents an interesting variation on "the Puritan dilemma"[5] as it was experienced by a sensitive, cultivated, and pious woman of early New England. "The Puritan was always trying to

---

[3]Ibid.

[4]*The Works of Anne Bradstreet*, ed. Jeannine Hensley (Cambridge Univ. Press, 1967), p. 241. All quotations from Bradstreet will be taken from this volume.

[5]See Perry Miller and T. H. Johnson, *The Puritans* (New York: Harper, 1963), II, 287.

Comments

The long quotation has been cut down by the two omissions indicated by the ellipsis marks (. . .). The words omitted are irrelevant to the point being made here. Since the second omission occurs within a sentence, three spaced periods are sufficient.

achieve a balance between this world and the next. . . . One could not safely turn one's back on this world, for the simple reason that God had made it and found it good; yet one could not rely upon . . . an earthly life which was, at last, insubstantial."[6]

Anne Bradstreet's dilemma was a little different but produced the same conflict between opposite impulses. Instead of loving the New World, she at first hated the harsh life it imposed on colonists, but this feeling went against her conviction that God's will demanded her to stay there and submit. Eventually she managed to strike a kind of balance: despite periods of doubt and depression, she bore and raised eight children in the wilderness near Andover and in intervals stolen from her scanty leisure time, she wrote five long didactic poems. With their publication in 1650, she became America's first poet.

The poems had been collected in manuscript as a present for her father, Thomas Dudley, an educated gentleman and future governor of the colony; they were not meant to be published.

---

[6]Robert D. Richardson, Jr., "The Puritan Poetry of Anne Bradstreet," _Texas Studies in Literature and Language_, 9 (1967), 317-318.

Comments

The spelling used in quotations is that of the original. Because seventeenth-century spelling is not expected to meet twentieth-century rules, there is no need to use [sic] or otherwise comment upon it.

Footnote 7. Note that the form of Footnote 4 has made it unnecessary to cite the edition again here.

But her brother-in-law took the manuscript with him on a journey to England and had it printed, as a family surprise for Anne, under the pompous title <u>The Tenth Muse, Lately Sprung Up in America</u>. His introduction is equally pompous and painfully condescending: "I doubt not but the reader will . . . question whether it be a woman's work, and ask, is it possible? If any do, take this as an answer from him that dares avow it: it is the work of a woman, honoured, and esteemed where she lives, for her . . . exact diligence in her place, and discrete managing of her family occasions, and more than so, these poems are the fruit but of some few hours, curtailed from her sleep and other refreshments."[7]

Anne Bradstreet's reaction to the success of <u>The Tenth Muse</u> was a witty reproach to those "friends, less wise than true," who had exposed to the public that "ill-formed offspring of my feeble brain."[8] She goes on to say that she had hoped to trim her "rambling brat" in better dress, "but nought save homespun cloth i' th'

---

[7]John Woodbridge, "Epistle to the Reader," in Bradstreet, <u>Works</u>, p. 3.

[8]"The Author to Her Book," p. 221.

Comments

Anne Bradstreet's poem, "The Author to her Book," is reprinted below. Note that the writer has selected from it just those phrases she needs and has fitted them smoothly into her own sentence structure. This technique creates a concise and effective summary.

THE AUTHOR TO HER BOOK

Thou ill-formed offspring of my feeble brain,
Who after birth didst by my side remain,
Till snatched from thence by friends, less wise than true,
Who thee abroad, exposed to public view,
Made thee in rags, halting to th' press to trudge,
Where errors were not lessened (all may judge).
At thy return my blushing was not small,
My rambling brat (in print) should mother call,
I cast thee by as one unfit for light,
Thy visage was so irksome in my sight;
Yet being mine own, at length affection would
Thy blemishes amend, if so I could:
I washed thy face, but more defects I saw,
And rubbing off a spot still made a flaw.
I stretched thy joints to make thee even feet,
Yet still thou run'st more hobbling than is meet;
In better dress to trim thee was my mind,
But nought save homespun cloth i' th' house I find.
In this array 'mongst vulgars may'st thou roam.
In critic's hands beware thou dost not come,
And take thy way where yet thou art not known;
If for thy father asked, say thou hadst none;
And for thy mother, she alas is poor,
Which caused her thus to send thee out of door.

Footnote 9. See comment on p. 230.

house I find." It is an odd phrase to describe the mixture of pedantic learning, dull moralizing, and poetic cliché that made the book popular in its own time. Modern readers are apt to pass over these once-fashionable quaternions -- rambling four-part exercises in poetic diction -- in favor of the genuine homespun of her later verses, written when her European heritage had faded from memory and she turned for material to the timeless events of a woman's personal life. These poems still stand, three hundred years later, as honest testaments of the human condition as seen from one woman's point of view.

Anne Bradstreet's poetic output is the more surprising when one considers the handicaps that a woman poet on the frontier had to overcome. At the very beginning of their new life, the Dudleys and Bradstreets, though among the richer founders of the Bay Colony, probably lived in wigwams or caves dug into the hillside. Anne Bradstreet's father reported that they had "no table, nor other room to write in than by the fireside upon my knee," and that they often lived upon "clams and museles and ground nuts and acorns."[9] Even when living

---

[9]Quoted in <u>Poems of Anne Bradstreet</u>, ed. Robert Hutchinson (New York: Dover, 1969), p. 4.

Comments

Note that the reference to *Paradise Lost* is not footnoted, since both the poem and its characterization of Eve would be familiar to anyone who is sufficiently interested in Puritan poetry to be reading an essay on Anne Bradstreet. As it is a book-length poem, its title is underlined.

conditions improved, the unending labor of feeding, clothing, and caring for eight children must have left little time for poetry or other diversions.

In addition, a good Puritan woman was supposed, like Eve in Paradise Lost, to base her life on submission to God and husband. It was her duty to love God and to subordinate her own interests to the welfare of her father, husband, and family. Anne Bradstreet was fully aware of "each carping tongue / Who says my hand a needle better fits."[10] Such critics held that it was an aberration for a woman to write at all, and that it was certainly unseemly, if not actually sinful, for a Puritan woman to write poetry.

To the Puritan mind, poetry represented attachment to the things of this world: to words rather than to the dogma words were meant to communicate, to the natural world rather than the Heavenly Kingdom, to loved ones rather than to God. Cotton Mather, the great Puritan preacher, announced magisterially that the poets were "the most numerous as well as the most venomous authors" in the Devil's Library

---

[10]"The Prologue," p. 16.

Comments

Footnotes 9 and 11. The phrase "quoted in" shows that the writer is borrowing a passage which was already a quotation when she found it in her source. Since both speakers, "Anne Bradstreet's father" and "Cotton Mather, the great Puritan preacher" are identified in the text, there is no need to put their names in the footnotes. For the correct form when it is necessary to identify the speaker, see Footnote 12.

on earth.[11] Any woman who attempted to join this company was apt to come to a bad end, like the wife of the governor of Hartford, Connecticut, who had lost her wits through devoting herself entirely to reading and writing: "If she had attended her household affairs, and such things as belong to women, and not gone out of her way . . . to meddle in such things as are proper for men, whose minds are stronger, etc., she had kept her wits, and might have improved them usefully and honourably in the place God had set her."[12]

There was also the example of her husband's sister Sarah, disgraced in her family for "Irregular prophecying"[13] and preaching in England, as well as her friend Anne Hutchinson, expelled by the Massachusetts Bay Colony for

---

[11]Quoted in American Poetry and Poetics, ed. Daniel G. Hoffman (Garden City: Anchor, 1962), p. 253.

[12]John Winthrop, The History of New England from 1630 to 1649 (Boston, 1826), quoted in Ann Stanford, "Anne Bradstreet: Dogmatist and Rebel," New England Quarterly, 39 (1966), 374-375.

[13]White, Anne Bradstreet, p. 176.

Comments

Here the writer is moving from the first main section of her paper, which dealt with Anne Bradstreet's earlier poems and with the background against which she wrote them, to the second main section, which will be concerned with a closer look at Bradstreet's later poetry. She makes her transition effectively, using one further quotation from Bradstreet's early work to support her point that "there is another voice in this first volume" which foreshadows the "more original, confident, personal voice" of the later poems. (Note that she concentrates her own and the reader's attention on the voice of the poem, which is relevant to the point she is making; she does not speak of the subject of the poem, which is less relevant.)

listening to the inner voice of God rather than to the elders of the Church. Such consequences of speaking out -- madness, heresy, banishment -- should have warned Bradstreet not to risk poetic fame and may have prompted her humble request to be rewarded, if at all, with a wreath of "thyme or parsley," rather than laurel.[14] And most of Anne Bradstreet's early poems are, indeed, too imitative and lifeless to merit a genuine poet's wreath.

Yet there is another voice in this first volume, a forceful, ironic, intelligent voice that has its wits about it, as in these lines from "In Honour of Queen Elizabeth":

> Now say, have women worth? or have they none?
> Or had they some, but with our Queen is't gone?
> Nay masculines, you have thus taxed us long,
> But she, though dead, will vindicate our wrong.
> Let such as say our sex is void of reason,
> Know 'tis a slander now but once was treason.
>
> (pp. 197-98)

As she set about revising her poems and adding to them in the second edition, Anne Bradstreet drew upon this more original, confident, personal voice. Instead of writing

---

[14]"The Prologue," p. 17.

Comments

The Sidney quotation is well enough known that it does not need to be documented. Note that this quotation, being run into the text, is put inside quotation marks and that therefore the words of the poet's muse, which would normally appear inside regular quotation marks, have been placed inside single quotation marks. Whenever possible, repeated citations from the same author should have their references incorporated into the text, as has been done here. A parenthetic (p. 224) is no more distracting to the reader than a superscript number[14]; and it is certainly easier on the typist. In general, you would not use this form if you needed to include a long title in it; but a short title could be given (e.g., "Contemplations," p. 205).

If a long poem were being quoted, a line reference (ll. 62–65) would probably substitute for the page reference. In a formal footnote, you might use both, with the line numbers preceding the page number. Some very long poems, such as *Paradise Lost,* are divided into books; then you would give book and line numbers (I. 49–50). For a play, you would give act, scene, and line numbers, with Act I, scene 3, lines 47–50 appearing as (I.iii.47–50).

what she thought was expected of a Puritan poet, she began to imitate the practice of her distant relative, Sir Philip Sidney: "'Fool,' said my muse to me, 'look in thy heart and write.'" The tension generated by the persistent conflict between the duty owed to God and the loyalty and love given to her husband and children gives strength and vitality to her later poems -- elegies on the deaths of grandchildren, verse letters to her absent husband, a meditation on the fire that destroyed her house and personal possessions.

"Before the Birth of One of Her Children" expresses her fears, well founded in the Seventeenth Century, of dying in childbirth. Her sadness arises not so much from terror of the after life, for she had the Puritan's confidence in salvation, but from imagined grief at leaving the husband in whose arms she had lain for so many years. The salt tears that dropped on her manuscript fell also for her "little babes" who might be left motherless or, worse, in the power of a "step-dame" (p. 224).

"Contemplations," by common consent the most successful of her poems, has as its underlying theme the truth that earth as well as heaven declares the glory of the Lord. Looking at the autumnal splendor of the New England landscape, Bradstreet asks

[illegible]

> If so much excellence abide below,
> How excellent is He that dwells on high,
> Whose power and beauty by his works we
> know?
>
> (p. 205)

Though the poem unflinchingly faces the passing of fragile beauty and human life into the everlastingness of God, the poet nevertheless lingers for a long, loving look by the river's bank, admiring the autumn color which "seemed painted, but was true" until her senses were rapt and she knew not what to wish. "Contemplations" has been called the first American nature poem, foreshadowing Bryant and the Romantics.[15]

Another theme that calls out the best in Bradstreet is the terrible mystery of the early death of children. Three of her grandchildren, including her namesake Anne, died within a period of five years, and Bradstreet's protest at this eradication of "plants new set . . . and buds new blown"[16] is at first bitter, revealing

---

[15]Hyatt H. Waggoner, American Poets from the Puritans to The Present (Boston: Houghton Mifflin, 1968), p. 8.

[16]"In Memory of My Dear Grandchild Elizabeth Bradstreet," p. 235.

Comments

On this page and the next, quotations from several poems are used to support single points. Since this part of the paper deals primarily with Anne Bradstreet's own attitudes, as revealed in her poetry, numerous quotations from her works are used, and fewer references are made to the works and opinions of scholars. The quotations remain brief and to the point.

a dark root of anger and grief that had grown during years of hardship, sickness, and the loss of loved ones. In the end, as always, she submits:

> Three flowers, two scarcely blown, the
>   last i' th' bud,
> Cropt by th' Almighty's hand; yet is He
>   good. . . .
> Such was His will, but why, let's not
>   dispute,
> With humble hearts and mouths put in the
>   dust,
> Let's say He's merciful as well as just.[17]

But one can still hear in the later poems, as on the Arbella, the rising protest of her heart against the desolation of life in this new world.

One of the senseless accidents of life that the Puritan was bound to accept as part of God's merciful Providence was the loss of worldly goods. When the Bradstreet house burned down, through the carelessness of a servant, Anne lost not only her shelter from New England weather but all the little personal possessions that had helped make life in the raw new world more tolerable. Her reaction was

---

[17]"On My Dear Grandchild Simon Bradstreet," p. 237.

10

SAMPLE PAPER

typical: sorrow at the sight of her treasures now in ashes, but

> . . . when I could no longer look,
> I blest His name that gave and took,
> That laid my goods now in the dust.[18]

Compared to the modest wealth she had known in England, her American treasures must have been paltry, but losing them was still painful, and her grief was real as she looked at the places

> Where oft I sat and long did lie:
> Here stood that trunk, and there that
> chest,
> There lay that store I counted best. . . .

The Puritan's answer to all this was well known to Anne Bradstreet. She had written some lines of stern comfort to her son Samuel when his wife died:

> Cheer up, dear son, thy fainting bleeding
> heart,
> In Him alone that caused all this smart;
> What though thy strokes full sad and
> grievous be,
> He knows it is the best for thee and me.[19]

---

[18]"Upon the Burning of Our House," p. 292.

[19]"To the Memory of My Dear Daughter-in-Law, Mrs. Mercy Bradstreet," p. 239.

Comments

The writer returns to a more general topic for her conclusion, summing up the points she has made in her paper. The early and late books are again compared, the experts once more cited. Now the writer returns to the questions of the reception accorded Bradstreet's poetry. She mentions again the "recognition that came with the 1650 publication," then brings the topic up to date by mentioning nineteenth- and twentieth-century critical responses. The choice of John Berryman, in particular, as a figure to end with—a contemporary poet now first brought in to join contemporary critics in speaking of a seventeenth-century poet—helps create a strong ending for the paper. Language as vivid and original as this is always a good note to end on.

The new poems published in Severall Poems were not intended for publication any more than those in The Tenth Muse had been,[20] but it is these letters, elegies, and prayers, in which the Old World and its old history are forgotten and the New World and its trees and small graves remembered, which assure her a prominent place in the American tradition. The recognition that came with the 1650 publication seems to have freed her from writing the poetry she felt a good poet ought to write and enabled her to write poems about what she saw and touched and held and lost.

Still it was not until the Nineteenth Century that literary historians began to give her the critical appraisal she deserved.[21] And perhaps not until 1956, with the publication of John Berryman's Homage to Mistress Bradstreet, did she become completely accessible to her literary descendants. Berryman confessed: "I did not choose her--somehow she chose me--one point of connection being the almost insuperable difficulty of writing high verse at all in

---

[20]White, p. 361.

[21]Josephine K. Piercy, Anne Bradstreet (New York: Twayne, 1965), pp. 116-17.

a land that cared and cares so little for it."[22] But whether we care for her or high verse or not, she is there, as Berryman writes, "a sourcing whom my lost candle like the firefly loves."

---

[22]Quoted by Adrienne Rich in her foreword to The Works of Anne Bradstreet, from an interview with John Berryman in Shenandoah, Autumn, 1965.

List of Works Cited

American Poetry and Poetics. Ed. Daniel G. Hoffman. Garden City: Anchor, 1962.

Bradstreet, Anne. The Works of Anne Bradstreet. Ed. Jeannine Hensley. Cambridge: Harvard Univ. Press, 1967.

Dictionary of American Biography. Ed. Dumas Malone. New York: Scribner's, 1928–37.

Hutchinson, Robert, ed. Poems of Anne Bradstreet. New York: Dover, 1969.

Miller, Perry, and T. H. Johnson. The Puritans. 2 vols. New York: Harper, 1963.

Piercy, Josephine K. Anne Bradstreet. New York: Twayne, 1965.

Rich, Adrienne. "Anne Bradstreet and Her Poetry." Foreword to The Works of Anne Bradstreet. Ed. Jeannine Hensley. Cambridge: Harvard Univ. Press, 1967. pp. ix–xx.

Richardson, Robert D. Jr. "The Puritan Poetry of Anne Bradstreet." Texas Studies in Literature and Language, 9 (1967), 317–31.

Stanford, Ann. "Anne Bradstreet: Dogmatic Rebel." New England Quarterly, 39 (1966), 373–89.

10

----. "Anne Bradstreet." Major Writers of Early American Literature. Ed. Everett Emerson. Madison: Univ. of Wisconsin Press, 1972. pp. 33-58.

Waggoner, Hyatt H. American Poets from the Puritans to the Present. New York: Dell, 1968.

White, Elizabeth Wade. Anne Bradstreet: "The Tenth Muse." New York: Oxford Univ. Press, 1971.

Index

4 5 6 7 8 9 10

Comments